INDIVIDUALS AND ENTERPRISE:
Creating Entrepreneurs for the New Millennium through Personal Transformation

Individuals and Enterprise:

Creating Entrepreneurs for the New Millennium through Personal Transformation

Colin J Coulson-Thomas

BLACKHALL

Publishing

BLACKHALL PUBLISHING
26 Eustace Street
Dublin 2
Ireland

e-mail: blackhall@tinet.ie

©   Colin J Coulson-Thomas, 1999

ISBN: hbk: 1 901657 71 X
          pbk: 1 901657 76 0

Printed in Ireland by
Betaprint Ltd

Contents

Acknowledgements

I would like to thank all those whose encouragement and support made this book possible, especially Hamid Aghassi and colleagues at Adaptation Ltd, ASK Europe plc, Attitudes Skills and Knowledge Ltd, the Business Development Forum, Cambridge Management Centres plc, Cotoco Ltd, the National Centre for Competitiveness, University of Luton, The Networking Firm, the Management Development Institute, The Results Partnership and Policy Publications Ltd.

I owe a particular debt of gratitude to Susan and Trystan Coulson-Thomas to whom this book is dedicated and to Tony Mason of Blackhall Publishing who suggested that I write it and has done so much to bring the project to fruition.

Last but not least, many thanks to all those business and social entrepreneurs whose imagination and initiative created the various products and services that have so enriched my experience of life.

Colin J Coulson-Thomas
March 1999

To Susan and Trystan Coulson-Thomas

THE DEMONS OF THE NIGHT

*Follow a trail of muck and you will
find a dung heap at the end of it.*

Storms that rage in the night terrify some while others sleep.
When gale force winds blow roofs and trees that are able to
cope with normal conditions can appear fragile and vulnerable. What has appeared strong and well-established may turn
out to have shallow roots and a tenuous hold on existence.

The taller trees in the higher locations that once dominated the forest are the most exposed. Willowy branches and
supple trunks may bend with the wind, while those less flexible and pliant snap and crack. The smaller plants keep their
heads down; some will escape and, in the morning, these survivors will have more space in which to grow. Others might
be less fortunate, being crushed by the falling limbs of stricken
giants.

Change and Continuity

Change, chaos, turbulence, insecurity and uncertainty are
typical of the words used to describe the age in which we
live. They are also evocative of our anxieties and the positions that many people feel themselves to be in. With extra
prosperity comes additional risk. The more we have, the more
that seems to be at risk. As with the bigger trees, those who
have reached the highest positions have the furthest to fall.

Many descriptions of the contemporary context portray
today's generations as uniquely challenged. It is simply assumed that those who are alive today face changes and
uncertainties of a different order and kind from those that
have gone before. For some this may be true; for others, such

conclusions could be misleading, and may reflect a partial analysis.

There are parts of the world, particularly rural communities in developing countries, where for centuries the pattern of life has continued according to the natural rhythm of the seasons. Reaction to snakes and spiders is part of daily life as well as an inheritance from the past.

Time travellers returning century after century would have recognized a continuing pattern of life, in some cases idiosyncratic and rich with local festivals. They would encounter multi-skilled people, peasants with a craft who could also play musical instruments and help each other at busy periods. On more recent visits, the impact of agrarian and industrial revolutions might have been evident.

During the 20th century the combined impact of cars, population movements, television and other developments has, in some locations, been dramatic. A way of life largely unchanged for centuries has become noticeably different within a single generation. Local customs and mannerisms have been dramatically eroded. Habits and products from other parts of the world intrude. People now steal from their neighbours rather than from those in the next village. They use drugs that have been processed in factories rather than indigenous substances.

Global trends and developments surreptitiously seep or, alternatively, blast themselves into remote areas. People drift, or are lured, towards city centres. Traffic noise drowns the calls of insects. The physical impact of such changes is all too apparent. Urban sprawl advances over the landscape. People breath fumes. Their eyes water. What they see is blurred by pollution. At night the twinkling of candles in lanterns and the glimmer of fireflies in the darkness, is replaced by a gaudy galaxy of neon lights.

Uncertainties and Insecurities

Discontinuities abound. Yet throughout the ages many people have faced changes as profound, and in many cases more so, than those confronting us today. Communities have been torn apart by conflict and dynastic strife. The experience of life of many generations, from the cradle to the grave, was dominated by hunger, struggle and disease.

Brute force has prevailed. Cruelty has been widespread. The ruthless have triumphed. Wars have, in many cases, been total. Salt has been ploughed into the land of the defeated to render it infertile. Whole populations have been put to the sword or transported into slavery.

Historic atlases record the rise and the decline of successive civilizations and the emergence of new faiths. There have been natural disasters, climactic changes, famines and plagues that have wasted and decimated populations. Human beings have demonstrated, over and over again, the will, tenacity and courage to confront great and profound challenges that would dwarf many of those which cause us so much anxiety today.

Hope and Despair

There has been hope as well as despair, the Renaissance and Enlightenment as well as the Dark Ages, and ages of darkness. We can dig into the dirt for the broken bones of communal graves or look skywards at the soaring arches of towering cathedrals.

Restless curiosity, the intellect, insight and imagination of inquiring minds, have led to the discoveries of new peoples and new worlds, scientific breakthroughs, technological innovation and fundamental changes in prevailing views of the world. These creative qualities form an integral and inherent element of our human inheritance. They are within us and part of us.

Regression as well as development has occurred. Through intention, or by accident, what some have built others will destroy. Great libraries and extensive collections of literature have been burned or destroyed. Centres of learning have been broken up and groups of scholars dispersed. Leading cities have been razed to the ground.

Changing direction, starting a new life and beginning again are as old as history. Such challenges have been faced by countless generations over many thousands of years. Families have been evicted. Tribes have migrated. Whole communities have been forced to abandon everything they cannot carry with them.

A proportion of mankind has always faced extreme and involuntary challenges. Most of those involved had no help

and were on their own. Only recently have the media of the
world been able to focus attention upon the plight of particular individuals, families and communities – and only more
recently still have aeroplanes been available to air-drop food
and medical supplies to those in need.

People struggled. They suffered – and they coped. In so
doing, many millions of them displayed a dogged determination to survive adversity and come through. At the heart of
the maelstrom, they discovered themselves and found meaning and purpose in life. In the midst of our prevailing climate
of whinging and grumbling, we can but marvel at their resolution. People should tread softly at ancient settlements lest
they disturb the spirits of heroes and martyrs.

We need to retain a sense of perspective. The contemporary sense of angst that appears to affect so many people is
being experienced by those who are well protected by the
standards of previous generations. It occurs among those in
all walks of life.

A degree of angst may be an inevitable consequence of the
melancholy side of our natures. A large part of what ails the
contemporary human psyche derives from our expectations.
Looking ahead, at the possible impacts of factors, such as
globalization and technological innovation, people have a feeling in their stomachs that in future their lives may turn out
to be not only different from, but less satisfactory than, that
which has hitherto been assumed or planned. The approach
of the millennium is viewed with trepidation rather than
enthusiasm.

A Spoiled Generation

People of the post-Second World War generation in developed countries used to have high expectations. They grew
from childhood to maturity at a time when steadily increasing material well-being was assumed and job security was
taken for granted. The students of the 1960s thought they
could live for today in the belief that tomorrow would be better.

Within organizations there were numerous layers of management and many different grades of manager. Going home
to the family with flowers, chocolates and good news about a
'promotion' was an almost annual event. Incremental salary

scales meant that people could take on financial commitments secure in the expectation that they would have the means to pay off any liabilities incurred.

It was a great time to be alive. Pay increases above the rate of inflation covered the cost of expanding families and greedy children. The range of goods in the average home steadily increased with mass production and growing incomes. An exceptional appliance or gadget in one generation would become commonplace by the next.

Graduates and professionals had social status and assured careers. There were far fewer of them than there are today. Many experienced the pride of being the first generation of a family to go to college or university. They were respected and treated as special.

The alumni of elite institutions moved effortlessly into 'blue chip' corporations. Those with the most prestigious qualifications went onto 'fast tracks' and were assured of steady progress to senior positions. Others looked up to them. Many differentiated themselves from the rank and file by adopting distinctive mannerisms, speech and dress. They looked and felt confident.

Career advancement was almost inevitable. A ratchet effect was in operation. People went up. Some went sideways but few seemed to go out. Almost no one went down. All one had to do to reap the fruits of ever greater seniority and higher standards of living was to stay alive.

Major corporations were benevolent and benign. They willingly assumed a range of welfare functions and also looked after many of their employees' social needs. Well-staffed personnel departments planned people's next move. Regular training courses were held at pleasant locations. All this was at the expense of the employer.

Many companies retained their own training centres. Some were smart and newly built with a gymnasium and floodlit fishponds. Others were formerly the country homes of the social elite of previous generations. There were also sports and social clubs, with subsidized bars at which the 'regulars' toasted Victorian founders.

For those in the mainstream, life was cumulative and portrayed in terms of ladders, escalators and a steady ascent towards the executive suite. On retirement people could join pensioners' clubs. There were alumni magazines to read and reunions to attend.

It was a relatively comfortable existence, almost as if life was being played in slow motion. Excessive haste was regarded as undignified. People smoked pipes and reflected upon thick reports. They took time considering issues and making up their minds. Ruminating was a valued activity. Decisions were sometimes postponed until another matter to ponder came along.

All that Glitters is not Gold

Spreading new ideas through an organization could take an age. Closed office doors, protective secretaries, job descriptions, functional divisions and demarcation practices limited shared learning. Achieving a significant attitude change might mean waiting for someone to retire and replacing him/her with a 'new broom'.

Salaried managers were not required, or expected, to succumb to an urge to be entrepreneurial. Directors dealt with the important matters. Managers ensured that formal procedures were strictly adhered to. Staff were informed that on most issues an appropriate response would be found in the corporate operating manual. Changes were discouraged in case forms might need to be redesigned.

Barriers to entry, vested interests, cliques and various devices to protect 'national champions' and particular occupational groups were widespread. New and small enterprises could find it difficult to break in and secure access to capital. Many consumers were nationalistic and avoided 'foreign goods'.

Inevitably there were outsiders, those without jobs and lacking in qualifications. However, it was assumed that many of them would be 'included' or 'absorbed' over time. For most people, life seemed to be a one way street to the good life. Hardly anyone seriously expected to have to move into reverse gear. For some, it was all a bit of a bore. Challenges were for those in movies and books.

Few were prepared for what was to come. Victims used to be other people, those 'across the tracks' or in other parts of the world which were written about in newspaper supplements. However during the 1980s, as markets opened up and competition intensified, the 'bad news' about 'lay offs', 'cut backs' and 'belt-tightening' began to creep closer. Now it was a friend who had been made redundant, the neighbour down the street whose mortgage was called in.

People who thought they had it made suddenly discovered that when the chips were down they and their peers were considered disposable. The real 'insiders' were those at the very top of the company. For a period they were able to isolate themselves from the forces of restructuring and re-engineering they afflicted upon others.

For over a decade, from the mid-1980s to the late-1990s, a succession of corporate policies and practices, from de-layering and downsizing to outsourcing and outplacement put people under ever greater pressure. In essence, most of the approaches that were adopted boosted short-term perform-ance, by either cutting costs or squeezing more out of people. Many initiatives used a combination of both. Each year the speed of the corporate treadmills was increased and people were expected to do more with less.

Millennium Blues

How much longer can this go on? Much depends upon the circumstances. ABB Daimler Benz Transportation emerged from dramatic downsizing as a more effective enterprise. The company is growing again and has taken on additional staff. BT found that its readjustment to changed market circum-stances required a succession of job-reduction programmes. Kodak thought it had downsized sufficiently to become com-petitive. Then having paused only long enough to draw breath, the corporation initiated a new round of cost cutting.

For many management teams the first job-cutting pro-gramme represents a crossing of the Rubicon. Once a beast has tasted blood it is more likely to return. So it is with de-layering and 'head count reduction'. Those who survive a first cull live with the knowledge that their number may come up the next time around.

Outside of the corporate embrace, life can be tough. We all seem to know, or to have heard about, former colleagues who have been unable to get work or people whose businesses have failed. Perhaps they lacked credibility or were not paid what was owed to them. Maybe they were optimistic in their forecasting or unrealistic in their expectations. They may have

been taken advantage of by colleagues or let down by suppliers. There might have been faulty decisions about people or
property.

Trials and tribulations, setbacks, mistakes, blind alleys and
rejections abound. There are so many things that can go wrong.
Listening to wine bar chat it can seem as if someone has to be
super-human in order to succeed. As markets become more
open, and previous imperfections are removed, people fear
that, unless they are outstanding, they will not be in demand.

Hopes and dreams can fall like autumn leaves. The cold
and damp of winter chills the spirit and weakens the resolve.
The rebirth of spring and the hot summer of achievement
can seem a long way off when there is frost on the ground
and it is too slippery to stand. The prospects of success may
appear too remote to be credible. No wonder people feel themselves to be between a rock and a hard place.

The layoffs look set to continue. Household companies such
as Kodak and Levi-Strauss plan further reductions in staff-
ing. Job cuts invariably follow major mergers and acquisitions.
Certain sectors such as banking and financial services look
ripe for further 'rationalization'. Developments such as European monetary union will encourage this process.

Pay-offs and Consequences

And beyond lower costs, where are the benefits? How much
extra value has been created for customers? Are people more
competent and organizations more capable? What about commitment, loyalty, morale and longer term relationships? Many
people feel they are treated with indifference, both as workers and as consumers. Social institutions, such as churches
and families, are also breaking up due to a lack of trust.

We come into contact with too many people who appear
primarily concerned with themselves. Directors who seem
preoccupied with their own benefits packages. Surgeons
whose first reaction to proposals for improving patient care
is to wonder whether changes will reduce their freedom to
play golf on a fine day. Consultants crowding around corporate business opportunities like vultures competing to tear
the flesh off a rotting corpse.

Of course, there are honorable and dedicated directors,
doctors and consultants who still put the company, patient

or client first – in deed as well as word. But there are enough self-seeking and greedy ones to ensure that those encountered for the first time are not automatically given the benefit of the doubt. Rhetoric and play-acting abound, but we do not expect people to be altruistic any more. Morality cannot be taken for granted. Integrity has become a pleasant surprise.

So many people and organizations don't seem to care any more. Try phoning an insurance company for advice about a policy that is about to mature or a train-time enquiry centre when you have an urgent journey to make. The lines are invariably engaged. Those who do get through face interminable recorded messages as they wait for the particular number, which they need to press to be connected with an apologetic operator. For the rail traveller armed with a departure time there is the further challenge of finding a lavatory that is not out of order on the train.

People sense that, as a result of relentless cost cutting and 'de-staffing', actual service standards are falling. In the age of the call centre and re-engineered processes, customers sometimes feel they are dealing with robots rather than human beings. Single sentence, standard responses have replaced individualized letters. Automated procedures supersede personal concern and responsibility.

In spite of over a decade of rhetoric from suppliers claiming to be focusing upon 'solutions', the 'technology push' continues unabated. Competing vendors offer what appear to be similar products. Yet each will stress the unique features of their particular products and services. The poor customer is left to work out how to assemble a combination of items and relate what is available to the requirements of a particular home or enterprise. There is much confusion and little guidance.

Exercise: Weathervane Analysis

Trivial ephemera and temporary conditions need to be distinguished from consistent longer term trends. Think about the cultural and operating climate of your orgnaization. Is it getting better or worse? Is it heating up or cooling down? Is the pressure rising or galling? How will you and others, cope

> **with any changes that are anticipated?**
>
> **In some corporations, people do not seem to know whether they are coming or going. A weathervane may prove more useful than a thermometer or pressure gauge. Which way is the wind blowing? Does it shift around or is there a prevailing direction? How strong is it? How long is it likely to last? What is coming with the wind and after it, rain or shine?**

The Elusive 'Feel-good' Factor

Many people today are anxious. They lack confidence. They feel vulnerable because they are not in control of their own lives. They are a pawn on someone else's chessboard and surrounded by colleagues selected according to someone else's requirements.

For millions who struggle to exist in developing countries, such as India, uncertainty is all they have ever known. Life on the edge is the norm. However, many pampered and protected members of the middle class in Western societies have not been prepared for an unexpected onset of insecurity. They were brought up to expect a higher degree of immunity from the relentless market forces that so dominate the lives of the rest of humanity.

In general, people feel powerless to influence 'the rules'. Things are done to them. They are reshuffled, reallocated and reorganized. The treatment of some individuals is tantamount to harassment and abuse. In return for the illusory prospect of continuing employment they are required to fit in, become 'team players', exhibit 'role model behaviour', mouth slogans, sign up to 'value statements' and generally subordinate themselves to corporate requirements.

'Big brother' is becoming all pervasive. Increasingly, telephone conversations and e-mail messages are being monitored. As companies embrace knowledge management, any original contributions of particular individuals are 'captured' to become part of the unattributed knowledge-base of the organization and a source of intellectual capital.

Many companies that profess a belief in the importance of people are intolerant of individuality. To be different may be taken as evidence of a lack of allegiance and inadequate commitment to corporate norms. Definitions of competencies, assessment checklists, the equipping of people with standard tools, can all wipe out diversity.

Members of some management teams develop the characteristics of clones. As a consequence of intense pressure to conform, they may develop a reluctance to challenge superiors directly. The safest course of action is to go with the flow. They use the standard jargon of 'insiders' and quote the same corporate rhetoric. They may even start to dress alike and exhibit similar behaviour patterns.

Much angst is being caused by various threats to the continuing viability of large organizations. Some management teams cling to the hope that standing, reputation, brand awareness or inertia will carry them through. Others sense they are struggling to keep alive organizations that have long since lost any sense of distinctive purpose.

When rapid change is needed in a dynamic context, scale can inhibit adjustment. 3M is both large and innovative. However, size and flexibility can be incompatible, simply because of the greater difficulty of managing and co-ordinating larger numbers of people. Within small groups, or family sized units, people can just sit around a table and sort it out. Instead of sending each other e-mail they talk and, more importantly, because of the much greater facility for two-way communication, they can also listen.

The Seeds of Rebellion

Of course, many people do adjust to new realities. Having survived restructuring and downsizing they become more confident about the extent and nature of their contributions to corporate employers. However, along with accommodation and reconciliation they often sense that their personal inputs are not fully appreciated.

Credit and financial rewards may well be given to consultants and senior managers. However, there is often little acknowledgment of the difficult process of readjustment that many other individuals may have gone through in order to deliver the successes that are claimed. Many may have borne the pain while the gains may have been reaped by a favoured few.

At senior levels, rewards tend to be more directly related

to perceived individual contributions. This principle of meri-
tocracy has its attractions for others, particularly those whose
services are in demand. There is frustration when such aspirations are not met.

At some point, rhetoric about how crucial people are needs
to be matched by appropriate action. Should incentives and
reward and development opportunities, which are available
to senior management, be offered more widely? Given the
reluctance of many corporations to be generous to employees, the process may start in those sectors with the most pressing skill shortages.

People long to be understood and treated fairly as unique
individuals. They want to be appreciated and valued for
themselves. Some aspire to playing in their own games,
according to rules they have devised themselves and with
colleagues of their own choice. They would like to be asked
about themselves not what extra commitment they could
make to their employer.

Electronic communication eliminates many traditional
differentiators. Those receiving e-mail messages may not
know, or indeed care, much about what the senders' job titles
are, what they look or sound like or whether they went to
this or that school or university. Seeming the part, or ap-
pearing to be the 'right stuff', is no longer enough. Speed of
response and relevance of content are more important. People want the beef not the wrapping. While unsettling for the
privileged, such developments are hugely encouraging for
others.

Frustrated individuals have qualities and potential that
are not fully tapped by their existing employers. They know
they could offer more, if only they could find a means of linking
up with those who both appreciate and need what they have
to contribute. They also sense that they cannot be alone. They
feel there must be other people with similar problems who
share their concerns and with whom they could co-operate.
Yet as a result of various restructurings and reorganizations
they may have lost touch with colleagues and customers with
whom they once had enough of a personal relationship to be
open about future trends, developments and opportunities.

Enough is Enough

After a time people may feel they have had enough. They are only prepared to give so much and to put up with so much. Companies that are financial 'high achievers' can become vulnerable when they do not adequately balance the interests of their various stakeholders. Even a worm can turn.

British Airways found that the middle classes too can go on strike. The airline had achieved high profits within its sector. Perhaps because of the strains which achieving them had imposed upon its staff, the company found itself in dispute with many of its people.

Similar situations have occurred in other parts of the world. General Motors also achieved a financial turnaround. However, according to striking workers at its truck plant in Pontiac, the performance renaissance was accomplished at the expense of the employees. The surviving members of the slimmed-down labour force simply felt they were being worked too hard. Many struggled to cope and felt the demands being made upon them were just not acceptable.

Not everyone wants to be an accomplice in a charade. United Airlines has come clean and acknowledged that, for many passengers, the reality of air travel does not match the rhetoric. The company is consciously investing serious sums of money in improving customer service.

Building an external image is one thing, focusing upon the inner aspirations of people is another. We may be approaching the end of the road in relation to number-driven approaches and corporate structures that make few concessions to many human needs. More holistic and people-centred approaches to management are needed.

Continuity of Relationships

Moving on or 'getting ahead' can present serious problems for social animals. Those who leave a job in one company to take up an appointment with another are expected overnight to drop one set of contacts and to start afresh at developing another. The whole family might be required, physically and emotionally, to relocate. Children at school have to say good-bye to their friends. They too are faced with the challenge of establishing a new set of relationships.

In the natural world, apart from fire, flood and other disasters, such dramatic changes rarely occur. Social evolution tends to be more gradual. The composition of the flock or herd changes, almost imperceptibly, as particular individuals come and go. Many people take control of their own lives in order to join or create networks or gangs that offer greater continuity of relationships.

Old-style, formal contracts and career progressions are giving way to more flexible and informal arrangements, as people are increasingly expected to assume greater responsibility for discussing and determining their future. Loyalty to an organization is being replaced by loyalty to the project group, immediate colleagues or the members of one's personal network. While, ultimately, such changes can be liberating for those concerned, people now face a succession of negotiations where once they had only to 'go with the flow' in order to progress.

'Positives' and 'negatives' often travel together. Greater choice is often accompanied by the instability and uncertainty that results from diminished loyalty. Customers have become more fickle. They flit from website to website, and from promotion to special offer, like flocks of birds moving from one watering hole to another.

When employers identify new possibilities, their existing employees will not necessarily be among the first to benefit. Instead, the oldest colleagues in their midst may become the first to be discarded. The skills needed may be bought in. The exploitation of an opportunity, or development of a new venture, can be contracted out.

Rather than change and re-skill an existing operation, a new one may be set up, as tends to happen with the introduction of 'direct line' selling or the establishment of call centres. When required skills can be obtained more cheaply from distant countries, or less qualified staff are employed to support an automated operation, older people know 'the writing is on the wall'.

Within many Asian countries age is respected. It is associated with experience and wisdom. Long service and loyalty are still rewarded. Elsewhere attitudes are different or changing. In a growing number of Western countries people are now regarded as expendable. They are retained only so long as they contribute to current priorities.

A 'hard-nosed' approach can have traumatic consequences for particular individuals. Following a heart attack, the jet-setting high-flier may be ejected from membership of an elite club for the employed. Overnight, the once pampered and fêted prima donna drops to the back of the status queue, shunned by former colleagues and perceived by neighbours as a burden upon others.

The widespread practice of ageism presents further problems for members of the 'baby boomer' generation who suddenly become the victims of 'delayering'. With the prevailing emphasis upon youth many find themselves labelled as a barrier to the progress of younger colleagues in a slimmer organization that offers fewer opportunities for advancement.

From their Measures you will know them

Performance objectives and measures have focused upon tangible factors, such as the volume of production or the quantity of money earned or spent. Crucial indicators, such as the quality of attitudes, values, learning and relationships have been overlooked. We have ignored behavioural issues and our inner selves.

As areas of the developing world rapidly industrialize, the planet's reserves of natural materials are further depleted. Car ownership, 'road rage' and deaths from traffic accidents continue to increase. What about the likely impacts upon the social fabric and the physical environment? Can it all be sustained?

Social and environmental issues are interrelated. Thus the growing mobility of people can lead to a loss of skills in peripheral communities while adding to the already chronic levels of congestion in the centres of cities. The fruits of development are viewed through watering eyes.

High rates of growth of physical production can be excessively demanding of finite natural resources. The external environment is plundered, while far too little is done to tap the enormous pool of latent potential within individual human beings. Reversing the trend, for example taking work topeople rather than have people travel to work, could benefit both the individuals concerned and lower the pollution count.

Exercise: Situation Analysis

You need to understand the situation you are in. Your company may have an issue monitoring and management system (IMS) which:

(a) identifies the developments in the business environment that are likely to have a significant impact upon it;

(b) assesses their implications;

(c) determines appropriate responses.

But what about you?

You could undertake a personal IMS. Alternatively, you could think about how you would describe your situation if it were a place. Are you in a swamp or a desert? Is the soil around you rich and easy to till? Are you lost in a thicket and unable to see the wood for the trees? Are you sheltered or exposed to the elements? Are the surroundings improving or deteriorating? Are you alone or with others? Do you have what you need to survive and prosper or should you move elsewhere?

Scope and Purpose

This book is about changing direction, identifying, grasping and creating opportunities to live a richer existence. It is based upon a decade of research (see the appendix on page 295) and wide-ranging conversations with a great many people, over a hundred of whom have founded an enterprise which has had a significant and lasting impact upon their lives. It attempts to distill and share the essence of what caused them to seek and find fulfilment. Its purpose is to encourage others to reflect, take stock and do likewise.

There are also lessons in the book for people holding positions of responsibility within traditional organizations. We can create the conditions and infrastructure that enable innovation, creativity and personal entrepreneurship to flourish. Major corporations can be transformed into thriving and vibrant enterprise colonies.

The book is not littered with tables or case studies. Many of those interviewed were emphatic that detailed exemplars can sometimes mislead. What one company or person did in a certain situation may not be relevant for another in a different context. Particulars can distract. While people may be encouraged by what others have achieved, they will need to think for themselves to achieve a breakout or breakthrough. Hence, the emphasis is upon capturing and presenting both essential advice and warnings about potential dangers.

The Research Programme

Arguably too much effort is devoted to analyzing the successes of exceptional individuals or lucky opportunists who have been in the right place at the right time. Although, inspiring, such examples may have less to offer others than the experiences of many 'unsung heroes' who live among us as living monuments to human endeavour. Many of the latter would be 'lost in the crowd' but they have all distinguished themselves by a willingness to have a go.

The individuals who have been interviewed represent a diverse group. They are drawn from the Americas, Europe, Asia and the Middle East. Some have been better placed than others to create new sources of wealth; others could not have had more humble beginnings.

The enterprises examined range from international corporations to local businesses employing only a handful of people. Because of their nature, many of the companies visited are likely to continue – well beyond the lives of their founders – to have a beneficial and global impact.

In selecting whom to approach imitators have been avoided in favour of innovators. At some point these people have consciously taken control of their own lives and in so doing have created new options for themselves and for others. They have been pioneers within their particular field or chosen arena of operation – and they have been promised anonymity.

In almost all cases, those encountered also retain an overview of a total enterprise: an overview that has a clear direction and purpose. In this sense their businesses are on a human scale. Their management liberates and fulfils, rather than consumes or destroys. Whether large and complex, or small and simple, the businesses that they have established, or are associated with, are certainly not drifting or aiming just to survive.

The focus of observation has been upon the less tangible aspects of corporate operation, particularly values, motivations and relationships. Against the background of various trends, which were observed in the business environment, these appear to be critical enablers of business development. Not all is what it seems. Many individuals do not practice their rhetoric, while many enterprises do not sustain their early promise. Hence contact has, in some cases, been maintained over an extended period of several years.

Journeys and Destinations

Some of those who have participated in the research for this book might not be considered 'successes' in conventional terms. Not all of them have impressive job titles or great wealth, but they are rich in wisdom and experience and have found great personal satisfaction through being entrepreneurs. In many cases the extent of their self-fulfilment suggests the traditional view of achievement should be challenged.

Particular portions of the journeys of most interviewees have been far from smooth. Many have been severely tested, some almost to breaking point. Yet all now view such periods of stress and adversity as opportunities to learn and grow, albeit with the benefit of hindsight. Having arrived at their destinations they now treasure the insights gained on their travels.

Most of those consulted have experienced periods of angst or crisis in their lives. During such episodes certain symptoms may recur, for example, physical and emotional exhaustion, feeling cornered by circumstances or fearing that time and energy might run out. Often certain activities or roles would drive out others, resulting in an unbalanced life. Their personal preoccupations would lead to an unhealthy degree of internal self-absorption and little time for others, thus prejudicing personal relationships.

In some cases corrective action was taken just in time. Had they delayed sorting out their lives for much longer the consequence could well have been physical or psychological collapse. Many spoke of friends, who had experienced similar situations, who had not been able to cope. The line between public victory and private collapse can sometimes be wafer thin.

When the Bell Tolls

The ringing of a bell could be a call to arms or an invitation to mourn. A personal challenge or the traumas of a colleague or a member of the family can be a catalyst of action. Many of those who now appear decisive and in control, admit to procrastination and indecision in the period leading up to the change of direction which has given them a new life. Most felt that their heart was telling them one thing, while their head seemed to argue a different point of view. Inner voices advocated change, while the consequences of a lifetime of social conditioning supported the case for staying put.

Having come to a decision and developed a passionate desire to change, some people find that those around them wish to continue as before. Others members of the family may not be swayed by inner reflection. Nor may they burn with personal conviction. If the situation is not resolved, a wife, husband or partner may come to be regarded as the main obstacle to a longed for move to the country, or whatever else represents the chosen route to fulfilment.

High status job titles often mask a mass of anxieties, frustrations and disappointments. Sometimes simply being seen to be successful is what is sought. 'Top dogs' may attract those who are lured by position power, while remaining stunted – emotional cripples in terms of what it takes to sustain relationships of choice. Individuals, who define success in other people's terms, can trap themselves into having to do whatever is necessary to achieve it. When an end is thought to justify the means, compromises and accommodations are rationalized. As a consequence, people can lose touch with their inner selves.

Just as muddy tyre tracks may lead to a dung spreader, so people arrive at certain destinations because of the paths they have chosen. They advance along particular dimensions while ignoring others. As a result, they may pay a high price in terms of the lack of balance and harmony in their lives.

A Manifesto for a New Millennium

In the main our interviewees are inwardly directed and self-motivated. While aware of others, and sensitive to their requirements, they live life on their own terms. Many set the rules of new games, which they themselves established. They can, and do, change these to suit new conditions and circumstances. They set their own objectives and standards and do not dwell over much upon comparisons with other people. They focus upon what they have, rather than dwell upon what they do not have.

Compared with 'position seekers', our selected community of entrepreneurs play to their strengths. They pace themselves, aiming neither too high or too low. In relation to others, they also appear at peace with themselves. They have a sense of perspective and proportion.

Many of those observed have evolved their own philosophies. While willing to take advantage of opportunities, most would not regard themselves as 'followers of fashion'. Nor have they been much influenced by trendy management fads. They have observed, reflected and formed their own conclusions, independently of others.

While a single life span may appear a mere flicker against the background of all eternity, it provides some with enough time to found not just one, but a succession of businesses. In the most unlikely of contexts there are those who transcend the limitations of their capabilities and resources and who overcome all manner of obstacles to both fulfill themselves and serve others. They rise above current preoccupations with external challenges by becoming more aware of their internal capacity to cope and create.

Technology has moved on a pace since the first wireless signal was sent across the Atlantic from Marconi's radio station at Poldhu in Cornwall. Operating from their own homes millions of people can now afford the means of overcoming the barriers of distance, time and nationality that divided previous generations and imprisoned them in their separate localities. Today individuals can reach out and contact like-minded people and kindred spirits around the world. They can build networks and create new lives for themselves and their collaborators.

Individuals can, and do have, an impact. The entrepreneurial spark is within people, even in the most unpromising circumstances. It can kindle the spirit and light the soul. The more modest the beginnings, the further individuals may need to travel in pursuit of their dreams. The longer the journey the greater the number of adventures that may be encountered en route. To set out on a personal quest we need hope. In the next chapter we will examine how many of our concerns hide opportunities to use our spark to light a fire.

Checklist

1. What uncertainties and insecurities do you face? Which of these are work related?

2. Of the things you really value, which are the most at risk?

3. How fulfilled are you in your current life? Does it have meaning for you? Do you have a purpose? What is missing?

4. Has your life turned out as you expected, or hoped, that it would? Are you satisfied or disappointed?

5. Is there a gap between where you are and where you would like to be? What would you like more of and less of?

6. What worries you the most? Who or what would you most like to be rid of?

7. Can you take more or have you had enough?

8. Has, or did, your chosen career live up to expectations? If you could start again what would you most like to do or be?

9. What do you feel you are most cut out to do or be?

10. What are the major developments and trends in the business environment in the area in which you operate? How will these affect your employing organization and your current role?

11. What is most likely to change?

12. Do you have a personal vision of where you would like to be? How does this compare with where you could end up if you merely 'go with the flow' and allow life to take its course?

2

THE DAWN OF A NEW ERA
OF OPPORTUNITY

The best pickings on the beach
are often covered by the stickiest tar.

Many a night of anguish has been followed by a sense of relief
and anticipation as a new day approaches. The darkness appears less threatening. Areas of opportunity emerge from the
shadows. It gets warmer. Birds begin to sing. People wake up
to new possibilities.

The storms of the night can leave their mark. Broken tiles
and scattered branches may impede the way. In severe cases,
wide swathes of woodland may appear devastated. Yet fallen
trees are good news for those species that feed upon decay.
Insects are busy. Fungi spread.

Once the worst affected areas have been cleared, it may be
found that a much wider variety of plants can flourish than
before. Small shoots may appear and thrive as new pathways
through the stifling canopies of giant trees allow sunlight to
reach the forest floor.

Similarly, business opportunities can multiply when giant
corporations lose their dominance. Although dependent suppliers may suffer, the managed march of the giant pines may
give way to a rich, chaotic and natural diversity. As market
conditions change so enterprise, like nature, reacts. The response can be varied and healthy, when and where natural
conditions allow.

On the Outside Looking In

Maybe what went before was not so great. Those on the 'inside
track' did well. However, many others were excluded from opportunities to put their noses in the trough. They lived in the

shadows. They looked backwards because they did not believe they had anything to look forward to. Some felt doomed from an early age to be 'outsiders' for the rest of their lives.

Barriers abounded, some overt, others subtle or hidden. They were difficult to overcome. Markets were closed. In many sectors preference would invariably be given to local suppliers. Significant domestic contracts were reserved for favoured 'national champion' companies. Big opportunities went to large firms. Government business was granted on cost-plus terms. There were restrictive practices, vested interests, closed shops and cabals to protect 'those that had'.

Newcomers and additional players were not always welcome. Potential members could be blackballed. Sincere, hard-working people, whose goods and services were in demand, found themselves excluded from opportunities by a host of obstacles. Those that tried hard and made some progress, could be subjected to a succession of further hurdles of ever greater magnitude.

It was difficult to break in. Outsiders were relatively isolated. Linking up with like-minded people was not that easy. Individuals could not afford the means of competing with major companies. Only large corporations could bear the cost of buying leading-edge technology, developing the latest management techniques or recruiting the best students from leading business schools. Few of the latter had much interest in working for smaller enterprises.

The Arrogance of Complacency

Choice was limited. In many parts of the world there were single suppliers or, at best, a cosy cartel. Such competition as existed might involve old rivals who had agreed some formula for sharing the available opportunities between themselves. The benefits of growth would be shared by a limited number of similar suppliers. Corporations could, therefore, afford a steady increase in corporate staff. They inflated the number of grades and levels of management and those concerned felt ever more important and smug.

Within the ranks, there was little personal accountability. People sometimes sleepwalked through the day. They were assessed and rewarded as groups, by grade or category. Few individuals were visible. Hence, the focus was often upon what one might get away with, rather than what one should contribute.

Assessment was tolerant rather than rigorous. Friends and cronies helped each other. Flattery and guile could triumph over insight and achievement when 'progression' decisions were taken. Advancement came automatically with each passing year, if only to dignified sinecures, comfortable positions created as a reward for long service. To be fired someone had to commit a grave indiscretion or get caught with their fingers in the till.

Towards the top of companies, pompous individuals hid behind grandiose, but meaningless, job titles. They mouthed slogans and platitudes. They engaged in organizational politics and participated in rituals. For corporate 'insiders' there were prizes of some form for just about everyone who stayed the course.

At the apex of the pyramid was the directors' suite. Corporate bosses aped previous generations of the leisured class as they booked country houses for 'away days'. They enjoyed the trappings of office, from drinks cabinets and keys to the executive washroom, to limousines and corporate jets. They walked tall when they travelled abroad to meet 'the locals'.

There were those who thought they had it made. Expense accounts could be used to sample 'the good life' – 'jollies' described as 'training' or trips to overseas 'conferences'. Budget surpluses were spent on improving the furnishings of corner offices. Even after a life-time of employment the benefits continued, from inflation-proof pensions to club facilities.

People became greedy. They took what they had for granted. Their collective protection societies were forever wanting additional rewards for less effort. The more pampered some groups of people became, the greater the levels of social protection they demanded. They campaigned through the political system to keep out foreign suppliers, who might offer their captive customers cheaper goods.

The End of an Era

This corporate life of arrogance, complacency and greed was built upon foundations of sand. Ultimately, it would not stand the gales of competition that would result from the opening up of markets and the erosion of privileges. Paradoxically the sheer scale of great corporations would prove their undoing. The coming age would favour flexibility and swiftness of response. The giants would sink under their own weight.

Corporate practices and procedures contained the seeds of their own destruction. There were simply too many passengers who contributed little of value. Too many bootlickers, crawlers and toads. Too many parasites who fed off the lack of opportunities available to those who were excluded.

Protection can be as bad for those who feel protected as it is exasperating to those who are excluded. A lack of challenge can deny people the chance to experience and demonstrate what they are capable of achieving.

Much of what was protected had grown flabby and slack. Inefficiencies and delays caused disappointment, anger and frustration. People, who were not subjected to the spur and challenge of competition, became sloppy and complacent. Certain public services appeared to be run primarily for the benefit of 'providers'. Customers were taken for granted. They had to take or leave whatever was offered.

Historic improvements in mortality and morbidity had occurred as a result of piped water, china dishes, better education and the conquering of contagious diseases. However, more recently some of the indicators began to tail off and go into reverse. Greater numbers of people were falling victims of the diseases of affluence, born of sedentary lifestyles, over indulgence and a lack of exercise. Psychological illnesses were on the increase. Ever more conditions were regarded as symptoms to be treated.

People overlooked, or chose to ignore, the fragility of nature. The environment existed to be plundered rather than safeguarded and renewed. Corporations took what they could, particularly for the benefit of those living in North America, who consumed a disproportionate share of the world's natural riches.

Consumption of energy and other resources had become wasteful. Obsolescence was built into products. If one element failed, the whole would be discarded. Some families regularly threw into their dustbins more than their equivalents in other parts of the world consumed. It was not efficient, nor effective. It was neither fair, nor moral – and it would not last.

The end would surely come. The talents and enterprise of the 'outsiders' could not be excluded for ever. They were people too, and they wanted a piece of the action.

Meanwhile the business elite enjoyed an Indian summer. Many of the most extravagant castles were constructed in the age of gunpowder. Some were completed as late as the 19th century and within a few years of the demise of the social roles of their owners. Many corporations also persisted until the end in building monuments to a previous era of dominance. City centres became dominated by glass towers of corporate head offices that would soon display 'for sale' signs.

Subsequent events have been dramatic. The scale and sweep of what has occurred suggests the era of corporate complacency could not have been sustained. Like the plantations of the old south the secure lifestyle of the salarymen has gone with the wind.

Few foresaw the coming social revolution. Following privatization, BT found it had twice as many people as it needed. Wave upon wave of restructuring, delayering and cost-cutting have cut a swath through the managerial class. Shell-shocked survivors have been subjected to an endless succession of initiatives to achieve yet more change and ever greater performance improvement.

Exercise: Volcano Analysis

Few jewels sparkle on the surface, most are buried in earth and mud. Entrepreneurs seek to penetrate the facades of life and uncover the true sources of opportunities. They put distractions aside and look beneath surface appearances for latent forces that may be hidden or blocked.

Think of the power that could be lurking within. Is there a fire at your core, an inner you waiting to burst out? Are there outlets for your passions and energies or are the vents blocked? Is the pressure building up? Will it be enough to break out? Could an explosion occur? Or are you all ash and gas? Are you an extinct volcano?

Emerging from the Shadows

Revolutions produce both victims and beneficiaries. Some inevitably cling to the past, while others look to the future. Within larger corporations, the insecure sometimes walk rather than wait to be pushed. Meanwhile, the quietly confident emerge into the light. While previously they may have been hidden and blocked, when the time comes they step forward and volunteer for new roles and further responsibilities.

While it lasted, corporate paternalism, although welcomed by many, irritated others. Corporate provisions, ranging from 'benefits' to training and development, was generally standard rather than tailored. Managers were required to take the model of car selected as appropriate for their grade, even though another might be more suited to their personal requirements. A host of status issues arose and procedural problems were created when individuals sought to be different.

Staff would be required to attend certain courses at particular stages in their career, irrespective of their individual job responsibilities or personal competencies. Training managers had budgets to spend. They selected programmes which they thought would benefit the greatest number of people. As a consequence, sessions might be offered that failed to meet the distinct requirements of any of the attendees. Those requesting an alternative ran the risk of being labelled as 'someone who is not a team player'.

Of course, not everyone in giant corporations rested on their laurels. Innovations still occurred due to the restless curiosity of certain individuals and teams. Some groups, such as those at Xerox PARC, used corporate cash flows to create the building blocks of technologies that would subsequently help to democratize opportunities. They sustained their commitment to pushing back the boundaries of what was possible, even as the weight of corporate bureaucracy and complacency sought to contain them.

New Organizational Requirements

The challenge is to create forms of organization that are better able to support knowledge workers, meet the individual needs of more demanding customers, exploit the potential of emerging technologies and reconcile competing stakeholder pressures. There are contending requirements to balance, such as those from employees for security and from corporate management for greater flexibility.

Organizations need the capacity to face in different directions while harnessing capabilities, sustaining relationships, creating value and serving customers on an international basis. Companies, such as Heineken, are adopting a network mo-del that allows people to collaborate with some colleagues for production purposes and others when serving the customer. Different channels can be used and resources accessed, depending upon the issues and priorities.

Where trust has been lost, there is an opportunity to re-establish it. BT, Dalgety and Reuters are endeavouring to re-build loyalty and relationships with their people, on the basis of greater openness, involvement, consultation and participation. Blue Circle Cement's 'way ahead' programme recognizes that employee 'buy-in' results from answers to 'why' questions.

Hierarchical boss/subordinate relationships are giving way to a shared sense of purpose. The distractions of internal conflicts are being replaced by a collective focus upon external customers and 'outputs' and 'deliverables'. Rather than watch each other, people are concentrating upon the collective opportunity.

Considerable effort is being devoted to putting frameworks of common and compatible values and mutual understanding into place. At British Aerospace, 15,000 managers are being encouraged to embrace 'core values' such as 'innovation' and 'partnerships'. The aim is to 'break the mould' and establish new attitudes and behaviours.

Companies are introducing more flexible employment practices, such as annualized hours, broadbanding, flexitime, job-sharing, sabbaticals and teleworking. Crèche facilities are being established for children. Pets may be welcome, provided they do not inconvenience others and their owners take responsibility for them. The aim is to make the workplace welcoming and warm. There is talk of 'new deals' and new 'psychological contracts'.

Inevitably, the changes being introduced will not please everyone. One person's enjoyment might become the source of another's irritation. The definition and pursuit of 'role model' conduct may lead some to conclude they would prefer to be themselves, rather than a senior management team's collective view of the sort of person they ought to be. In relation to more flexible working options, why settle for half a loaf when the whole could be obtained by 'going it alone'?

The New Entrepreneurs

The new age creates a host of opportunities for people all over
the world. Exclusion is becoming a matter of choice. Individuals can acquire the means of communicating with the world.
Relevant information is available on-line. Government programmes champion the 'small business'. A growing proportion
of ambitious business school students want to join small companies when they graduate. Many aspire to becoming entrepreneurs.

The seeds of many entrepreneurial opportunities lie in the
consequences of the policies and practices which have been
pursued in the past by major companies. Consumers are reacting against poor services and standard products. They are using their new found freedom of choice to experiment with alternatives and to punish poor performers.

Customers are also more willing to try out new products
and different suppliers. They are prepared to reward those who
are more responsive to their needs. As a consequence new entrants are able to break in.

Around the globe, when constraints are removed, enterprise
has been found to flourish. In societies at very different stages
of development, people seek a purpose and yearn for identity. Economic, political, religious and ethnic outsiders desire a place in the sun. They want to participate and make a
distinctive contribution. People who have been down stand
up and walk.

Assembling the elements, which are needed for effective independent operation, has never been easier. People can plug
into electronic databases and bulletin boards, join electronic
conferences and enter electronic marketspaces. They can send
and receive memos and files. They can access and participate
in, via the internet, a wide variety of activities that are available on the World Wide Web. All this, and more, can be done
from a terminal at home or a portable device. A new and independent lifestyle for the price of a Christmas present.

Some succeed beyond their wildest dreams. Great effort may
be required to bring about an initial movement against the
forces of resistance, whether real or imaginary. However, once
some momentum is built up, each successive acceleration often appears easier to achieve. The length of time it takes for
companies to reach certain thresholds of turnover continually falls.

Change as Opportunity

The struggles of the 'old guard' for renewal and transformation represent new opportunities for the enterprising. Demanding and painful change can give rise to requirements for various 'support services' that may help people to cope. People under pressure might need counselling. There may be meetings to facilitate and conflicts to reconcile. As delayering and downsizing scale down internal resources, managers become more dependent upon external assistance. Insiders look beyond the walls for those who can refresh their gene pool.

A focus upon core competencies generally leads to outsourcing and 'hiving off'. These can create possibilities for people, who set up new businesses, to provide relevant and specialist services. Innovation, capability building and organic growth are replacing cost reduction and internal restructuring as corporate priorities. New preoccupations mean new requirements for consultants and contractors.

Corporate drones can undergo a metamorphosis. They can become busy worker bees when given the opportunity to run their own businesses. Some have not waited to be asked. They felt the breeze and smelt the salt. They sensed the turn of the tide and have sought freedom.

Helping others to take advantage of emerging trends, such as the adoption of more flexible models of operation, creates opportunities for companies new and old. Regus has assembled a worldwide network of offices containing work spaces and meeting rooms. These allow its clients to rent space, as and when required, in cities around the globe. Established businesses such as Marks & Spencer and McKinsey use this facility, as do start-up companies.

Business fashions can and do result in the emergence of 'new industries'. For example, the use of call centres has spread rapidly. They quickly became a significant source of employment, and many enterprises were set up to support their introduction and operation.

Many emerging areas of opportunity are equally open to long-established corporations and sunrise ventures. Among the successful pioneers of retailing over the internet are major companies such as Dell, whose past experience of the direct selling of computers enabled it to jump at the chance of a further channel and new enterprises, such as Amazon the bookseller. As a sign of the times, IBM offers a 'one-stop shop'

service for enterprises of any size that wish to establish and
operate a website on the internet.

Certain individuals may still experience problems in lo-
cating others with whom they could discuss business opportunities and share concerns. Entrepreneurs are identifying
the need for new electronic meeting and marketplaces that
bring interested parties and potential collaborators together.
The Networking Firm, abfl and Attitudes Skills and Knowledge have already introduced relevant services and facilities.

Opportunities for New Relationships

For the adventurous and far-sighted there is an historic opportunity to redefine the form and nature of work and employment, and to transform relationships between people and
organizations. Never before have so many individuals had so
many options for making a difference and leaving their mark.

Managers should not assume something cannot be done.
Rather they should begin with the attitude that what people
would really like ought to be possible. This is especially so when
an expressed need comes from within and is deeply felt. People are often expected to select their careers at a relatively
early age, when their experience of the world of work, and the
options available, is limited. Not surprisingly, many subsequently discover a mismatch between the demands of a job or
role and what they believe to be their 'true selves'.

The challenges faced by large and established organizations
can present new opportunities for redefining and renegotiat-
ing their relationships with individuals and for people to get
out from underneath past constraints. Restless souls can escape to become intrapreneurs or entrepreneurs. They can re-
build their lives around their own attitudes to work, their personal reasons for wishing to work, their values and what they
feel are their distinctive attributes.

People can be both simple and complex. They may long for
change in some areas and yet seek continuity in others. They
may want to develop in new directions while retaining a link
with an existing organization. Such dilemmas are faced by many
individuals. They create opportunities for imaginative employers to devise new concepts of employment and models of operation that offer a different mix of opportunities.

Invariably, there are alternatives. A part, rather than the

whole, of someone's time could be contracted. A sabbatical period could be offered, during which individuals might assemble complementary portfolios of activities that would benefit both them and the organization. People could be helped to face the future in the knowledge that there would be someone behind them. In return for the support provided, those who are enabled to venture out might be expected to share the spoils of their success with those who have assisted them.

Increasingly, people want sufficient autonomy and discretion to allow and enable them to make an identifiable contribution. Personal fulfillment results from making a difference through the exercise of individual responsibility. People are becoming less tolerant of dull, repetitive jobs. They no longer want to be regarded as extensions of machines or as mere activities within a process.

BT's personal communications division released its staff, who respond to customer queries, from the constraints of 'operating by the rule book'. The staff's satisfaction increased and customers began to feel that thinking individuals were working to tackle their particular problems. BT could have further reduced the discretion of its people by automating more aspects of their work. Instead it opted for greater freedom, trusting the judgement of its staff to do the right thing for each customer.

Customers as well as employees can be empowered, for example giving them the means of designing their own products. Examples, range from furniture design to the selection of tracks on a CD. Some farmers allow customers to go into the fields themselves to select their own fruit and vegetables.

Opportunities for the Environment

Environmental and social pressures strengthen the case for introducing new ways of working. The physical mobility of those whose skills are in demand, can split up families and impoverish communities made up of those who are 'left behind'. Instead of expecting people to travel to a 'place of work', information and communications technologies could be used to take the work to the people.

Commuting can be expensive in a number of ways. Apart from the vehicle, fuel and congestion costs, there are also accommodation and other charges to be taken into account. Moving to an out-of-town location and establishing a 'home office' in an area of cheaper housing could allow important aspects of lifestyle to be maintained, perhaps even enhanced, at a lower level of income. Some prefer the scent of flowers and the ripple of the stream to the smell of tarmac and the roar of the traffic.

Many of the challenges we face are interrelated. So too are potential solutions. Replacing physical commuting with teleworking offers individual, environmental and social benefits. The time saved could also be used to relieve other members of the family from chores, thus enabling them to develop portfolio careers or lives. People could even help their neighbours.

Individuals who are confused by technologies represent possible clients for those who could help them to understand the options that are feasible and make a relevant selection. Investigation and relating what is available to personal requirements and a particular context could take some time and require reflection. Such a brief might be difficult for the busy full time employee but ideal for someone seeking a less hectic but more thoughtful existence.

Exercise: Storm Analysis

You need to assess the resilience of the roots and foundations of your life and the extent to which you will be able to withstand current and future pressures and challenges. You need to identify areas of weakness and take steps to strengthen your defences.

If a storm were to wage through your life, what would be left standing and what would be swept away? Would the trappings or the fundamentals be blown away? What is most exposed and what is most secure? If the going really got tough how many of those around you would remain by your side? Who or what is dispensable and who or what could you least afford to loose? Are the latter at risk? Overall, how well placed or vulnerable are you? What needs to be done to strengthen your position?

Falling Barriers

A common feature of many technological changes is that they are reducing certain barriers to involvement and participation. In an age of teleworking and electronic commerce, no location need be too remote. Invitations to contribute can be sent in seconds to all those who could be interested, wherever they might be.

Work can be subcontracted and outsourced. Jobs are now more geographically mobile than ever before. When making a selection, we are no longer limited to those people, technologies and other resources which are physically at hand. We can search on a global basis for who and what we consider to be the best.

The internet, and other emerging technologies of electronic commerce, are democratizing business opportunities. Companies do not, necessarily, need to spend decades, and relatively large sums of money, building up an international distribution system by such means as establishing offices or acquiring companies abroad. Using the internet and the World Wide Web, it may be possible to establish within weeks a steady flow of visitors, from many countries, to the company's site.

A growing range of services, from brochure design and printing to accountancy support, are now available on the internet. Organizations may no longer need their own 'in-house' departments when specialist services are available on demand and whenever required. For example, small businesses without any internal design and production facilities can issue documentation as smart as that provided by major corporations.

In fields, such as education and development, traditional league tables of student numbers are being turned upside down. New suppliers can enter the global market as a result of offering internet, accessible versions of programmes that have hitherto only been available locally or to particular organizations. Institutions that for generations have only operated within a national context can – overnight – find themselves global players.

As some barriers fall, we need to be vigilant in ensuring that others are not created to take their place. In relation to government policies and regulations, whatever frameworks and measures are put in place should encourage rather than reduce flexibility and enterprise.

Increasing Choice

No generation in history has had so many options in terms of where, when, how and with whom to consume, earn and learn. For example, we can choose between continuity and change,

between routine and variety or between prescription and
spontaneity in many areas of life. And with lower transaction costs, cancellation charges and 'crawl-out' penalties, we
can afford to change our minds. We are not locked in. We are
spoiled for choice.

Increasingly, areas of knowledge, money, basic skills and
core technologies are becoming commodities. They are accessible, like the air we breath. Thousands of continually up-
dated sources of information and live conferences involving
international experts, are equally available to anyone with a
modem connection, for the price of a local call. Higher level
capabilities can be bought, borrowed or licensed.

When beginning the process of reassessment, people should
not assume that certain 'trade offs' are inevitable. There may
be opportunities to resolve inner conflicts and to lay personal
dilemmas to rest. Thus, those who feel torn between emotion
and reason, desire and logic or the heart and the head, could
set down the essence of each and then search for lifestyles and
relationships, or combinations of roles and activities, that might
satisfy both.

People should be sensitive and attentive to both their feelings and their intellects. They should seek to fulfill different
facets of their character. A new edifice could be composed of
many elements. The foundations could be broad and deep. There
might be a number of main pillars and a network of intercon-
necting beams. A single column lacks lateral support. It is much
more likely to topple over as a result of sinking under its own
weight.

There should be a pillar for whatever each person might
consider to be a fundamental element of their life. Personal
passions should not be left out of the design. If they are ignored,
the new existence that is built will turn out to be incomplete.
The building may well stand. However, because something important to the inhabitants is missing it may not be considered
a home. The occupants may be dry and warm without feeling
attuned or at ease with themselves.

People generally fail to realize how much freedom they have
to create their own world and to determine their individual
place within it. For example, the arena in which one person
decides to operate could be a village or neighbourhood, while
another might seek to play a part on the international stage.
The first might define his or her role and significance in rela-

tion to local community needs and opportunities, while the perspective of the second could be global.

Problems as Opportunities

Having got thoroughly wet while madly packing up, many people leave the beach just as the last of the summer shower is moving on. They leave more space for those who remain.

Entrepreneurs often view situations and trends differently from others. For example, they may not cut and run the moment a financial indicator begins to fall. Declining markets and dying industries have provided lucrative opportunities for people who have asked such questions as why is the market declining? Why are customers going elsewhere?

Bert Claeys confronted what appeared to be an inexorable decline in the cinema audience with a very different approach to the defensive strategy adopted by other cinema providers. Whereas they introduced multi-screens into existing sites, he built the Kinepolis cinema complex in Brussels, containing no fewer than 25 screens and as many as 7,600 seats. Within a year the new site, with its extensive car parking facilities, was attracting a half of the city's cinema audience. It is also used by the European Commission as a venue for conferences and other events involving large numbers of participants.

The origins of many new enterprises and lifestyle changes lie in contemporary problems. Bill Cran recognized that many aspiring entrepreneurs find it difficult to secure flexible access to the volume of accommodation which they need. He formed the Birkby Group to provide premises which are conveniently located and contain workspaces that can be increased or reduced as a business expands or contracts. Credit facilities are also made available for those who might need them.

The growth of electronic commerce, the adoption of outsourcing and virtual operation create new areas of opportunity. They also produce new challenges and entrepreneurial companies have focused upon particular management problems which are emerging. Attitudes Skills and Knowledge equips people to 'manage at a distance', Conduit Communications helps companies manage key business relationships, while The Networking Firm supports the process of building virtual teams.

As gaps between the actual and the possible widen in many walks of life, people seek ways of bridging them. The desire of developing countries and emerging companies to 'catch up' creates a demand for products and services that can 'short circuit' the time and cost of evolution and expansion. Thus, instead of laying down an expensive network of cables, use could be made of mobile phones.

Notwithstanding other changes, certain basic human drives continue. Like the poor, they seem always to be with us. For example, people still seek recognition. They crave esteem and personal identity. Individuals like to feel that they are wanted and that their lives have a meaning. Many hunger for the counselling and support, that would enable them to cope with age-old questions relating to human existence while surviving in the contemporary social and economic context.

Development Opportunities

Corporate, group and individual learning represent a business opportunity of heroic proportions. American Express, Apple, Harley Davidson, Intel, Motorola, Sears and many other companies have developed 'corporate universities'. There are visions and values to shares and competencies to develop.

As companies become more aware of the importance of learning and individual knowledge creation, the necessity of producing future intellectual capital creates new opportunities for redefining the relationships between talented knowledge workers and the organizations that seek their services. Corporations are becoming less paternalistic and prescriptive in areas such as training and development. Individuals are assuming greater responsibility for their own provision.

Universities and other external providers are responding with more flexible course frameworks, including degree programmes that enable students to select themes and topics and determine their own preferred mode of assimilation. Opportunities are created for the creation of individual learning accounts and establishing relationships and mechanisms for lifelong learning.

With so much material captured electronically and accessible via the World Wide Web, educational institutions, occupational associations and training providers no longer find their lives dominated by the provision and transfer of content. The emphasis can shift to the facilitation of learning.

As individuals increasingly define their own subject matter, identifying areas relevant to personal interests and development needs, the role of the educationalist or trainer becomes that of mentor and guide. People may need advice on where to find relevant material and how best to access it. They may need help in determining how they might best learn and build their understanding.

Providers of learning support services can avoid the risks involved in selecting which programmes to offer and the time consuming and costly task of assembling standard packages of material. Instead they can concentrate upon supplying frameworks, support mechanisms, assessment techniques, quality processes and learning management systems.

As electronic and international intellectual property markets become better established, and people work in a variety of ways, they are likely to become more aware of their market value and less tolerant of contracts of employment that automatically vest property rights in employers. They may increasingly expect some form of equity stake in the value which they are creating. The worker, rather than the church or the feudal lord, may expect a 'proportion of the take'.

More people are likely to set out consciously to create distinct items of 'intellectual capital'. Greater opportunity to exploit 'know-how' on an international basis is increasing the value of potential income streams from the use of intellectual property. David Bowie has raised money using future royalties from his songs as security. In the case of a product selling in large quantities, small royalty payments per item can quickly amount to a fortune. The great wealth of the Rausing family derives from exploitation of its patent rights in the production of Tetrapak milk and juice cartons.

Trends as Opportunities

Most people are preoccupied with themselves and the present. They are passive and largely concerned about what is happening to them as individuals. Entrepreneurs are more sensitive to the problems experienced by others around them. Technological, social, economic and other developments can all impact upon people in so many different ways. How are other people handling the situations they are in? What would enable them to cope more effectively? If people are under pressure and experiencing stress what could be offered to them to help them relax?

Corporations, such as AT&T, Boeing and Xerox have brought in very different kinds of people and services to help their employees to become more reflective and creative. Poetry readings in the executive lounge or poems on the London Underground, can take people outside of themselves and enable them to find meaning in new connections and relationships. Oriental gardens and running water can help people to unwind. Poets, gardeners and spiritual counsellors, as well as fitness trainers for the corporate gym, can all find new opportunities for their services.

Different groups of people can be impacted by developments in diverse ways. Trends, such as the growth of part-time work involving women and the spread of two career families, give rise to questions. How convenient are shopping facilities and banking arrangements? What will the children do when school finishes? Who will look after elderly parents? How will people wish to use their leisure time at the end of a hard day or when they decide to take a break?

Many trends are interrelated, for example the emerging social costs of an ageing population and the steady withdrawal of State welfare cover. A variety of new services will be needed to replace public provision. The nursing home sector expanded in the UK to fill gaps which emerged in local government services.

Lifestyle changes can create a variety of opportunities for those who are alert and aware. Take the increasing awareness of the importance of diet and exercise. Within the City of London lunch used to take the form of a lengthy and heavy three course meal accompanied by alcoholic drinks. Typically the main course would consist of 'meat and two veg', while a variety of stodgy and calorie-rich puddings would be served. Little wonder people aimed to do the 'real work' in the mornings.

Times have changed. There has been a steady trend over many years towards lighter and quicker eating, accompanied by mineral water. At the same time, customers have become more discerning, for example sending people out to seek outlets that offer a wider choice of sandwiches. Once a traditional formula is discarded people may become more open to new ideas. They may be willing to try practices adopted in other countries. There is scope for experimentation.

As a result of such changes, new outlets have spread throughout the City offering food and drink which meet the emerging needs of customers. Health centres have opened as well, for those who opt to use their 'lunch break' to work out. In many cases, the opportunities have been seized by new entrants, people without a background in the areas concerned. They were astute, attentive and agile. They spotted a gap in the market and quickly moved in. They innovated while existing players stayed with old formulae and strove unsuccessfully to make them work by such means as cost cutting and 'efficiency drives'.

Opportunities for Individuals

The power of giant corporations cannot be dismissed, but neither should it be exaggerated. Individuals can be smart where corporations are stupid. The qualities of many talented individuals are neutralized when they are brought together in a collective entity. Many market opportunities, such as that for small motorbikes in the US, have been spotted by particular employees, when the weight of corporate opinion, expert advice and market research has pointed in another direction.

Throughout history, pioneers have asked questions which others have either not thought to ask or have been afraid of asking. Discoveries rarely result from the use of 'me-too' management approaches, the adoption of standard tools or people viewing the world as others see it. Innovators think 'outside of the box'. They challenge the status quo.

Entrepreneurs look beyond the immediate and beneath the surface. They see opportunities while those around them are inhibited by problems. While others on the beach may be put off by the tar and seaweed, their own assessment might be that the plank which has washed ashore could be cleaned and used. Rather than worry about today's dirty hands, they already have a vision of a fine timber forming a central feature of a seaside room.

Checklist

1.   Why do you work? How does work relate to the inter-
     ests, concerns and relationships that are most central
     to your life?

2.   Are there things which you would still like to accomplish
     in life?

3.   What new areas of opportunity are opening up around
     you?

4.   Among those you know are there people who are chang-
     ing direction or establishing a new enterprise? Might any
     of them need some assistance? How might you help?

5.   What obstacles, barriers or restrictions have recently been
     removed in the area in which you operate? What could
     you now do that was not possible in the past? What might
     you be able to do in the future?

6.   How much freedom of action do you have? What are the
     main constraints upon you and how might they be re-
     moved?

7.   What are the main problems faced by those with whom
     you work, whether as a colleague, supplier or customer?
     What do these people most need?

8.   Which of them would you most like to work with?

9.   Which of the problems and requirements are most likely
     to give rise to business opportunities?

10. Who around you is considering the opportunities which
     you have identified? Who is planning to exploit them?

11. How are patterns of earning, learning and consuming
     changing in the areas in which you operate? What are
     the implications?

12. What new services are required? Which of these interest
     you the most? What are you going to do about them?

3

HOW WILL ALL THIS AFFECT ME?

Pilchards can rot or see stars.

Storms affect people differently. Some keep their heads down or hide. Others venture out to see what is happening. Going out too soon may be dangerous. However, those who stay under cover for too long may miss some of the more interesting sights.

When looking around us, what we observe will depend upon who we are and our mood. One person might focus upon problems, such as the shed that will need to be repaired, while another may see opportunities, perhaps for a new entrance where the fence has blown down.

Where electricity lines are blown down people are plunged into darkness. Those without candles may be forced to provide their own illumination from within. Some may start to recreate the world in their minds, selecting some features and discarding others. There may be time for thinking and talking.

People who react tactically to what is happening to them, rather than thinking strategically about what is occurring around them, can become victims rather than beneficiaries of change. Over time, a succession of short-term accommodations and responses can lead to a dead end. While preoccupied with immediate issues people may not notice the 'white water' ahead.

Change and its Implications

Change is rarely neutral in its impacts upon both individuals and groups, however it may be dressed up. Many of the restructuring, cost cutting and productivity initiatives introduced in recent years have been entirely driven by narrow corporate objectives. Improving the quality of working life, the reduction of stress or allowing people more time for thinking, have not been among the primary objectives given to re-engineering teams.

Companies employ people, or hire consultants, to 'sell the benefits' of change. Their role is to 'secure acceptance' through portrayal of the 'positive' factors. They play down those aspects that disadvantage the people of the organization. 'Implementation' is viewed in terms of 'getting people on side'. 'Aligning goals', getting everyone pointing in the same direction, often means that individual concerns are ignored.

Organizations use a variety of ploys to encourage people to put their own interests and personal concerns to one side or on the 'back burner'. Great emphasis is placed upon teamwork. Appeals are made for visible demonstrations of commitment, such as long hours of work. Role model managers become the modern equivalents of the heroic tractor driver who regularly exceeds norms of performance. Those who burn themselves out are thanked and disposed of.

Putting people under pressure may give them little scope for thinking about themselves and their families. The immediate prevails. Those suspected of reflecting upon the personal implications of corporate changes are made to feel selfish. They are accused of not 'seeing the big picture' or of not being 'team players'. They are made to feel guilty for not putting the group first. Persist and they may be thought to lack managerial qualities.

On occasion, the extent to which people subordinate their own interests to corporate purposes borders upon the perverse. In the natural world, individual animals of several species will sacrifice their lives to distract, or hold up, a predator so as to allow others of their group to escape. But the circumstances in which members of re-engineering teams work themselves out of a job, or people join project teams with little prospect of continuing employment on the completion of their work, are hardly 'life threatening'. Yet in most major corporations in recent years people with a variety of personal and financial commitments to others have 'committed job suicide'.

Breaking the Bonds of Dependency

It should not be wrong for people to question. Those with family obligations who are cautious, and who behave as responsible adults, should not be disadvantaged. A healthy level of self-interest is sensible. If people do not respect themselves, who else will? In many organizations it would be naïve to believe there are still people in personnel and other departments whose prime duty is to look after the interests of individual employees. The main focus of those who remain in these areas is likely to be upon the achievement of corporate objectives.

Individuals need to look after their own interests. Many should, and some must, make the journey from dependency to autonomy. Benign employers are few and far between among organizations of a certain size. Tough ones are widespread and ruthless ones are becoming more common.

People need to assess, realistically, where they stand. Most employees are not on the 'fast track'. With fewer positions at the top, whether or not one is a totally committed 'high flier' or belongs to an inside group or elite network – such as being an alumnus of l'ENA or l'Ecole Polytechnique in France – can become a more significant determinant of whether a person is destined to become a beneficiary or a victim of delayering. In the family-owned business, are the top slots already earmarked for certain close relations?

Open and confident organizations welcome a degree of scepticism and self-interest among their employees. Many corporations would have been spared the consequences of ill considered and half-baked initiatives if these had been subjected to greater questioning and their implications thought through. The best team to undertake a challenging mission is one made up of sturdy individualists with complementary skills who come together through choice, because they understand that through collaboration they can achieve both their individual objectives and a collective purpose.

To build an intelligent capability for facing the future, companies need to retain access to the skills and commitment of those who know what they are about. They need to ensure both their own continuing relevance and help their people to remain employable. Longer term success is more likely to occur where there is a community of fulfilled people who are learning and growing together.

Companies, such as Motorola and Canon, have consciously sought to create the conditions in which innovation can occur. Many others have a long way to go. The importance of initiative is not championed by those at the top. No one feels responsible for encouraging different alternatives, let alone breaking the mould. People are not inspired to dream. They are not networked together or equipped with the tools and processes to be inventive.

Becoming More Aware

In corporate contexts, people should reflect carefully upon what is happening to them. For example, the 'multi-skilling' that is ostensibly 'broadening' them could actually be de-skilling them. The 'workflow' systems and processes being installed, with their 'menus of options' and prescribed responses could deny individuals the opportunity to develop their own particular competencies.

As a result of becoming 'jacks of all trades and masters of none' people may lack a distinctive skill that would enable them to develop a successful second or third career as a consultant. By focusing upon their obligations, pleasing others and being dutiful and loyal, many people lose sight of their individuality and may act against their personal long-term interests.

Many employees feel over-worked, undervalued and ill-informed. People should be helped to become more aware of what is happening around them. Marks & Spencer and Willmott Dixon hold lunch-time discussion meetings at which current issues are considered and their impacts assessed. Xerox shares the results of internal and external assessment activities with its managers.

People should be told about the rationale and purpose of corporate initiatives and encouraged to think through what the implications for them are likely to be. They should be urged to assess what they will need to do in response and to articulate the nature of the support they will require from senior management in order to cope and prosper. Issue monitoring and management are not just for the big company. They are for individuals too.

In particular, people should assess whether they are a member of a 'natural' or 'family-sized' community. Units on a human scale are less likely to impose stress upon their members. Can people be themselves? Are knowledge and understanding easily shared? People have evolved over centuries to undertake certain forms of work most effectively in particular types of groups. The nature of the team that is most appropriate, and how focused, fast, flexible and fearless it needs to be, will depend upon the circumstances.

A structure, roles and responsibilities, and a mode of operation should be instinctively right for the particular context and the tasks to be undertaken. Thinking people do not passively assume that relevant questions have been asked. They actively critique the capability of their employer to cope. Is a company proactive or reactive? For example, does it go out and choose its customers? Is it standardizing or tailoring? How much emphasis does it place upon values and the quality of relationships and learning?

Often the companies best able to cope are those with the strongest beliefs, consistent standing and cherished values. People who buy a Coca-Cola know what to expect. The strength of a 'classic' brand is continuity not change. In contrast, customers purchasing 3M products may be confident that these are likely to represent 'state of the art' solutions. The corporation has a reputation for making innovation a normal activity.

Assessing Potential and Latent Qualities

An alien from Mars would have great difficulty explaining the existence and operation of many large organizations. The visitor would observe the denial of individuality, the imposition of corporate approaches to working and learning, the focus upon structures and systems rather than feelings, relationships and values and would struggle to find a plausible explanation.

Do earthlings aspire to become more like machines? The problem with this suggestion is the very different patterns of behaviour observed when people have some time for themselves and engage in various activities, ranging from sex to sport, that engage the senses. Many also enjoy solitary pursuits, such as walking, fishing or gardening. They become more individualistic.

Why is it that reluctant followers of a 'corporate line', become proactive champions of their favourite causes after they have left the office? People who would not say boo to a goose at work, brave all sorts of adversities to deliver charitable supplies. Known procrastinators become decisive when tackling a blaze as members of voluntary fire services. Quiet professionals have served in war zones while called up for military service. Either mice become lions or many more people than one might think have the potential to become heroes.

Do people have so much potential that organizations feel obliged to frustrate, inhibit and constrain them so that certain rewards, such as being distinctive through the possession of an impressive job title, may only be enjoyed by the few? Given the untapped reserves and latent qualities of most people and the many obstacles which organizations place in their path, this could be a plausible explanation.

Distinguishing Between Contributors and Parasites

Our sojourning Martian might also notice individuals in parasitic roles who do not appear to contribute value. For old-style organization-machine politicians who creep and crawl and slick and slime, the writing is on the wall. As more companies adopt various means of monitoring individual performance there are fewer places to hide.

Tracking who actually contributes and adds value can reveal many surprises. It can also highlight those upon whom the corporation depends and whose allegiance needs to be retained. On occasion such people are identified too late. They may have already decided they have 'had enough'. Some may have 'turned off'. Others may be planning to leave.

Teamwork sometimes provides the last refuge of scoundrels. However, when team performance bonuses are awarded and peer review systems are in place, teams can be robust when dealing with individual non-performers. Increasingly, people are expected to assume individual obligations and answerability. While supportive of those who are doing their best managers should not be reluctant, or ashamed, to be firm with free loaders.

Personal accountability attracts some and unnerves others. There are those who cling to the belief that greater responsibility will be for other people, perhaps the disaffected or foolhardy who 'jump ship' to establish their own companies, rather than themselves. They believe that by sitting tight the wave may wash over them leaving matters very much as before.

Over time there are likely to be fewer sinecures. Those who remain as salaried staff in larger organizations are increasingly likely to face many of the same challenges as independent operators. People will be expected to become intrepreneurs, negotiating with colleagues for a role in future projects. As a consequence, the distinction between employment and independent contractor status is likely to become less clear cut.

Training and development is an area in which many independent operators have felt themselves to be at a disadvantage compared with full-time employees, who go on various courses at the expense of their employers. Increasingly, this distinction is becoming blurred. Both employees and contractors are now expected to assume responsibility for their own development.

Where staff are mobile between employers and projects, companies question why they should be expected to pay the fees for MBA and other programmes, which may benefit an individual more than the organization. Many companies expect employees to pay part, or all, of the costs of such courses. Thus employee and non-employee are having to take similar decisions about the value and costeffectiveness of different development options.

Companies are also realizing that it is in their best interests for contractors and business partners to be competent and up to date at what they do. A value chain is only as strong as its weakest link. Hence all its members may need to remain at the cutting edge. Learning processes and shared learning should embrace all those responsible for delivering value to customers. Hence, contributing independent contractors should also share in corporately funded development opportunities.

Old and New Careers

Some people aim to benefit from both corporate and independent lifestyles by periodically moving between employment and self-employment as opportunities arise. Experiencing one allows people to appreciate the benefits of the other. How each is perceived will depend upon the individual. One person might regard a period with 'a job and a boss' as equivalent to a stay at an oasis after a term of exile in a barren desert. Another might regard it as a necessary evil, rather like having to walk off the beach for occasional visits to a lavatory.

Traditional careers were based upon linear thinking. They consisted of a succession of discrete steps. Some progressed quickly, gaining the fly wheel momentum to carry them forward. A few shot up like the trajectory of a rocket. Others moved more slowly, like the latter stages of a meandering river en route to the sea.

Professional development, and the collection of years of pensionable service, were cumulative activities. Life was viewed
in terms of ladders, escalators and steady progress, rather than
as an ever-changing context that provides multiple challenges
and opportunities.

In the real world regression can occur. Life is a game of
snakes and ladders. A person might be up at one moment and
down the next. Employability can be a constant worry. Without work today, how can an individual acquire and hone the
skills to be employable tomorrow?

Dead ends abound. So do difficult trade-offs. People may
want, indeed long, to break free to achieve a more balanced
life. At the same time, their desire for financial security can
cause them to hang on to their jobs. Many are not proud. Any
job that could help to pay off a housing loan or fund retirement
is welcome.

A ratchet effect used to operate. What one had was not taken
away. Although future progression might be uncertain, past
achievements were preserved. In our more competitive world
companies are finding it increasingly difficult to act as welfare
organizations.

As people physically, and in some cases morally, decay they
can deceive themselves in so many ways that they are still
'getting ahead'. Within the military, there are promotions to
'desk jobs' for those who can no longer handle front-line roles.
University staff have their academic designations, titles and
robes. There are also honorary degrees which, like State hon-
ours, are often conferred when an individual is at the point of
bowing out.

Many of the old notions of 'making progress' were based upon
a con or collective self-deception. Mechanisms abounded for
sustaining the illusion of advancement. For example, many
professional bodies had undemanding criteria for the award
of Fellowships. In return for paying the higher subscriptions
that filled organizational coffers individuals secured 'senior
grades of membership'.

For those interested in trappings, there are many devices
for securing voluntary input ranging from additional job titles
to fancy clothes. In time, those who undertake the 'donkey work'
of serving upon committees may obtain badges of office on rib-
bons which they can wear around their necks. They attend functions and are toasted.

Some people devote so much emphasis to attaining an alluring final destination that they manage to lose sight of important aspects of their journey through life. They are focused on tomorrow rather than today. Their preoccupation with the next move, prevents them from enjoying where they are at any moment of time.

Exercise: Likes and Dislikes

Objective and impartial analysis of a situation may be the right thing from a corporate perspective. However, those intent upon taking control of their lives should form a personal view of what they like and dislike about the alternatives open to them. They should pause, look and think before they jump.

People should not aim for theoretical solutions. Each person should determine the best course of action from their own individual perspective. The chosen option should be based upon what someone enjoys doing and, as a consequence, does well.

What do you most like or dislike about the situation you are in? What is missing? What could you do without? What would you like more of? Who do you most like or dislike among those around you? Which of them would you associate with, if you were free to choose your own colleagues?

Internal Markets

People can no longer afford to behave like privileged passengers who are along for the ride. Employees too have to manage their careers and proactively make contact with those likely to manage forthcoming projects. Internal markets are coming into operation. Individuals and groups are expected to seek out opportunities to contribute and to market and sell their skills and capabilities to other parts of the same company.

The extent of market operation may allow individuals to set the price at which they will offer their services. Inevitably there is a trade-off between fee rates and the volume of time that is bought. Personal incomes will reflect the forces of supply and demand. Such an approach fosters competition alongside collaboration and the efficient use of scarce talent. The better qualified gravitate to those projects that yield the highest margins, as these are more likely to be run by managers with the budgets to afford the most expensive people.

Corporate markets, and the signals they generate, encourage a more responsive and gradual adjustment to changing circumstances. Those, whose services are less in demand, find themselves with the time to acquire new skills in those areas experiencing shortages of qualified people.

On the other side of the coin, internal markets also put people under greater pressure. As with an independent consultant seeking to retain a valued relationship with a client, future prospects can depend upon perceived contribution to a current project. This can engender greater rivalry between people and lead to an unwillingness to share and help each other.

For many people, companionship is the most highly valued aspect of collective work. It can be undermined when each person seeks to 'play up' the importance of their particular inputs. Effective partnerships between people and organizations depend on trust. This needs to be earned and can rapidly erode when people feel their every move is being subjected to scrutiny and evaluation. Defensive, justificatory and risk-averse behaviour can result.

Some specialist individuals and groups may experience a steady decline in internal demand for their services. In response, they could seek the freedom to offer their services to non-competing organizations. The Shandwick Group grew out of an internal PR team that took such a step.

Selling services externally can spread 'overhead costs'. The host company can benefit from privileged access to a team, to the extent required, while the people concerned can develop their competencies as a result of a wider range of experience. Working for other companies may also give them a comparative understanding of how different organizations deal with similar issues.

In time, the volume of work done elsewhere may suggest a change of formal status and the transition from employee or internal unit to independent operation. Such a mutually agreed step can be both pragmatic and incremental. It is less traumatic than the traditional practice of enduring a prolonged period of anxiety, during which various attempts are made at concealment, work creation or protection, followed by redundancy and the need to rapidly retrain and find alternative work at a time of maximum vulnerability and pressure. The individual is forced to become reactive and may feel a victim. The nature of the 'termination' itself can be emotionally draining and may prejudice a continuing relationship between the parties concerned.

In many companies, 'purchasers' of services are no longer required to buy exclusively from within. They are able to look outside and obtain what they need elsewhere, as and when it is appropriate to do so. Increasingly, internal providers find themselves in direct competition with external contractors. Whole departments are required to justify their continuing existence as corporate entities in the face of various purchasing and outsourcing alternatives.

Assessing Lifestyle Options

Increasingly, people should think in terms of activities rather than 'work'. If tasks, such as shopping, gardening or cleaning, cooking and washing within the home, had to be paid for the Gross Domestic Product of many countries would double. Where 'markets' or 'exchanges' for such personal services are established, and people arrange to help each other on a reciprocal basis, dependence upon paid work is significantly reduced.

Some people build a business out of a hobby or a passion. George Davies developed Cambridge Management Centres and designed a purpose built training facility, to offer the type of programme which he enjoyed delivering. Import/export houses can grow out of a fascination with particular products or countries. James Hobbs and Graeme Love, the founders of the Indian Ocean Trading Company, import teak garden furniture from Madagascar. Snapdragon retails craft products from various exotic locations in Asia, which its founders love visiting.

Paid work, which dominates so many lives, needs to be kept in perspective. It is not the whole of human existence. Yet many millions of people find it difficult to 'package and market' themselves. They feel trapped. They are dependent upon their jobs, both for a salary to meet today's bills and for a pension to cover tomorrow's expenses.

The good news is that while large companies have been busy shedding staff, smaller enterprises have been quietly hiring people. In the United States the health of the emerging business sector is such that net employment levels have increased. While not all the new jobs are full-time, or as well paid as

past corporate sinecures, they can offer people opportunities for more balanced lives.

Responses from students on MBA programmes, who have
been asked to describe where they would like to be within five,
ten and fifteen years suggest that smaller entrepreneurial companies are growing in attractiveness at the expense of giant
corporations. Energetic individuals are, increasingly, viewing
jobs with large companies and leading consulting firms as an
interim period of valuable preparation for eventual leadership
roles within their own organizations.

Many people underestimate the extent of the discretion and
choice which they have. Whether because of inertia, modesty
or not being aware of alternatives, they become passive reac-
tors, rather than active directors of their own destiny. They
are so preoccupied with survival and coping with stress that
they have little opportunity to develop sufficient self-worth
to take control of their lives.

There are many moves which can be made at most stages of
the game of life. Some consider all the available options at
every decision point. Others adopt a 'me-too' approach. They
simply follow the flow, perhaps by climbing upon an escalator
that is going in a desired direction or which has what appears
to be a sought after goal at its end.

Some options may be incremental, they could be added to
existing roles without replacing them. Thus someone could
become a non-executive director, take on a voluntary activity
with a professional body or charity or agree to lead particular
sessions at a local college or university. Time could also be
devoted to activities that do not involve adoption of a formal
position. For example, learning a language, pursuing a hobby,
travelling or playing a sport.

The alternatives may vary in attainability. Many people are
attracted by the prospect of one or more non-executive directorships. However, there is usually a huge imbalance in
the supply and demand. Typically, many hundreds of people
are chasing each available vacancy.

Well-qualified individuals with golden careers sometimes
find themselves waiting for years for the right directorship
opportunity to come along. And when it does, they may quickly
realize the full extent of their legal duties and responsibilities.
These are onerous and daunting in relation to the relatively
modest fees which are often offered. In comparison, consul-

tancy may appear to offer more generous levels of remuneration for substantially less risk.

Lifestyle Strategies

Certain options could be undertaken on a part-time basis in order to sample the lifestyle concerned. Putting a toe in the water can enable people to know themselves better and 'the market'. It can help them prepare more effectively for the 'big one'. Over time, a particular activity could grow into a full-time commitment. For example, the occasional session on a weekend MBA could lead to a permanent appointment at a local university.

It is possible to experience a number of quite distinct, and alternative, careers during the course of a life. One option does not necessarily need to be forgone to pursue another. Thus a person with a penchant for both university and commercial life could move between academic and consultancy roles or pursue both concurrently, perhaps through a visiting appointment. Many of the associates of Attitudes Skills and Knowledge have visiting or part-time university appointments among their multiple roles.

Some individuals move periodically into and out of full-time roles, with consultancy or interim assignments in between. An enlightened company is aware of the benefits of bringing on board experiences from the outside world. It might welcome a periodic 'fix' from someone who appreciates its particular requirements. As a result of understanding the culture, the regular visitor – like a migrating bird – is more likely to know what to expect and what is relevant.

Some people take to self-fulfillment to such an extent that they become 'serial entrepreneurs'. They may establish a succession of businesses, interspersed with periods of reflection or a change of scene, such as sailing a yacht. One form of indulgence may lead to others or make them more possible. It might require the solitude of a jog along the Great Wall of China and the time this would take, to think through fully the next business concept.

Different patterns of work provide their own distinct challenges. The flexibility and relative freedom of the portfolio life-style has to be balanced against the sense of isolation that can arise when people sense that others regard them as outsiders. Those who naturally attract similar opportunities have to be sensitive to possible conflicts of interest and competing claims upon their time. The greater the income that is sought the more intense these pressures can become.

The team that founded The Networking Firm consisted entirely of people with significant stakes in two or more enterprises. The overlapping areas of operation of the companies concerned could have led to divided loyalties. Instead, recognition of similar and complementary perspectives and objectives formed the cement that held the group together. It produced a whole that is greater than the sum of the parts.

Great opportunities do not always arrive on the doorstep clearly labelled. If they were that obvious they might not be so precious. In reality, they can be elusive. Sometimes they are concealed or disguised. It is possible to tramp through the jungle, oblivious to hidden temples that may be only a few feet away. Those who hurry, or are harassed or preoccupied, may not notice what is under their noses.

Some individuals prepare a life plan at an early age. They set out on a particular journey with such confidence, dedication and premonition that they could attempt to write their obituary on day one. Others are more flexible. They move unexpectedly and spontaneously between different worlds, as if attempting to live more than one existence. They wander off the beaten track, as the fancy takes them, and discover the temple in the jungle.

Many options are not mutually exclusive or self-contained. Thus one could be an owner/director, with a part-time contract of employment or a consultancy arrangement with the company concerned. Certain combinations of roles can be complementary. They may also vary over time. Sometimes a change can be as good as a rest.

Exercise: Impact and Reaction Analysis

Various challenges and opportunities are coming your way. Like rain clouds or a shower of meteorites, you know they are approaching. But you may not be sure about what their impacts are going to be or how you will react. Forewarned is forearmed. You need to think through their likely impacts and your possible reactions.

What is coming your way? What are the consequences likely to be for you personally? How are you likely to react? Are there other options? What would improve your ability to cope? Are there impacts which you could deflect or avoid? How might you benefit from what is about to happen?

Meeting the Requirements

The observant may notice a variety of different development paths and routes through life. Some will be more frequented than others. Various institutes and associations offer guided tours. Progress can depend upon understanding the 'rules of the particular game'. Mentors and counsellors may advise upon what it takes to succeed in this vocation or that profession.

Career patterns, and their requirements, will depend upon what it is that people set out to do. Some aim to become outstanding or pre-eminent. Others are content to be acceptable or respectable. Individuals can measure themselves against the performance of others or in relation to their own potential. Inwardly directed people may only have themselves to satisfy and their own self-respect to sustain.

Some ways of working are easier to adopt than others. People do not always match their aspirations to their personal strengths and weaknesses. Thus, some seek to become independent consultants with little or no experience of defining work in output terms, negotiating a contract or planning an assignment.

Many people operate as if subject to a law which states that prospects and clients have to be corporate entities. Those with an interest in helping others could develop practices to provide counselling, mentoring or advisory services to private individuals.

People can, and do, subject themselves to all manner of tests in order to determine their prospects and potential. They assess the compatibility of their natures and attributes with the assumed requirements for excelling in a particular field. Often this means benchmarking themselves against some notion of a typical, or average, practitioner – not exactly a recipe for standing out or becoming an exceptional talent.

Members of the public display certain attitudes towards established professions or harbour particular preconceptions

about them. Those in some roles may find themselves acting a
part. An important rationale of formal qualifications is that
'others will know what to expect'. Professional bodies establish
standards and codes, while those working independently, or in
other fields, may have to determine these for themselves. Some
individuals are lazy customers and hide behind certificates and
kitemarks when making purchase decisions.

Inevitably a degree of compromise is involved when people
seek to adjust to, or fit in with, whatever is demanded or expected of them. Such accommodation can be avoided by those
who play according to their own rules. They recognize their
own individuality and distinctiveness. They accept that they
do not need to conform to stereotyped images or norms. They
set out to be true to themselves and to be judged on their own
merits.

Someone, who cannot be categorized easily, may find it more
difficult to secure recognition. This dilemma is often faced by
those who aspire to act as a much needed link between distinct
areas or recognized roles. They fall into a boggy wasteland of
uncertainty between islands of activity that are better understood. It is sometimes necessary to make a choice, for example
between the pursuit of that which is easy or that which is actually needed.

Single or Multiple Activities

Different lifestyle options have their own distinct advantages
and disadvantages. Thus, in comparison with a portfolio of specific assignments, a single project or interim appointment might
provide a greater depth of immersion and a more holistic learning experience. It may create an opportunity to secure a more
intimate understanding of a particular organization and a more
extensive exposure to contemporary issues and concerns. Links
could be forged with a wider range of contacts within a single
organization.

However, the benefits of total and monogamous involvement
may be secured at a cost. One may lose touch with contacts in
other areas and not follow up alternative prospects. Certain
opportunities may fall by the wayside. While heavily engaged
in a particular project there may not be time to develop new
relationships. A period of intense involvement may be followed
by a stretch of inactivity. While some may prefer to work in

concentrated bursts, others might find the time between as-signments unsettling and may prefer a more even spread of work.

Maintaining a portfolio of roles reduces the risk of depend-ency upon a single income stream. However, it can be very difficult to achieve when individual clients demand a full-time commitment. If there is a steady turnover of projects, with fresh ones coming on stream as others are completed, peaks and troughs in workload may not be so extreme.

With multiple activities, it may also be possible to avoid the 'feast and famine' syndrome. Marketing initiatives can be more easily built into the normal week. There are more likely to be existing tasks that one can be getting on with while waiting for 'final decisions' in relation to future work.

Current or past employers should not be overlooked. Inter-personal skills sometimes lead to contracts and continuing in-come. For example, a company could retain one or more former employees to help counsel a cadre of managers. A part-time role could supplement other earnings.

Much depends upon the nature of the individual assignments that are taken on and how compatible they are with each other. Where different projects make inconsistent or contradictory demands, or too many of them run alongside each other, a de-gree of overload may be experienced. Even temporary periods of distraction, or individual clashes of dates, can lead to a cli-ent feeling disappointed. It may not prove possible to keep all the balls in the air at the same time. At its worst, they may all be dropped.

As with non-executive directorships it is possible to become over-loaded as a result of taking on an excessive number of parallel appointments or activities. The last straw may break the camel's back. The stress and unravelling points come ear-lier for some individuals than for others. People need to be realistic when assessing how many commitments they can take on and effectively discharge at any one time.

Realities of the Marketplace

Those with a penchant for the individual lifestyle of the inde-pendent contractor should think carefully about the likely market for the services which they would like to offer and how they might set about reaching it. They should also assess opportunities from a customer perspective and reflect upon whether or not they have what it would take to succeed. Just because a gap or requirement exists, it does not follow that every entrant into the marketplace will 'make a go of it'.

Identifying trends and opportunities is one thing, reacting appropriately is quite another. Major corporations, with all their resources and extensive advice at their command, make mistakes. They respond inadequately, misunderstand requirements or misread signals, as happened with the Ford Edsel car. Individuals can also get it wrong. All or nothing strategies are high risk.

Aspiring to a high income can become a source of anxiety and strain. There are only so many chargeable days in the year, and self-employed sole practitioners may need to be personally involved with their clients. Time has also to be allocated to marketing and development activities. While a comfortable existence may be possible, some find that, unless they are superstars and able to sell their time at high fee rates, it is difficult to become seriously rich.

There may be practical limits to what one person can achieve. Those wishing to realize large capital gains and join the ranks of the very wealthy, may need to consider the establishment of a business that sells the time of others or some form of manufactured product. If it is ultimately to be sold, the business will probably need to become independent of its founders and able to continue without their involvement.

To take charge of one's life choices must be made. Ultimately, these will depend upon personal preferences and qualities. It is up to us. We can be observers or participants. We can avoid or engage. We can dither or act. Pilchards can be left on the quay to rot or they can be taken home and made into a star-gazey pie.

Checklist

1. Why are you engaged in what you are doing today? Are the reasons still valid? Is it because of necessity or choice?

2. Will your business, or the organization that employs you, still exist in five or ten year's time? What is there that is distinctive or special about its vision and values?

3. What major threats are looming in the background that could possibly turn your world upside down? Where are the areas of vulnerability?

4. How secure are you in what you have accomplished? Have you already succeeded in attaining cherished goals? Do you feel good inside?

5. What is your own self-image? How does this match, or differ from, the image that others have of you because of your work?

6. How are your job and employing organization likely to change over the next few years? Will your own profile match likely future requirements and your personal aspirations?

7. Do you anticipate something different or more of the same? How will your development and perceived value be affected? Will you become more or less marketable?

8. Are there areas or roles from which you have been excluded? Who else could perform your current job as effectively, if not more so?

9. How much control do you have over your life? If you continue as before, is this likely to increase or decrease?

10. What do colleagues think of you? Are you perceived as plateaued or as having potential?

11. How much freedom of action do have? How adequate is your pension provision? For how long could you survive on whatever level of redundancy payment you might receive?

12.   What is most likely to happen to you? For how much longer will your current contract(s) run? Who will decide your fate or what will resolve it?

13.   What has already been determined? Are you likely to become more or less fulfilled as a result?

14.   Who, if anyone, is really interested in your prospects? Who would send you a Christmas card a year after you have left your current role? What about the cards that 'come from the past'? What are their senders up to?

15.   Are there other roles, patterns of work or lifestyles for which you would be more suited? Has something which someone else has recently done 'caught your eye'?

4

WHAT DOES IT TAKE TO SUCCEED?

Primroses stand out from the weeds.

Chickens peck about. They huddle together but do not really notice each other. They seek security in numbers, like dependents upon an organization. Their futures are determined by others and their options are limited. So long as they continue to lay they receive a regular and standard ration of food. The chickens are insiders and yet vulnerable.

The fox is on the outside, but free. It is more focused and single-minded than the chicken. While it can be spontaneously opportunistic, it also thinks through how to take advantage of particular circumstances. It is quite happy to be outnumbered by the chickens. The fox can survive on its own. Its security does not come from external fencing but from its inner resourcefulness and cunning. Those it cannot outwit, it aims to outrun.

Ascendant Attributes

Many companies have, traditionally, rewarded loyalty. People have been encouraged to 'fit in' with corporate requirements in return for some expectation of continuing employment. Like chickens, if they remained in the coop they were fed. However, corporate assumptions, expectations and practices are changing.

New qualities are required to succeed and sustain relationships, in the age of interdependence and connectivity which is emerging. The nature of these will evolve over time, according to changes in the situation, circumstances and context and what particular individuals are seeking to achieve. They may not necessarily be the attributes which many organizations have, in the past, been eager to encourage and develop.

Vanguard is in the pharmaceutical business. Similar to other companies which have adopted a virtual model of operation, it has encountered an additional range of management problems that can result from building relationships with a network of subcontractors. These range from managing the contractual process, to resolving disputes and the establishment and protection of intellectual property rights when multiple parties are involved.

Many corporations have bred a certain restlessness into their people. The relentless search for greater flexibility and speed, has created an automatic assumption that change is desirable. Perhaps too much emphasis has been given to novelty at the expense of ensuring a degree of continuity of those factors which can enable people to cope successfully with innovation and uncertainty. As in many other areas, a greater sense of proportion is needed.

Perhaps, above all, what is required is the ability to strike a balance or equilibrium between forces and pressures which may have hitherto been regarded as contending rather than complementary. Thus, in order to build upon their natural strengths, people may have to become more individualistic and self-aware, while, at the same time, showing greater sensitivity and empathy towards fellow members of collaborative networks.

Companies that fail to 'move up the value chain' will find themselves losing opportunities to competitors in lower wage economies. To generate greater value they need to tap more of the potential of their people. They need more foxes, people who can both co-operate and think for themselves, those who are prepared to go out and to look for and create opportunities. They need the self-contained, savvy and streetwise, rather than drones, deadheads and dependents.

The Age of the Corporate Clone

Past agendas, determined by those at the top of many organizations, discouraged individuality and dulled entrepreneurial instincts. The 'rules of the game', the same procedures, were applied to all. Corporations used standard policies, whether on assessment, 'benefits' or the size and decor of offices, regardless of individual circumstances.

In the search for economies of scale, the emphasis was upon long manufacturing runs of homogenous products. Tools and techniques were employed to 'reduce variation'. Those who used their imaginations and did things differently were disruptive. They generated waves. They created problems for systems and confounded customer expectations of uniformity.

The subdivision of labour, with its attendant job descriptions and organization charts, meant that people thought they were needed. They could see where they fitted in. Head office executives felt secure in the belief that their 'long experience', and their knowledge of corporate mechanisms and expectations, would always be required.

It was assumed that one's 'seniors' were older and wiser. Competition for promotion was largely against lateral colleagues, other individuals within the same organization. These were people who were known. There was less chance, than is the case today, of a person's prospects being frustrated by the sudden arrival of new faces.

The bureaucratic model of organization proved effective throughout the duration of whole management careers. Controls were in place to reduce the prospect of unwelcome surprises. Competitors were known. Size appeared to be a distinct advantage. The logic of economies of scale and 'learning curves' enabled domestic companies to replicate themselves in a succession of overseas markets. In the process, the largest of them became multinationals.

As corporate staffs at head offices increased, and more support and co-ordination roles were created, even those on the slow track had opportunities to progress. Length of service in certain countries, such as the UK and US, brought the protection of inflation-proofed pensions in old age. Individuals were seen to benefit directly from the improved performance of their employing organizations. Desired corporate behaviour led directly to individual rewards.

More recently, this model of operation has started to break down. The process of transition is more advanced in some sectors and markets than in others, but the trend is clear. More emphasis is being placed upon tailoring, diversity, flexibility, empowerment and multi-skilling.

Clones can struggle when conditions change and past certainties no longer apply. Big company managers are often naïve when confronted with new and unexpected problems and opportunities. Entrepreneurs need the ability to look ahead and the instinct to distinguish between initiatives that will cover today's costs, and those that will build value for the future.

The relationship between IBM and Microsoft, a small enterprise to which responsibility for developing the operating system for the computer giant's first PC was outsourced, is a much quoted example of a minnow darting where a whale would wallow. IBM's highly paid executives handed one of the global opportunities of the century to a start-up enterprise.

Changing Requirements for Corporate Success

New agendas need to be established. Yesterday's critical success factors may not be relevant in tomorrow's world. Indeed, great success can lead to arrogance, complacency and inflexibility. People come to believe they have 'got what it takes'. As a consequence, they may be reluctant to listen to others and to learn from them.

Too much can be made of the advantages of scale. Usinor Sacilor, the steel producer, was one of the first companies in France to adopt 'total quality management'. With its reputation for quality, and protected by its size in the marketplace, it felt secure. Its managers were not prepared for the challenge of 'mini-mills', which could produce good quality steel from scrap, while requiring a quarter of the capital investment of a traditional integrated mill.

Around the world, new entrants quickly established profitable operations based on 'mini-mill' technology, while traditional suppliers, which had failed to adapt to a 'discontinuity' in the development of technology, struggled to break even. The scale of investment in a previous generation of technology proved to be a barrier to the evaluation and adoption of new alternatives.

The value of knowledge is often exaggerated, while the significance of learning and innovation are frequently overlooked. A stock of 'commodity knowledge' can quickly become out of date. It may also be easily accessible to others. More important is the ability to apply quickly understanding to the process of value creation and the capacity to learn and to develop the know-how that will be relevant for future opportunities.

In order to both think and act, the knowledge company needs a body as well as a brain. Intellect must also be accompanied by imagination, insight, inspiration and intent. As the Learning Systems Institute has pointed out, in uncertain and changing times knowing how to do things can be more important than knowing what to do. However, much of the work being devoted to developing competencies is equipping people to do things in a particular situation and context. When these change, the skills of those who are supposedly competent may no longer be relevant.

In the past, excessive emphasis was placed upon rationality. Empathy, instincts and feelings were unfairly maligned. Bright people can develop intellectual capital, but commercial value results from its deployment in the context of a relationship with a paying customer. Intellectual abilities, such as quantitative and reasoning skills, need to be accompanied by emotional, social and relational intelligence. Companies and headhunters, such as Egon Zehnder, increasingly take these factors into account when selection and recruitment decisions are made.

BP and Kellogg have found that the qualities needed to obtain regular promotion and to climb to the very top of a corporation, may be different from those required to lead it into the future. Some people find it difficult to alter their leadership style as issues and priorities, and those around them, change. Our models need to be dynamic and organic, rather than static and mechanical.

Exercise: Eclipse Analysis

The qualities and competencies of people should be compatible with their present roles, and also any future ones. The degree of overlap between personal and role profiles can reveal the extent to which there is a match or mismatch. It may help to think in terms of an eclipse.

There needs to be some overlap or compatibility, for an eclipse to occur. However, a total eclipse requires careful interpretation. It could indicate a perfect matching, or that a person has been taken over completely by a role and that any distinct individuality is likely to be blacked out while the eclipse lasts.

Draw personal and role profiles, in the form of circles around attributes and requirements, upon sheets of acetate. When they are put alongside, or on top of

each other, is there a degree of overlap? Is it just discernible or clearly apparent? Is there a natural fit or does the matching appear contrived? Is your employer pushing for a greater or lesser degree of compatibility? What are the implications of this? Will your personal profile continue to meet the requirements of the role?

Recognising and Reconciling Conflicting Interests

Ambitious corporations, and staff seeking advancement, face challenges from unknown competitors. Steady incremental progress and job security can no longer be assumed. Staying solvent and remaining employed have become more of a challenge.

When people and organizations are under pressure, relationships between them can suffer. Their respective perceived self-interests may diverge. Contemporary approaches to management often achieve improvements in corporate performance at the expense of the people in the organization. Employees are subjected to ever greater demands as a consequence of the twin drives for greater productivity and lower costs.

Both organizations and individuals are having to refocus, and establish roles for themselves in new games. If their respective concerns and requirements are not reconciled, they may come into conflict. Corporate actions sometimes undermine the very positions they are designed to protect.

Some companies are keen to encourage dependence upon their particular systems and procedures, and to establish their own identities as suppliers. They may not wish to empower people to such an extent that individuals develop reputations and a standing in their own right. Moving them around the organization or across accounts, and a subdivision of labour within teams, may all be designed to reduce the risk of staff setting up their own businesses and perhaps taking one or more clients with them. However, customers may react against these policies. For example, they might poach staff in order to secure a greater continuity of relationship or look elsewhere.

Teamwork is a corporate defense mechanism that may not be in the best long-term interests of those seeking to build portfolio careers around distinct competencies. People can become lost in a featureless swamp of ever changing groups and teams, their individual identity submerged beneath the weight of 'tick list' approaches, the firm's methodologies, standard competencies and role model behaviours. Over time, and as a consequence of not being required to take an individual position on issues, they may lose any strong sense of who they are.

At the same time, one should not underestimate the power of effective teamwork. Innovative teams respect individuality and encourage diversity. With more parties to accommodate, systems to integrate, and knowledge to assimilate, assembling the right team is likely to become more rather than less important. Great teams, as well as outstanding men and women, contribute to the advance of human civilization and improvement in the quality of our lives.

Establishing Common Ground

Members of industrial and information societies are often alienated from their employers and from themselves. The hectic pace of modern corporate life does not provide them with the time, space, motivation or freedom to think. For some, the only opportunity to 'get away from it all' maybe to break out. Yet more companies could provide their people with scope and opportunity for reflection and self-discovery. Some do. They recognize that personal exploration and development can benefit an organization as well as those directly concerned.

A succession of innovations have emanated from Bell Labs and Xerox PARC. While the initial sparks of creativity may ignite in individual minds, interaction with respected colleagues, possessing complementary qualities, can fan the flames of inspiration. Participation in an inventive culture, and a supporting infrastructure, may enable promising lines of enquiry to be followed up more quickly and effectively.

The cartoons that brought some magic into the lives of millions of unemployed people during the inter-war period were the result of collective effort. Individuals could not have generated the great number of drawings required. The were produced by creative teams working together within studios founded by Walt Disney and other pioneers.

The design consultancy Elmwood provides its people with a meditation room, a secular equivalent of the private chapel in a cathedral. They can escape from bothersome colleagues and the hubbub and frenetic distractions of office life. For a few precious moments they can be at peace with their inner selves. They can simply stop and think.

Many people focus upon personal differences rather than common interests. They fail to campaign from within for more creative and fulfilling working environments. They miss opportunities. They live or hide behind prison bars that have either been erected by colleagues or are self-imposed. In some cases, the barriers may be psychological, shackles of the mind.

Not all companies are equally receptive. Constraints and inhibitors can vary from the mild and subtle, to the painfully overt. However, people should try. Cell bars may be rigid, but they can also be permeable. A wide range of external messages and influences, some threatening and others comforting, may pass between them.

A realistic assessment should be made of how fertile corporate soil is likely to be. People are frequently naïve. They may not realize they have become trapped by circumstances or market forces. The cause might be innocence or a lack of awareness. Perhaps they are too busy. Some endeavour not to notice, or they refuse to accept, how vulnerable their employing organization may have become.

Others overreact against restructuring and 'head count reduction' programmes. They regard themselves as victims, abused by corporate power. They view their superiors as jailers. They feel trapped, as if condemned to a Siberian labour camp from which there is no escape. They sense they are doomed to working ever harder to maintain a current standard of living.

Both viewpoints can lead to unhealthy responses to personal and corporate challenges. Successful transformation, for both individuals and organizations, requires that each should recognize the importance of the other. So long as there is a prospect of mutually beneficial collaboration, both sets of aspirations should be accommodated in the responses of each party.

Glaxo Wellcome sets out to equip its people with whatever it takes to succeed within the company and elsewhere. While the company recognizes it might be developing researchers for rival pharmaceutical companies, employability now and in the future is a priority concern of the most talented researchers it seeks to attract.

Pacific Bell and the Communications Workers of America union formed a partnership based upon commitments to update skills and provide career counselling. The aim was not to guarantee people's jobs but to enhance their continuing employability.

The Frontier Spirit

Whether in jail or gently punting and blissfully unaware of a weir ahead, people are increasingly on their own. Colleagues are just too busy to notice someone else's burdens and anguish. Besides, dependency cultures are on the way out. Companies are becoming more like frontier towns. Sturdy and self-reliant people who respect themselves, and are prepared to look after themselves, have the best chance of surviving the winter.

Increasingly, people are expected to take responsibility for their personal careers and development. Those operating as sole practitioners, whether through positive action to take control of their lives, or as a consequence of redundancy, have little option but to determine their own future. They cannot assume that anyone else is looking after their interests.

The self-employed should think of themselves in terms of capabilities and aspirations. A balance needs to be struck between the two, based upon an honest assessment of personal strengths and weaknesses in relation to the challenges and opportunities that are faced. Many people are having to face up to marketing themselves for the first time, not just on the occasion when they are seeking a new job, but throughout the year.

Employees operating within organizational contexts, can find themselves in a similar position. Corporate structures and arrangements tend to be temporary and subject to frequent review. As situations and circumstances change, against a backdrop of drives for greater performance and lower costs, employment resembles a game of musical chairs rather than steady progress up a corporate escalator. Those at the top decide which music to play and when to switch it on and off. The players are left to find a place on a diminishing number of seats.

There is greater delegation and more emphasis upon tailoring, getting it right for the individual customer. Those, who hitherto found that important matters were decided for them by their seniors within the corporate structure, are now in the front-line. They are empowered, grouped with others in self-managed groups. The 'centre' gives them direction, goals, objectives and targets, and they are expected to determine themselves the best means of achieving them.

Each employee is asked to display initiative and add value. Instead of merely operating within a standard and prescriptive corporate framework, people are invited to come forward with suggestions for improvements. In theory, they are counselled, advised and mentored, rather than controlled. They are expected to be visible and accountable. They are encouraged to take ownership of relationships with their particular customers.

People are expected to be self-motivated, to build relationships and to look for incremental business opportunities. They need to be self-starters when it comes to their own development, proactive users of whatever corporate learning support is provided. They are required to negotiate their own roles with colleagues within the framework of project teams and activity work groups.

Each individual is under perpetual pressure to demonstrate relevance. Continuing employment cannot be assumed. It has to be earned or justified. When tasks and projects are completed people re-enter the 'internal' or corporate labour market. Like the self-employed, they have to think ahead, anticipate, network, position themselves for a role in the next round or game.

Blurring of Boundaries

The distinction between the security and rigidity of employment and the uncertainty and flexibility of working for oneself, is becoming less clear cut. Many people have a greater say over the terms upon which they are remunerated and the nature of the benefits they opt to take. Increasingly, rewards reflect individual and team performance rather than corporate grade.

As corporate entities restructure into smaller units, each of which is given a variety of performance targets and made responsible for its own destiny, they increasingly resemble portfolios of separate businesses. Many corporate centres now act as bankers. Business units are provided with certain resources and are expected to generate a rate of return that will reflect an assessment of the challenges and opportunities they face.

Increasingly, management teams within companies are expected to display many of the qualities and characteristics of independent entrepreneurs. So much is made of the divide between employment and self-employment that other distinctions are overlooked, such as that between those who seek and readily take personal responsibility and those who avoid it.

Those who accept personal and collective responsibility for their futures and acknowledge accountability to those who have provided them with resources, or are dependent upon them, generally find it easier to move from one form of employment to another. Where there is the possibility of a management buy out, a team of people may find themselves undertaking a journey of transition from dependent employee to owner manager or director of an independent company.

The Right Stuff

People do not necessarily need to be exceptionally talented or gifted to take control of their own lives. Simple, indeed quite ordinary, individuals sometimes have great empathy with their customers. People of talent are sometimes so self-absorbed as to be insensitive to the requirements of others.

Significantly, many of those who have succeeded through political skills, and a mixture of dedication and cunning, in climbing the ranks of bureaucratic corporations make poor entrepreneurs. When setting up their own businesses they discover certain hard truths. While a subordinate can be ordered about, the customer with a choice cannot be compelled to buy.

Often it is the 'lesser lights', those who have done their best to be helpful to others, perhaps to the disadvantage of their own careers, who are more successful when establishing their own professional practice or setting up as an independent tradesperson. Potential customers may sense that they will be concerned with delivering value, rather than squeezing the maximum of benefit for themselves out of every transaction.

Increasingly, individuals who are intensely competitive may be at a disadvantage. They may see life in 'black and white' and 'zero-sum' terms. Their concern is more likely to be with whether they, as individuals, win or lose compared with their arch rivals when promotion and other decisions are taken. Ultimately, until one has had a chance to assess their capability, every colleague encountered in a pyramid bureaucracy is a potential adversary. To succeed in collaborative relationships, a different mind set is required, one that is concerned with benefits for all the parties that are involved.

Individuals who are perceived as 'wheeler dealers' may find themselves less in demand when the emphasis switches from 'doing deals' to building longer term relationships which depend upon trust and mutual respect. While a longer term strategy may build for the future, a focus upon quick returns from frequent transactions can erode value. This could be as true for personal relationships as it is with investment portfolios. In the financial arena, the best advice may be to select carefully and hold for the longer term.

Ethical awareness, and qualities such as integrity, are likely to become more important. In short-term cultures, in which people are under continuing pressure to perform, they may feel tempted to 'cut corners'. Some might do whatever is necessary to 'get the business'. This is not the best recipe for building longer term relationships.

In an era of collaboration and shared learning, both between partners and along value chains, people are opting to work with those on whom they can rely. Those suspected of being 'sharp' may find themselves limited to being suppliers of commodity products that are bought upon the basis of price. Moving up the value chain may require collaborative relationships that involve the sharing of risk and the exposure of intellectual property. Too much is at stake to take risks. Only parties that trust each other are likely to co-operate.

Exercise: Personal Balance Sheet

Companies undertake strengths, weaknesses, opportunities and threats (SWOT) analyses. The significance and relevance of strengths and weaknesses depend upon how they relate to opportunities and threats. You could undertake a personal SWOT analysis. Alternatively, if you have already identified the challenges which you face and their likely impacts, you could draw up a personal balance sheet. This might enable you to identify areas of relative deficiency. What, or who, are your major assets or liabilities?

List them. Distinguish between those which are temporary (i.e. current) and those which are more permanent or are likely to persist for some time (i.e. fixed). If you were to strike a balance, would you have net assets (assets exceed liabilities) or net liabilities (liabilities exceed assets)? Is there sufficient of a positive margin to enable you to succeed? What steps could you take (e.g. build or acquire assets and reduce liabilities) in order to strengthen your balance sheet?

Age Considerations

Many companies in Western societies, which have ageing populations, excessive emphasis is placed upon youth. These companies overlook the benefits of age and experience. Older employees are assumed to be inflexible and set in their ways, rather than a source of knowledge and experience that could benefit others.

Corporate policies often fail to distinguish between individuals. Those beyond a certain age may be automatically excluded, regardless of their personal qualities, when hiring and promotional decisions are taken. Such an approach could be based upon the mistaken assumption that companies get less of a return when training older employees. In practice, a higher rate of turnover of younger staff may actually mean their development is more likely to benefit competitors.

Younger employees may be more willing to be mobile, but they can also be anxious, competitive, headstrong and impulsive. They are still searching and striving. Many become obsessed with getting ahead and making an impact. They perceive life as a race against time. Burn out often results.

Older people can often afford to be more relaxed and laid back. Life may have given them a more balanced perspective. They may be better able to handle lateral moves. Some will have 'seen it all before'. They think before rushing in. They have got youthful enthusiasms out of their system, and they know who they are. As a consequence, they can be more patient, open minded and tolerant. They may also be more willing to share.

Certain physical capabilities can, and, do decline with age, although the extent and impact will vary from person to person. Many cognitive abilities can remain effective to the age of retirement. Areas of deficiency can also be compensated for by learning how move closer to the limits of one's potential.

Crude information, processing power is of less value in an age of widespread access to information technology. The ability to relate information to experience, the perspective to understand its significance, and the recognition of links and patterns, may actually improve with age. An older person may have a greater pool of different, but related, cases or situations to draw upon.

Older people sometimes appear to be slower learners. This is often because they can also be more careful learners. They may be more willing to question and reflect upon what they read or are told. They may also be more conscious of, and interested in, the 'inner person'. They can be more sensitive to others, and more concerned about them.

B&Q stores have positively recruited older staff. They find that many retired people have greater empathy with customers than 'youngsters' who simply regard their 'job' as 'a way of getting some money'. Mature employees are prepared to take the time to talk through requirements with customers. With homes of their own, many of them will have undertaken 'do-it-yourself' type jobs over the years. Hence they understand what is required. They are better able to relate what is on offer to the particular requirements of individual customers.

Many companies are striving to make the 'quick in, do the deal, out and onto the next one' culture a thing of the past. As the emphasis switches to the building and nurturing of longer term relationships, the greater wisdom that often comes with age may no longer be perceived as a penalty. It may come to be valued and might actually attract a premium.

In the meantime, personal planning should take account of the reality of whatever age discrimination exists, rather than what ought to be. Many employers are not enlightened. People who are victims of ageism should seek to build an alternative lifestyle that would enable them to play to their strengths.

Self-assessment and Personal Obligations

The extent to which someone needs to change will depend upon the personal aims of the individual in question. After reflection, many people conclude that they still have career ambitions in certain organizations or that 'while the going is good' they should buckle down and earn as much as possible to pay off a mortgage or reduce other outstanding debts.

Within current generations the puritan ethic remains a resistant strain. People still feel they should be strong and silent. Longings, and other distractions, are put to one side until children have graduated, retirement or even the next life. Older relatives remind us of our 'duties' and 'obligations'. Meeting family and other commitments or working for a cause that one believes in, may appear more worthwhile and less self-interested, than retreating into personal gratification.

The family can represent a core set of interpersonal dependencies and relationships. The state of these at a particular moment in time will reflect what has gone before and could be a positive or negative factor for the individuals concerned. The support of a family can be a great source of encouragement for those seeking to change direction. However, opposition from family members has prevented many people from pursuing their dreams.

Many individuals experience varying degrees of tension, if not conflict. They are torn between what they would really like to do and what they feel would be right, or preferred, from a family perspective. In such cases, different people react in different ways. At one extreme is selfish opportunists who 'jump ship' and renege on their responsibilities. At the other are those who sacrifice personal opportunities of a lifetime in order to avoid domestic strife by acquiescing to the irrational reactions or unfair demands of others. Neither of these outcomes is satisfactory.

Each case needs to be considered on its own merits. One should endeavour to secure a balance between the reasonable interests of all those involved. A proposed change of direction can sometimes put relationships under stress. Separate family members may take a different view of its desirability or implications. In other situations, a new opportunity may bring latent divisions to the surface. It may be necessary to 'clear the air' or 'grasp the nettle', rather than pretend a problem does not exist.

Every effort should be made to isolate points of difference and secure a mutual understanding of their likely impacts. Extra weighting needs to be given to the interests of those who cannot represent their own case, especially dependents.

In some situations, those in dispute may put an issue on hold. For example, they may defer until children 'leave the nest'. At this point, the parents might separate and the new business is set up. However, more fortunate people set out on an enterprise journey with the full backing of those close to them and their capital intact.

Concentration Upon the Essentials

Customer/supplier relationships should also be sensitive, intimate and vital. Corporate entities can be unduly constrained by what they have. They are often blinded by their strengths and are slow to change. They may be mentally locked into the consequences of past investments, existing people and current contracts and relationships.

IT companies sell 'boxes' and 'software' because this is what they do. Banks have branches because these have always been there in the living memories of today's employees. Cars are sold through independent distributors rather than direct because most motor manufacturers operate this way. Yet the longer the pressure for change is resisted, the higher the reservoir of unfulfilled requirements and the more destructive the consequences are when the dam bursts.

For those changing direction, or attempting something new, such constraints may not exist. There might not be existing arrangements or careers to protect. Perhaps they do not own assets whose values they are keen to protect. Because of what they do not have, and the company they do not keep, they are free to react to what customers actually want.

The requirements for business success are shrouded in the mist of many myths. Government initiatives are devoted to innovation, whilst almost every consultant who is encountered appears to be offering a range of 'change management' services. Sensitivity and intuition are needed rather than rules and tools. Entrepreneurs understand how people feel.

In certain sectors, rapid technological developments are occurring. Customers may demand the latest versions of whatever is available. Hence, a continuing commitment to product and service innovation may be essential if an enterprise is to stay ahead of the pack. However, change for the sake of it can alienate a user base.

Some customers may find change unsettling. Continuity,

being able to rely upon the familiar, could be important to them. 'Traditional' formulae, decor and recipes attract visitors to hotels and restaurants and buyers of products ranging from cakes to cough sweets. Brand valuations depend upon continuing attributes and qualities in relation to ongoing expectations. A key challenge within many businesses is the determination of what needs to change, (when and to what extent) and what needs to be maintained.

General trends and assumptions may not apply to a particular case. People can assume too much, for example that a business has to be international. Or, that what works in one context is likely to be appropriate in another. Tastes can be quite local. Exploiting them could provide a fulfilling, and profitable, opportunity for a local business that might not need national, let alone international, ambitions.

Just because something is possible does not mean it will be relevant for particular groups of consumers. There is no substitute for empathy and perception of what really matters to customers. In service, and especially face to face situations, people like to feel they are understood and that suppliers are genuinely interested in what they are seeking to achieve.

Many companies strive to provide ever more 'features' to such an extent that their customers become confused by the range of options available. Indeed, many find it difficult to operate certain equipment. A focus upon essentials could result in products which are easier to use. Perhaps a menu of alternatives should be provided, from which people could select the combination of features that best matches their requirements.

Problems invariably create business opportunities. Thus entrepreneurs have created enterprises to help consumers handle the increasing range of choice which they have. Examples range from internet bookshops to the provision of a service to enable companies with various premises to assess from which utility, or utilities, to buy their energy.

A common feature of such businesses is their focus upon particular difficulties which people have. The more imaginative solutions are often developed by either individuals who are from outside of the sector concerned or those who have left one of the established providers within the sector to start a new business. Too many existing suppliers focus upon what they produce rather than the value that is sought by their customers.

Natural Entrepreneurs

A willingness to shoulder personal responsibility and the flexibility to adjust and respond to the demands of an individual project or task, should not be assumed. Large company managers often inhabit worlds in which they 'benchmark', behave as role models and use standard tools. As a consequence, many lose the ability to think for themselves. Their 'me too' approach to life makes it difficult for them to create or establish an enterprise that is distinctive.

There is a certain bond that links all those who 'have a go'. In the company of entrepreneurs, no amount of creeping or crawling around the carpeted corridors of corporate head offices can earn the respect commanded by those who set up in business. Whether or not they succeed is less important than that they have had the courage to try. Rather than hide behind big company job titles, they were prepared to put their names, and reputations on the line.

Entrepreneurs are human. They experience moments of doubt and encounter stressful situations. However, they do not become immobilized by negative thinking. They identify and tackle obstacles and barriers. They take steps to overcome inner fears, insecurities and other inhibitors. They face up to challenges.

Entrepreneurs release latent potential. They see prospects rather than snags. They are optimists rather than pessimists. Where others hesitate, they will try. If all they have is a fire and a muddy pool, they think about using a hot stone to boil the water and make it safe to drink. The wiser ones among them also learn how to relax and play.

The success of an entrepreneur should not necessarily be measured in terms of the amount of money made. Within a free market of voluntary exchanges, great satisfaction can be derived from modest transactions that may have a very significant impact upon the customer.

The proprietor of a small and unexpected wayside hut dispensing drinks and simple fare to thirsty and tired walkers on a hot day may bring more joy to customers than the manager of a gourmet restaurant whose diners expect what they receive and take it for granted. Anyone setting up in business, however modest the enterprise may be, has the potential to bring some magic into the lives of others.

Entrepreneurs create wealth. Chisellers, who merely 'cream off', only consume it. The unscrupulous, at least for a period and until they are 'found out', can make a great deal of money. 'Intermediaries' in many parts of the world earn large sums exploiting family or other relationships. Hustlers and manipulative con artists feed upon human frailties.

Some individuals derive personal satisfaction from 'playing the system', 'pulling one on others', being 'streetwise' or 'making a fast buck'. As word gets around, such individuals need to seek out new territories or arenas in which there are still gullible people to be found. Many come unstuck because, having 'got things sown up', they become complacent and reluctant to move on.

There are others for whom such conduct has little appeal. Being 'poor but honest' yields them greater self-respect. It can also be an effective strategy for securing repeat business and also new business as a result of 'word of mouth' recommendation. Many of those operating in service sectors survive and prosper largely on the basis of positive referrals from others.

There are many corporate chickens who doubt their ability to survive on the outside. 'Employment' has been a central 'issue' of the present century. It has become an obsession of public policy and yet, in historical terms, the daily commute to a job is an aberration. From time immemorial people have worked for themselves, either at, or close to, their homes. As recently as the 18th century only one in ten were employees. Within many individuals there lurks the natural instincts of the fox.

Taking control of one's life is tantamount to returning to human roots. It also involves thinking for oneself. Pioneers do not follow the crowd or passively consume existing approaches. They develop new ones. They are positive. They believe in themselves and that anything is possible. They aim to be distinctive, to stand out like spring flowers along a hedgerow. A drip on the end of a nose may be noticed. The dew drop on a primrose petal can touch the soul.

Checklist

1. Have you thought about what will be required to succeed in the new millennium?

2. What are the critical success factors likely to be? Do you have them? What is missing?

3. What are your greatest strengths and weaknesses? How do these relate to the qualities that are most likely to be in demand?

4. What is there about you that is particularly distinctive?

5. Have you experienced age discrimination? When might employers begin to hold your age against you? How long have you got to prepare for an alternative lifestyle?

6. Do you have particular fears and anxieties? Have you already coped with a major challenge or transition in life?

7. Who around you has 'got what it will take'? What do they have which you don't?

8. Do others see you as a potential winner or loser? How concerned are you about their opinions? Are you sensitive to criticism or relatively self-contained and thick skinned?

9. What would they say you should most concentrate upon?

10. What is there about you that others do not see? Are there areas of latent potential which could be exploited?

11. Do you have interests and hobbies outside of work? Do these utilize qualities or involve aspects of your character, that are different from those demanded in your current role?

12.   What are the foundations of your life? Do you have a loving family, close friends or a deep faith? Do your current roles strengthen or erode these foundations?

13.   How important are ethics and integrity to you? Are there certain areas of business which you should consider and others that you ought to avoid?

14.   Are you entrepreneurial material? Have you a capacity to give in order to receive? Do you instinctively endeavour to create value or would you prefer to consume it?

15.   Do you give a lead or stand back and let others take the initiative? So far as your own life is concerned, do you intend to be a driver or a drone, a pioneer or a passenger?

5

WHO AM I?

*Pumpkins can be used to make
pies or halloween lanterns.*

A glimpse of oneself in a summer rock pool can be both unexpected and a trifle surprising. It may be noticeably different from the last observed reflection from a winter pond. It may differ again from the formal portrait in the company magazine or the face seen every morning in the bathroom mirror. Which image captures the essence of the spirit of the person concerned?

After years of 'fitting in' or 'playing the game', many people no longer know who they are. So much effort has been spent striving to understand and meet the expectations of examiners, become a member of this occupational group or satisfy the performance assessment criteria of that organization. Any sense of self may be limited to the few remaining areas in which adjustment and compromise have not occurred.

The Person Within

Our true selves can become concealed beneath a succession of veneers as people seek to portray what others would like to see, rather than project what is within. There always seem to be role models, or exemplars of best practice, that one should seek to emulate and imitate. Where people recruit and promote others like themselves, advancement can depend upon conforming and removing evident traces of individuality.

Those who are unable to knock the rough edges off themselves employ image consultants to do the job for them. Having sorted the mannerisms and the clothes, the really ambitious get to work on the body beneath. They lie under sun lamps, hire personal fitness trainers and spend hours in the gym. Some resort to the surgeon's knife. Changing the way we are to match a stereotype of how we think we ought to look, sound and behave can become an obsession.

Many people are unsure of themselves and their own positions. They lack confidence in their personal opinions. They defer to others who are more senior or who present themselves as having greater or more relevant expertise. So much emphasis is placed upon support systems and the use of methodologies that it may not occur to them to think for themselves.

Most educational systems have encouraged a dependence upon experts and authorities. People are told. They are given answers. They are not encouraged to discover for themselves. The role of teachers has been to communicate content, rather than to support the voyages of exploration of individual students. Factual information is poured into pupils' heads, as a consequence of which, they become passive recipients rather than active investigators.

There are also requirements to be met, or tests to sit, at various stages of the educational process. Instinctive leanings are viewed as distractions. People with a particular bent, whether artistic, musical, literary, sporting or entrepreneurial, are discouraged from building upon their natural talents. Instead of following their innate curiosity, they are expected to listen and learn, to follow a standard curriculum that will enable them to be assessed according to the same criteria as their peers.

All are expected to play the same game, regardless of individual differences and inclinations. Personal passions are put on hold until after the examinations. They are subsequently deferred until the individual has got a job or sorted out a mortgage. People then become ensnared with financial commitments. Next comes the demands of careers and families. These can take over one's life until retirement. For many, the pursuit of personal fulfillment is postponed forever.

Of course, some people break free. They derive satisfaction from formulating questions rather than receiving answers from others. They avoid packaged solutions and think for themselves. They seek out challenges and fresh problems to solve. As issues are resolved, their enquiring minds and restless spirits set out in search of new mountains to climb.

Many of those who achieve distinction in worlds, such as music and sport, have fond memories of the few individuals who encouraged them to remain true to themselves and pursue a personal passion. What, at the time, was probably viewed as evidence of feckless behaviour and lack of moral fibre is later regarded as an early sign of what was to come.

From Conformity to Dependency

Within many corporations, a trinity of Ps (procedures, processes and professionals) are used to determine the nature of responses to a wide range of circumstances. Absolutist views of what is right or wrong underlie a wide range of procedures, from the quality manual to the 'tick lists' of criteria used to evaluate individual performance. Membership of occupational and professional groups is usually dependent upon demonstration of the mastery of a body of knowledge and accepted practice. Becoming 'qualified' is often a rather passive process.

People were encouraged to believe that those in more senior positions, and holding certain formal qualifications, knew best. Not just corporate direction, but detailed policies and criteria for assessment and selection, were determined by those at, or near, the top of organizations. Such individuals were often far removed from the varying contexts in which their rules and procedures had to be put into place.

Deference to experts has extended to many other areas of life. General medical practitioners are expected to know the answer, even though they may not have encountered the condition in question before. People listen to pundits who tell them what is safe to eat. They rely upon consultants who suggest courses of action and the use of particular management approaches.

Accepted knowledge, standards, experts, codes, norms, laws and many other aspects of the societies in which we live should not be taken for granted. When used appropriately, and if not taken too far, they can be an essential precondition for civilized life. They allow us to build upon the labours of previous generations. We can pick up where others have left off.

Without a framework of law to protect their interests, people may be reluctant to trade, accumulate and build. Without constraints, rules and disciplines more people might pursue their own interests at the expense of others. When they are removed, as a consequence of man made wars and revolutions or natural disasters, communities often melt down into chaos. Resulting activities, such as looting, destroy both personal and social capital.

Maintaining a Balance

It is a question of balance and legitimacy. When helpful support becomes a straight jacket, it can be counter-productive. An excess of constraints can infringe individual liberties and suffocate enterprise. On occasion, rules, norms and practices appear to be, primarily, for the benefit of some groups rather than others – the enforcers rather than citizens, the corporation rather than its people, the 'haves' rather than the 'have nots'.

When certain groups push too hard to protect their own interests and enforce conformity upon others, their practices may come to lack moral authority. People may 'switch off', withdraw or 'opt out'. The perceived oppressor is denied the benefits of their wholehearted commitment and contributions.

In many corporations, certain recent management practices have arguably been taken too far. They are no longer fair nor reasonable. Legitimate individual interests have been overlooked. As a consequence, such companies have failed to harness the full potential of their people.

Too much effort has been devoted to maintaining the trappings of high office, while too little attention has been given to those in the engine room of value creation who are working with individual customers. Status and success in corporate environments has been associated with plush and expensive offices. Yet creative work is often done in relatively basic surroundings. The technological equivalent of the manger is the 'skunk works' or shed.

Marconi worked in a damp hut on an exposed Cornish cliff. Many innovations in the aviation world were the product of sustained effort in bare, cold and windowless buildings on bleak windswept airfields. Both Apple and Hewlett-Packard were started in garages. In such cases, the conditions may have been primitive but those concerned were totally absorbed. They were not 'playing a part'. They lived and slept for the challenge of making something happen.

The Spring of Liberation

Times are changing. Diversity, individuality and exceptions have their champions. Educators are becoming more aware that we are not all equipped to learn in the same way. An approach which is right for one individual might not be appropriate for another. The roles of teachers are being redefined in terms of the facilitation and support of learning.

The relevance of professional knowledge is increasingly questioned. In dynamic environments, the situation, requirements and expectations are constantly shifting. Customers are demanding tailored rather than general or standard responses. There is less emphasis upon the possession of knowledge and greater concern with the competence to use and apply it in individual cases.

Organizations are evolving or being transformed. Managers are more aware of the value of delegation and empowerment, although some remain determined to prevent either becoming more than rhetoric. Past structures and mechanisms were unable to cope with multiple challenges. Collective entities that survive for centuries, such as colleges, livery companies and guilds, do so by becoming living communities of people who share and sustain the values and traditions of fellowship and mutual support.

People have been told that their views are sought. They have been equipped with problem solving tools so that they can themselves identify and tackle problems. They are expected to question, assume responsibility, take ownership of tasks and add value. Greater support is being provided. Buckman Laboratories' intranet allows people to tap into the expertise of colleagues in 80 countries and seek their help.

Many individuals do now have greater discretion. Within companies such as Xerox, enterprise teams are given objectives and then left to themselves to determine the best means of achieving them. Organizations as varied as the BBC and ICI have introduced flexible benefits schemes which give individuals a wider choice of options to adopt. In coming to their decisions, people are having to think through their personal requirements, preferences and aspirations.

Flatter structures and the introduction of broadbanding into various organizations, from HM Customs and Excise in the public sector to Citibank in the private sector, are reducing opportunities for vertical career progression. As a consequence, people are more alert to the possibilities for lateral moves. They are also becoming aware of the implications of this.

Being locked from an early age into one career ladder prevents people from pursuing other options. Mouchel Group has
introduced opportunities for staff to switch roles. It finds people are attracted by the prospect of being able to swap horses
as their interests evolve. However, along with the extra freedom to change course comes the need to think through the direction in which one wishes to move.

Liberation releases the energies and talents that build value.
Individuals and small groups of collaborators – free, liberated
and creative people – produce the insights and knowledge which
corporations seek to package as intellectual property. Skandia,
the Swedish insurance company, has pioneered the measurement and reporting of intellectual capital. Investment in the
development of skills, making people more capable, is a key
performance indicator.

Adjusting to New Realities

The scale of the changes occurring within companies is such
that their full implications for roles, careers and patterns of
work are not always clear. The nature of the ultimate adjustment that may need to be made by both individuals and organizations is profound. We cannot be entirely sure how either
will react. There could be both winners and losers.

Some respond positively and assume greater personal responsibility. Those who are closer to the customer, or the context concerned, frequently find they know more about the situation than remote experts and senior executives. They begin
to question the relevance and practical value of much of the
advice and guidance that has been offered in the past.

Invariably, following 'research' or 'experience', the advice
changes. Yesterday's safe food becomes suspect and vice versa.
Last year's management fad is 'rubbished', while its successor
is aggressively marketed. Yet many people still take on board
whole packages, from management tool kits to religions, rather
than think for themselves.

Many organizations are in a state of transition from one
model to another. In the process, there are some who have
travelled further along the path to individual responsibility
than others. Some remain naïve, eager to believe. They still
search for panaceas and single solutions. Others have become

cynical. As layers of management are removed, and as organizations open up and become transparent, certain flaws are more apparent.

Corporate intriguers, fixers and conformists may technically do a good job, however, like those who energetically drive others to achieve results, they may lack what it takes to become strategists and entrepreneurs. They may be able to quickly absorb the directions of others and may excel at playing politics, while lacking the imagination to devise new games by bringing together new combinations of elements. They may be adept at hiring those they can control, and who do not represent a threat, whereas effective entrepreneurs seek to recruit those who are more talented than themselves in order for their business to grow more quickly.

Within any professional group, not everyone will be equally competent. There is often a skewed distribution of ability, with perhaps a few superstars and a long tail made up of the ordinary and some who are barely acceptable. By 'going direct' to those who contribute most, it is possible to punch through the concealment of status. Observing the pattern of traffic on networks can reveal groups that appear to be sidelined. There are a growing number of ways of distinguishing those who are adding value, from colleagues who are merely passengers.

Certain changes occurring within corporate organizations are like 'honest mirrors'. They confront people with their own worth and significance, their own strengths and inadequacies. People are having to face themselves, warts and all. It is becoming more difficult to live a lie.

Reality can be painful for those who become dependent upon the trappings of status and office. When people were compelled to consult them they felt they had a role. When the telephone falls silent and the e-mails no longer arrive, they learn the truth about their irrelevance. The people who once came to them now have a choice. They are going elsewhere.

Some find their value suddenly declines. People may not need to contact an expert anymore. Maybe they can find what they want, indeed more than any individual could provide, via their own desktop PC simply by accessing a website or the corporate intranet. Why pay a fee or a salary for information and knowledge that is accessible for the price of a local call?

Those who add value can find themselves in greater demand. People respect them and seek their contributions. They receive invitations to join project groups and networks. Some become so busy they hardly notice the disappearance of job titles. More junior staff may not mourn the loss of descriptions and designations that made them feel 'second class' corporate citizens. However, it does not matter any more. They are now valued for themselves.

Exercise: 'More of' and 'Less of' Analysis

Many people lack self-awareness. If may help you to better understand who you are, if you work through the different facets of your life and identify those aspects you would like more of and those you would prefer less of. These can then be ranked in terms of the strength of your preference for more or less. The relative positions of the various items listed could give you a clearer insight into the sort of person you are. When considering alternative roles and lifestyles, you could compare the profiles of each option with your current requirements.

In relation to your current activities, roles and life, select those aspects you would prefer to have either more of or less of. Which of the 'negatives' would you most like to be rid of? Similarly, which of the 'positives' would you most like to have more of?

Prioritize your 'more' and 'less' requirements. Is there a pattern? Are any of the 'mores' and 'lesses' related? For example, are they opposite sides of the same coin? Does the profile which emerges match your current situation or are you 'a square peg in a round hole'?

New Possibilities for Individuality

When the flow of one way memoranda and top-down orders begins to dry up, people become more aware of the potential of corporate and other networks for supporting other forms of interaction. Many channels can support two-way or 'all channel' communication. Those who have something to share or say, and the will to become proactive, can initiate communications, make suggestions and canvas support.

People who are given greater discretion can become more confident. Whereas they used to accept with resignation the roles which were allocated to them, or tasks imposed upon them, they might now push for those they would prefer to have. They may explore the limits and possibilities, trying out different roles, testing whether or not there are others who might benefit from their inputs and welcome their contributions.

Many managers now play their employers at their own game. They are becoming mercenary and focus upon their personal 'bottom line'. They are more willing to move to a different company for better experience or a higher salary, anything that will clearly benefit 'me plc'.

Suddenly it helps to stand out, to have a reputation and to be different. Conformist clones merge into the decor. Those who mouth slogans become background noise. Rough edges are more likely to leave a mark.

People have an incentive to discover their relative strengths. In doing so they need to be aware of the many arenas in which there are opportunities to excel. An individual could have particular linguistic or spatial skills. A person might be emotionally sensitive or physically robust, good at quantitative tasks and problem solving, or have what it takes to establish and sustain relationships. In these and many other areas, someone may stand out from their peers.

Those who just aim to 'fit in with the team' become targeted for elimination. Why tolerate a passenger? Why bring into a group, a person who does not add some distinctive value over and above what is already available? As for the clones, one is more than enough. In today's global business environment, an international perspective, sensitivity to cultural differences and a belief in the value of diversity are valuable qualities.

Management fads come and go. Wait long enough and today's emphasis upon decentralization may well be followed by another wave of centralization. However, many of the trends affecting the roles and perceived value of individuals within organizations appear likely to have a more lasting impact. They are deeply rooted in the growing power of customers and their demand for more tailored products and services.

Past qualifications, job titles and salaries are becoming less important than personal competencies, current relevance and future contributions. People are being questioned less about who they reported to, what benefits they received or what clubs they belong to and more about who they have worked with, what they achieved and learned and what value they have added. The emphasis is shifting from past trophies to future contributions.

When Roger Enrico learned he was to become Chief Executive of PepsiCo he decided to take time out from the normal day to day pressures to reflect upon the new role and to prepare himself for it. He spent several months away from the office, thinking and holding discussion sessions with groups of senior executives in order to share experiences and discuss ways of building the business. The sessions helped those involved to review and refine their own leadership styles in the light of the contribution they could make collectively to the development of PepsiCo.

Doing it Our Way

People should be encouraged by the changes which are occurring. As a consequence of delegation, empowerment and the replacement of prescriptive rules with enabling frameworks, there is greater scope for individuality, more opportunity for people to be themselves.

We are ourselves: and we are living creatures. Scratch us and we bleed. Each person has a particular genetic inheritance, and life to date has exposed each of us to a particular combination of circumstances and experiences. There is no point trying to be someone else.

Making comparisons, always looking over our shoulders at others can be a fruitless exercise. We see what is on the surface rather than what is within. In any event, what we observe is often the result of past constraints rather than an indication of future possibilities. Besides, what enables one person to succeed might not be available or desirable for another.

The lessons of success can be very misleading. The conditions in which they occurred may have changed fundamentally. Producers of case studies based upon situations with which one is familiar invariably ascribe favourable outcomes to the wrong causal factors. Often this is because post event rationalizations are accepted. What actually caused a particular result may be very different.

Relevance is relative. Much depends upon situation and circumstance. What is regarded as standard or absolute may not be appropriate or acceptable in a particular context. Because of the inherent diversity of people there is great potential for tailoring to personal requirements and different cases. More opportunities are being created for individuals to make a distinctive contribution than many have appreciated.

Siren voices need to be resisted. New age visions can lead to the squatter camp and welfare dependency. Potentially healthy developments may not suit everyone. Teleworking has its passionate advocates among the self-motivated and inwardly directed. However, for the gregarious it can mean a solitary existence. Community involvement may be needed to prevent social death.

In spite of the extra pressures, work at an office or plant can meet a range of interpersonal needs. In comparison, teleworkers, and especially homeworkers, can feel isolated, stultified and cramped. They may be surrounded by reminders of chores undone. Children that were 'delightful' when rarely seen can become 'noisy' when underfoot for several hours each day.

Families can be even more demanding than work colleagues. Neighbours can be more troublesome. Bores at the office can sometimes be avoided: at home one is stuck with them.

Individual footprints should lead social blueprints. Ideally, people should be allowed to achieve a mixture of home and office-based activity that enables them to be true to themselves, while at the same time meeting their work and family obligations. The bothersome family may be a consequence of a previous lack of balance in a working life.

The criteria for success are changing. Following fashion, aping others and fitting in with identikit profiles, whether real or imagined, are becoming less important. Of greater significance are judgements about the matching of people to situations and contexts. Germination may only occur under certain conditions. These can vary from person to person.

People should search for opportunities to be true to themselves. The quest is easier for positive, self-contained and internally driven people than it is for uncertain and reacting conformists. The former may have a sense of purpose in life that is both independent of and broader than their current role. The latter are likely to take cues from their employer about what their aim ought to be. They may take an organization's mission or rationale as their own.

Looking for Clues

Interviewers and selectors often ask people to identify their most significant accomplishment. Impacts achieved rather than positions held are relevant for independent operation. What did someone actually do that made a difference? Do the results attained suggest any special qualities or distinct competencies? Was the achievement an individual or collaborative one?

Perhaps the most important area of self-knowledge concerns the things one most enjoys doing and feels strongly about. People should identify those events and activities at different stages of their lives that brought the greatest satisfaction. Moments of joy, important events and periods of great fulfillment, are often buried under the weight of baggage accumulated over many years of 'fitting in' rather than 'being oneself'.

People should go back as far as early childhood memories in their search for the 'high points' of life. The challenge in transition planning is to make such moments the norm. Unexpected tragedies, not personal achievements, should be the exception. Many who rewind and review their lives are surprised, both by what is remembered and what is conveniently forgotten. The 'high points' tend not to include the delivery of the 'urgent report' about which so much fuss was made by so many people at the time.

Exceptional gifts can go unnoticed. 'High points' yield vital clues about what really matters to people, their peculiar characteristics and the talents they may have. Were they 'public affairs', involving others or private and personal? Did they involve a mental, emotional or physical challenge? Were the activities practical, creative or managerial? Were they paid or voluntary?

Individuals can use such questions and various tests, to help them discover what sort of people they are: leaders or followers, loners or socialites, performers or groupies, catalysts or conciliators, warm or cold, driven or open, etc. People should attempt to draw up personal profiles of themselves, covering their personality type, personal qualities and particular skills and competencies.

Self-awareness

Self-awareness is essential in an entrepreneur. People need to understand their personalities and motivations, as well as their attitudes, skills and knowledge. Particular attention should be devoted to attributes or characteristics relevant to success as an entrepreneur, such as whether one is inwardly directed, goal-focused and proactive. Those setting out to build a business should be able to influence and inspire others and integrate their contributions.

Caution is sometimes a rationalization of inaction. The dream of victory may be more appealing than the pain of defeat. People need to think through their attitude to failure. How would they, and their friends and families, react to it? More important perhaps, why should failure be painful or have negative connotations?

Some believe it is better to avoid challenges than to confront them and be found wanting. Not necessarily so. Testing can lead to greater self-knowledge. People learn about possibilities and limits, what can and cannot be done. Areas for improvement may be identified. Then there is the 'buzz', the sense of satisfaction that one has had a go.

People should learn about themselves warts and all. The process of self-examination should not be rushed. There is more to most people than meets the eye. There are different dimensions of capability: rational, emotional, spatial, moral and many others. In any one of these, or a combination of them, individuals may find themselves well-placed. It is a question of knowing where to look and what to look out for.

People need to assess how they prefer to interrelate with others. For example, are they natural leaders or instinctive facilitators? Are they preoccupied with their own point of view, or can they draw out and integrate the opinions and contributions of others? Are they thinkers or doers? Are they strategically or operationally inclined? How hard do they drive others? Is their focus upon relationships or outcomes? Answers to these and other questions can enable people to determine whether they should operate alone or as the focal point of a team; and, if the latter, the sort of people and personalities to seek out as collaborators.

Being True to Oneself

Harmony and balance result from honesty and awareness, being true to oneself. They are becoming increasingly important. This has not always been the case. Many have benefited positively from being unbalanced and abnormal. In competitive sports the struggle occurs within a framework of rules and regulations. It may help to be outstanding in particular dimensions. A desire to feel wanted, perhaps stemming from emotional dep-rivation while a child, can spur the politician to greater success.

Even in such specialized arenas, the unbalanced can come unstuck. Psychological preparation is essential in certain sports. Participants and contestants need to be 'together'. In politics, when rolling cameras capture the body language involved in interpersonal relationships, it can help if there is a human being beneath the biography, a person behind the poster.

Priorities need to be reviewed. How important are money, material possessions, work and career goals in relation to the quality of life and one's health, family and friends? Are inner peace and personal relationships valued? Do you have time for the activities you most enjoy?

Timescales must be established. How many years are there until retirement? Will there be future opportunities for a change of direction? Is one looking to 'gear up' and take on more onerous responsibilities or is the aim to 'wind down' and secure a more balanced life?

Not being realistic and self-aware can be a recipe for disaster. For example, individuals who are similar in many other respects, may have very different energy levels. Those who find it difficult to sustain high levels of input for long periods of time should avoid activities that could lead to stress levels that might impair health. Instead they should seek out other possibilities, perhaps those requiring varying, or intermittent, levels of input.

Some people are more consistent than others. Those who have 'good days' and 'bad days' should go for options that involve a higher level of discretionary activity. Certain tasks can then be tackled when the individual feels so inclined. Those who experience a variety of moods could assemble a portfolio of activities to suit the differing facets of their personality.

A sense of balance can be created. Reconciliation can occur.

The traditional Chinese garden breaks down barriers between inside and outside, earth and water, light and shade. A variety of environments are encountered within a relatively small and three-dimensional space. People, fish, birds and insects live in harmony. Natural materials abound. The routes taken by visitors enable rocks weathered by the elements to be appreciated to the best advantage. Such a relationship with nature is increasingly precious in an era of sound bites and cryptic and functional electronic communications.

Exercise: Personal Accountability Exercise

Good managers do not necessarily make effective founders of entrepreneurial enterprises. Setting up a company and becoming a director involves legal duties and responsibilities. People with boardroom aspirations should consider the differences between the roles of directors and managers and reflect upon what it takes to be a competent director.

Are you willing to become accountable and ready to assume legal responsibilities? Do you understand the distinction between direction and management? What is different about directing an enterprise as opposed to leading other teams? How would you rank yourself in relation to the qualities, knowledge and experience required of an effective director?

Personal Development Plan

Companies could do more to encourage reflection and self-analysis. Once a quarter, Motorola asks its employees about their career plans and the extent to which the corporation supports, and is enabling, their achievement. The grandly named Individual Dignity Entitlement Programme assists the realization of personal aspirations.

Corporations could also help people establish mutual support networks and transformation partnerships with each other. Just as the State does not have to be involved in every aspect of human endeavour, so the organization itself does not always need to be a provider.

An honest review of where someone is, in relation to where they would like to be, can lead on naturally to the drawing up of a personal development plan. Aspirations could be expressed in the form of aims and objectives. Identifying the qualities, skills and competencies needed to achieve these, and comparing them with one's own attributes, allows gaps to be identified. Appropriate learning and development activities may enable these to be bridged.

Undertaking a personal SWOT analysis can help individuals to take stock of where they are. Examining personal and professional achievements to date can result in the identification of both strengths and weaknesses. In relation to opportunities, there may be particular roles the person would like to undertake or particular organizations they might aspire to join.

People should not be afraid to seek out the opinions of others. The involvement of colleagues, or a counsellor or mentor, can help someone establish aspirations and objectives that appear attainable in relation to what has been achieved to date. While no one should sell themselves short, impossible missions, which can only result in disappointment, should be avoided.

A timetable for development will need to be established, along with some form of monitoring and review, to ensure that activities undertaken are contributing positively to personal objectives. In the case of ambitious goals and large gaps, it may be advisable to set some shorter term or intermediate aims against which improvement can be measured. Achieving them may encourage further progress.

When setting development objectives the focus should be upon what is most important. At the same time, putting all of one's eggs into a single basket should be avoided. A balanced development plan with a mix of elements is generally the most fulfilling. Enjoyable activities can counterbalance those which are less to one's liking.

Both Ford and Xerox help individuals to acquire new personal skills. Even though these may not be in areas directly related to jobs, the learning experience usually results in a more questioning approach to life in general.

Enlightened companies ensure staff have an opportunity to draw up personal development plans. Where counselling and mentoring support is provided, individuals should actively seek them. They are for the proactive as well as those who have lost direction. Such help can enable an individual and an organization to enter into a more mutually rewarding partnership during implementation and thereafter.

Room at the Inn

Fulfilment is not limited to the outstanding or exceptionally good. There need not be, and should not be, any expectation or assumption of perfection. Offering customers what they would like may require little in the way of special skills. On occasion, it may just be a question of becoming aware of an opportunity and being willing to respond.

People are becoming more aware of the differing levels of competence among members of particular occupational groups and it is becoming easier to identify and communicate with 'high performers'. Inevitably, such individuals will be in greater demand and they may charge a premium for their time.

However, those with lower levels of capability may also be required. Some customers will not be able to pay 'superstar' rates. Nor need they. For activities that are not critical, or do not differentiate, adopting a workable option at an affordable price may be preferable to waiting for a more optimal solution.

Particular capabilities may be more relevant in some contexts than others. With greater diversity and tailoring, there are more opportunities for people to carve out niche reputations for themselves. When electronically held information and advice is available to all practitioners, those, whose standing depends upon possession of scarce knowledge, may find their positions eroded. The ability to adapt for each requirement may be more important.

There are also many dimensions of competence. Empathy might be crucial for certain relationships rather than technical ability. Different people may find themselves regarded as 'superstars' depending upon the facets or qualities which are most relevant in each case.

No one should feel permanently excluded. Conditions can change. We can overcome the barriers of distance and time in the search for customers and clients. Plateaued managers faced real barriers in old-style organizations. If someone's face did not fit, or if a boss was likely to be in post for many years, future prospects were limited. This is not so in today's company with a continuous flow of projects. For those whose hat is in the ring the next assignment could be just around the corner.

It Could be You

Many people are imprisoned by doubt, immobilized by indecision or neutralized by pride. They may refuse to accept the need for development. Success in a former role can make it more, rather than less, difficult to establish a new one. It may result in an unhealthy attachment to a past lifestyle which can no longer be maintained. The consideration of options may be constrained by unrealistic assumptions and expectations concerning levels of earnings.

The insecure are forever trying to please or impress others with material goods or job titles. As most other people are pre-occupied with themselves, this effort can be largely wasted. It makes better sense to be true to oneself. Also, contributions to recent tasks and projects are becoming more important than qualifications and job titles. Playing to one's strengths can help sustain a flow of remunerated activity. Obtaining a role for which one is not suited, through exaggeration or deception, can be counter-productive when it leads to other members of the team becoming disappointed with your performance. There may not be a second time.

People whose sense of who they are is dependent upon the opinions of others and who value themselves according to car type and other symbols of status, are very vulnerable when such props are taken away. They risk the loss of dignity and self-respect. The self-contained, who know who they are, people at ease with themselves, and find it easier to weather life's storms.

Throughout history, extraordinary deeds have been performed by quite ordinary people. Victorian and Edwardian encyclopedias were full of such positive role models. Whereas world-weary contemporary journalists focus upon 'exposure', 'muck raking', and spreading cynicism and distrust, their authors sought to communicate a sense of the awe, wonder and excitement of being alive. Readers were invited to delight in practical solutions to problems.

Our generation has so many opportunities to explore new worlds and for self-discovery. By donning the virtual reality helmet, or jumping on an aeroplane, we can experience alternative lifestyles in diverse locations. We can experiment with different surroundings and evaluate various combinations of work and play. Periods spent in other contexts enable us to better appreciate our own. We sense our feelings, insights and reactions under divergent conditions.

Which course of action is the right one for us? Until we undergo a process of reassessment we cannot be sure. One person could develop a passion for growing organic vegetables. Another might emerge with a hard-nosed desire to start a business in the hope of creating capital for a comfortable retirement. Both are united by their desire for greater independence.

Even on an island, where all routes lead to the sea, we may have a choice of which path to take. Given a pumpkin, one could either opt for the pie and a fuller stomach, or the Halloween lantern that would bring magic and fun into the lives of others. Which is it to be?

Checklist

1. Who are you? What do you most enjoy doing? What has brought you the greatest satisfaction during your life?

2. What have you achieved to date? What is your most significant accomplishment? What particular competencies have you developed?

3. Do you have an aim or purpose in life? Is this independent of your current employer and your present role?

4. How positive, cheerful and optimistic are you? Do you experience moods and periods of self-doubt?

5. Does anyone actually know you? How much do you really know about yourself?

6. How self-aware are you? How realistic are your assessments and impressions of yourself?

7. To what extent are you able to be yourself in your current role and lifestyle? Who, or what, gets in the way? What ends up being suppressed?

8. Do you adjust how you would like to appear, dress or behave to fit in with those around you? Which aspects of this accommodation or compromise would you most like to ditch?

9. Are there currently pressures upon you to conform to a greater or a lesser extent? In future, are you likely to have more or less opportunity to express your individuality?

10. What balance between change and continuity would you like to see in your life? Are you a risk taker or risk averse? Do uncertainties make you insecure? Do they put you under stress?

11. Are you capable of more? What else could you achieve? Would you like to assume greater personal responsibility and take more control over your life?

12. In recent years, how true have you been to yourself? Reflect upon your life. Where have you sold yourself short? Are you still doing it?

13. Do you have a retirement or development plan? Do you reflect upon the alternatives? Have you identified other options?

14. Would you like to be someone else or somewhere else? What lifestyle, and form and pattern of work, would be most in tune with your preferences?

15. How satisfied are you with past personal development activities which you have undertaken?

16. Are you willing to undergo whatever further development may be needed to effect a successful transition from where you are to where you would like to be?

6

THE NEW DAY

It is better to be warmed by the
sun than burned by it.

Seasons come and go. Every night, as the sun falls petals, close and each morning when it rises they open again. The tide ebbs and flows. The cycle may be annual, daily or more often, but it is inexorable. Regeneration and rebirth are all around us.

Yet many people regularly and persistently deny themselves opportunities to be reborn into a different life. Fulfilment is forever postponed. They survive and accommodate, rather than prepare for a tomorrow which would enable them to live for today. Some have got themselves into an unnatural groove. Others are reconciled to an inevitable decline into senility and death.

Organizations cannot afford to be complacent. As transaction costs fall and purchasing processes become more effective, changes of arrangements can be achieved more quickly and with less disruption. People find it easier to become aware of alternatives and to take advantage of them.

The cycle of ascent, decline and fall has speeded up. In part, this is because the media have greater reach and sharper teeth. They can bite – and bite quickly. Within minutes, if not hours, bad news can be projected into homes all over the world. If an incident is sufficiently damaging, a reputation that has been painfully acquired over a long period of time may be quickly lost.

The rhetoric of quality has played its part in raising expectations. People are less tolerant of lapses in performance. They demand the best every time. A succession of future improvements is taken for granted. The perceived existence of a group that is resting upon its laurels may be sufficient to encourage new, committed and more sensitive entrants into a marketplace.

Rediscovering Hope

Risks and threats need to be acknowledged. However, they should not be exaggerated. Each board and management team needs to undertake a realistic assessment of how much change is needed, and by when. It might be possible to take corrective action before it is too late.

Not all existing organizations are doomed to die. Some, such as churches and orders of chivalry, look set to survive for further centuries. They endure. They meet deep seated needs that continue for generations. Nor are major corporations compelled to be unimaginative. 3M and Merck have creative cultures. Over their relatively short lives, companies such as Canon, Honda, Intel, Sony and Xerox have produced innovations that have had a significant impact upon the lives of millions.

Corporations can, and do, reassess their rationale. They emerge from the tunnel of analysis into the light of a more inclusive strategy that seeks to understand and meet the needs of a wider range of interests. Even the best of relationships go through periods of strain. Bonds and commitments that have grown loose as a result of a lack of reciprocity can sometimes be reforged.

Even those organizations that lack a sense of purpose and drive may continue to operate for some time. They might not necessarily fold. Existence generates its own momentum. Companies are listed in directories: even the worst of suppliers may receive random orders.

Not all customers will switch allegiance overnight. Some are too lazy. 'Crawl out' or 'set up' costs might be incurred if alternatives were sought. Also a public image may lag behind the reality of decline. The reputations of many companies and brands ensure a degree of repeat purchasing, while certain contracts may still have some time to run.

Employees continue to turn up each day. They may not be happy and they might lead unbalanced lives as a result of the long hours they are putting in. But for reasons of financial dependence and economic self-interest their heads overrule their hearts. They stay put rather than look elsewhere.

Sweeping generalizations and dire predictions are often made about the future prospects of companies. Such assessments attract attention, but fail to recognize the capacity of people to learn and change. Organizations like individuals can have an in-built desire to survive. A collective drive to remain relevant can lead to adaptation to meet emerging requirements.

A sense of will and purpose is essential. Where it is absent, the end may be sooner or later but it will surely come. Where it is present, there is still hope and scope for action.

Invariably there are options. The extent of the opportunities is rather like the night sky. The longer and harder one looks, the more that becomes apparent. Escape from the pollution of trendy jargon, and corporate atmospheres of denial and distrust, and they are even sharper.

Retaining Desired Relationships

A proportion of today's organizations will successfully make the transition to more flexible and responsive forms. They will reinvent themselves and re-establish relationships through new appeals to both the head and the heart. Some have already demonstrated a capacity to survive dire challenges, and they may do so again. Societies would 'melt down' into collective insecurity, chaos and confusion if it were otherwise.

Millions of current livelihoods, and future pensions, depend upon the renewal, transformation and continuance of existing organizations, institutions and relationships. We are not all cut out to be internet pioneers. Many people do not have the desire, drive or capability to establish enterprises or form networks. We are not all natural born innovators and entrepreneurs. Some want to join and belong, rather than initiate and instigate. They wish to be 'employees' or 'members'.

However, organizations should not take the continuing allegiance of their most talented staff for granted. A younger generation of managers is emerging whose primary loyalty is to themselves. They are more self-confident than many of their predecessors and more willing to change employer to obtain new skills. Glaxo Wellcome needs to retain its researchers. The company explicitly gives them opportunities to develop and rewards them for acquiring new competencies.

Sir Montague Burton established a chain of men's outfitters. He expressed the view that a business should have a conscience as well as a counting house. Increasingly, managers who are under pressure to focus more narrowly upon corporate objectives ignore his advice at their peril.

The founders of confectionery suppliers Cadbury and Rowntree believed employees should be well-treated. They created social and physical communities. The total experience of relatively pleasant working and living conditions, training, fairness, trust and respect made people and their families feel valued. It gave them a sense of well-being.

More recently, The Body Shop and Ben & Jerry's have attracted staff and customers as a result of their public identification with social causes. Relatively hard-nosed companies, such as Ford, find that shifting the emphasis from costcutting and squeezing their people, to investing in them and rewarding them, pays dividends in terms of reduced staff turnover and absenteeism and greater commitment. Generosity, where it is due, can also entice new blood.

Companies today can create a sense of living community for those who might otherwise be limited to electronic contacts with various members of their networks. At the same time, people want fair recompense for their personal contributions. The elimination of layers, and the replacement of regular increments with individual assessments within broader bands may reduce the prospects of advancement for manual and clerical staff. However, it gives greater flexibility to recognize 'high contributors'. Volkswagen rewards its people according to the impact or influence they have.

Sensitivity to Impacts, Concerns and Requirements

While many companies may have the potential to survive, their continuing existence can depend upon a degree of change. This is particularly important in relation to the various groups that have an interest in a company, especially employees, customers, suppliers and business partners. Stakeholders are becoming more aware of their bargaining strength.

The greater choice, which people have, continues to erode corporate power. As a consequence, companies are finding it more difficult to impose their standard terms and conditions upon others. In an age of diversity and tailoring, value comes out of relationships. Their creation results from listening to, and understanding, individual customers and each employee.

Seasonal staff are often insecure. They can lack a continuing link with those for whom they work. McKay Nurseries understands this. It is owned by its employees, many of whom are only on the payroll for a few months each year. All those who have worked for more than 1,000 hours are eligible to join the company's employee, stock-ownership plan. Larger companies, such as Allied Signal, also encourage employee share ownership as a means of building a community of shared interests.

Companies need to become more sensitive to the impacts of their own actions. For example, downsizing may have reduced costs, but what about those who left? Where are they now and what view of the company are they spreading? Moreover, what about those who remain?

Staff who survive culls in organizations such as BT, which has shed large numbers of people, can experience various traumas. They may be left to cope alone, while at the same time adjusting to heavier workloads. Those who are expected to counsel and support them may be too busy to help. People in survivor cultures often feel helpless and powerless. They keep their heads down and become more focused upon immediate tasks. Such reactions can cut across a company's drive to encourage people to become more proactive, questioning and entrepreneurial.

Exercise: Compatibility Analysis

Many people dwell on issues in dispute, rather than focus upon areas of agreement. This approach can lead to suspicion, defensive behaviour and conflict. Instead, they should endeavour to build upon what they have in common with others.

In the case of your organization and its people, what are the main points of difference and dissonance? What are the major interests which both have in common? What concerns or objectives do you share with your employer?

Separate the areas of disagreement from the mutual interests. How important and critical are each group to those concerned? What could be done to build

upon the areas of joint interest? Could people [or you] sideline some areas of dissension and simply agree to disagree, rather than pursue arguments that are getting in the way of more positive developments?

Appealing to the Economic Electorate

Yesterday's corporations used power to impose, protect and coerce. Successful companies today derive their purpose, potential and power from the promise of satisfying the aspirations of those who associate with them. Like a democratic politician, a corporate manager has to go out and 'get the support of the people' by winning the votes they cast each time they make a purchase.

The size of the potential economic electorate has increased massively. In many sectors, it spans the globe. The consequences of a successful appeal can be dramatic and can arise more quickly than ever before. Companies have experienced consumer boycotts that spread with the speed of a forest fire. If corrective action is not taken they can be just as devastating. In Shell's case, plans to dispose of an oil platform by sinking it in the North Sea had to be publicly abandoned.

The number of electors, and the multitude of different forums for choice which occur every day, create unprecedented opportunities for minority parties. An individual enterprise may only need to secure a minute proportion of relevant transactions in order to succeed beyond the wildest dreams of those involved. Those in business today have everything to play for.

Every vote counts. A cash flow is an accumulation of individual decisions. With each negative vote a company weakens. Those that become too anaemic die. Conversely, every prospective relationship is a possible source of new strength and life. With each positive vote and new commitment a company grows in capability and potential.

To engage the economic voter, stand out from other messages and appeal, it is necessary to be focused and relevant. People need the ability to listen to, and learn from, groups that may be very different from themselves. Those without these skills should endeavour to develop them quickly.

In the past, customers, employees, suppliers and business partners were often regarded as statistics, described in terms of trends or ratios and treated as targets for various corporate initiatives. They were viewed through the distorting spectacle lenses of corporate advantage. They must now be seen for what they are, individual human beings each of whom can vote with their feet or their credit cards.

The Internal Constituency

Levels of loyalty have eroded in many companies. Steadfast and faithful troops cannot be taken for granted. Allegiance has to be earned rather than assumed. People need to be treated as adults if they are to stand on their own feet and assume greater responsibilities.

Increasingly, people seek recognition of their personal contributions. They demand respect as unique individuals with particular interests and distinct qualities. They actively look for opportunities to acquire the experiences that will help them to develop their competencies further. They favour employers who allow them to acquire and share knowledge.

Companies are responding with a variety of initiatives. Anglian Water has developed an Aqua Universitas and an encyclopedia of water. British Aerospace has a virtual university. Organizations as varied as Xerox and the University of Glasgow fund non-job-related courses. They find that any learning experience can result in a more questioning attitude to work.

Cable & Wireless encourages its employees to think in terms of projects, and 'contracting' with colleagues to provide defined outputs, rather than jobs. Instead of occupying slots, and waiting for tasks to drop into their in-trays, they focus upon the 'deliverables' they have negotiated. 'Career action centres' support those who proactively seek out opportunities for roles with future projects. Enabling people to move between different companies within the group helps to create an internal market within which people can steer their development.

Internal contracting makes companies aware of the unpaid overtime being worked by many long-suffering employees. It can shift the emphasis from the quantity of work to its quality. For those whose skills are in greatest demand, one of the benefits of independent operation is the prospect of being paid for all those extra hours that are put in.

Measures taken to stimulate imagination and creativity

can create a healthy scepticism. They may invite challenge. Unions may press for opportunities to use a corporate intranet to canvas opinions. The rhetoric of 'involvement' and 'participation' may have to be matched by the reality.

Companies should expect more 'why' questions from their people. Before 'voting' their commitment, they may feel entitled to an explanation of why a particular course of action is being advocated. They may reasonably expect an honest and straightforward explanation of what the consequences for them, personally, are likely to be.

Staff no longer want to be 'ambushed' by the consequences of corporate activities, to be half way through a re-engineering exercise when the truth dawns that they are working themselves out of a job. Companies that conceal their true intentions and deceive are likely to be punished by a withdrawal of commitment, limited only by the loyalty of those concerned to the individual customers for whom they feel personally responsible.

People should be engaged. They should feel they are involved participants in decisions which affect the future use of their experience and skills. They also represent a rich pool of potential ideas and initiatives. But people will not suggest new concepts if, once these are tabled, they are not taken seriously.

Confident companies are likely to become more democratic, and more open about the rationale of decisions. Certain customers, suppliers and business partners, and more staff – perhaps all of them – could be involved in the decision making process. Thus, an examination of the situation and possible options could be presented and people invited to comment upon, or contribute to, the analysis, suggest further courses of action or vote upon the options.

The Legitimacy of Authority and Relationships

Voluntary co-operation and commitment are far superior to coercion if companies are to tap the full potential offered by emerging technologies and a greater sharing of experience. People are prepared to respect the exercise of authority which they regard as legitimate. A key test of legitimacy is the extent to which there is a fair allocation of rewards between the parties concerned.

Relationships should be viewed in 'positive-sum' rather then 'zero-sum' terms. They ought to generate benefits for all the parties involved and need to be approached with such outcomes in mind. Take childcare for example. Concerns about conflicts between parental and employment obligations can impact adversely upon work performance. IBM has worked with professional providers of childcare services to ensure that suitable facilities, with appropriate opening hours, are located adjacent to their major facilities. Lloyds/TSB provides its staff with workplace nurseries and childcare vouchers, while play activities are arranged for school holidays.

Certain opportunities may appear to offer one's own organization an overwhelming and disproportionate share of 'the benefits'. However in some situations they should perhaps be avoided on the grounds that they are unlikely to reach fruition. The projects to pursue, in terms of their longer term potential, may be those which offer more balanced and equitable outcomes.

People who believe they will derive value from a relationship are more motivated to ensure the interests of other parties are satisfied. They may prolong an investigatory stage in order to help a prospective partner clarify the possible rewards better. A company should want its suppliers and employees to benefit. If they do well, it is more likely itself to prosper. If they do not, the relationships concerned will probably not last.

Companies are recognizing that too much emphasis has been placed upon changing structures and processes and not enough upon changing attitudes and behaviour. For culture change to occur, people need to understand why change is needed. They should also be helped to adapt.

The changes of perspective required are far from trivial. In a particular context they can have a profound impact upon the qualities that are sought in managers. Many will have built their careers and reputations upon their tenacity to the point of ruthlessness in squeezing benefits for their own party out of every transaction that comes within range of their influence. The high flier who has generated results by 'screwing the last drop' out of others during the course of negotiations can become a liability when the emphasis shifts to the identification of mutual benefits.

Another test of legitimacy is responsiveness. Are those leading the company listening? Are they sensitive to the interests of others? It is particularly important that a company is aware of the changing preferences of those employees who are likely to be in greatest demand. Insensitivity can be measured in terms of the number of staff leaving to go elsewhere.

Communications need to become two-way, or 'all channel', rather than one-way. Too many people are drowning in memos and messages which are of little relevance to them and their immediate priorities. Those who are well-placed and able to take the initiative should do so in the form of invitations to enter into a dialogue. Companies, such as Deeside Furniture and Rechem International, have found that conscious effort to achieve more inclusive and pertinent communication and more active staff involvement has contributed significantly to performance improvement and greater employee satisfaction.

The Erosion of Dependency

Relationships, both formal and informal, between many organizations and those who work for and with them need to change. Past arrangements have been too heavily stacked in favour of organizations. The main rationale for the 'small print' has been to protect corporate interests.

Employees have been regarded as a 'human resource', or factor of production, to be exploited. Taking advantage of their fear of loss of income and status, many corporations have been able to make 'take it or leave it offers' and impose standard terms and conditions. In a less competitive age, they also generated the revenues to pay for the costs of enforcement. At some point, right or wrong, any individual in a dispute would most probably concede or withdraw when faced with the deep pockets of the corporation.

With far fewer alternatives, and various barriers to 'going it alone', those who simply 'needed a job' had to swallow their pride and 'eat crow'. Managers were able to force employees to live and work on their terms, in environments and conditions which they imposed.

The management of people in some corporations in recent years has involved principles which most farmers would understand. While employees lactate, they are fed, sheltered and put out to graze. When the flow of milk dries up, or demand falls, they are sent to the abattoir.

Companies have employed a wide range of approaches and methodologies designed to squeeze more out of their people. Various professional groupings, and numerous consultants, have prospered in the search for better ways of extracting the very last drop of liquid from human pulp.

Enough is enough. Companies are recognizing that more employees can now 'shoot back'. Increasingly, people are no longer resigned to the bleak prospect of becoming a bloody carcass on an abattoir floor. They can sell their services to a higher bidder, or perhaps they could go around the corner and operate themselves, without the deadweight of yesterday's overheads.

In some sectors, panic reactions have set in. Those who are thought to have most to offer are positively wooed with 'golden hellos', share options and the like. In many cases, such largesse may not be sustainable. Neither may it be necessary.

Getting Each Relationship Right

Relationships and mutual benefits are becoming more important. Compared with productive labour, the knowledge worker or professional is often less dependent upon the capital of the organization. The proportion of 'cases' involving new or unfamiliar elements is also increasing as a consequence of greater tailoring. They may, therefore, be less dependent upon corporate norms. Increasingly, they may find themselves working as individuals and for particular customers.

People are becoming less dependent upon an employer's technology. They are able to afford their own. The device needed to extract relevant information, and work up and communicate a response, may also be so small as to be portable. Increasingly, work can be done in a variety of locations, including the home. If need be, individuals can make direct contact with end users and cut out a corporate intermediary. The user, or end consumer, may be more concerned with the relevance and quality of a response than the source from which it has been obtained.

When standard solutions were offered, it was important that people followed corporate procedures. Standardization encourages coercion and control. Departures from norms can be identified and reported. Certain solutions come to be regarded as better than others.

When customers increasingly demand tailored solutions to

their particular problems and requirements, the emphasis needs to change. Comparisons between solutions are less important than achieving the most relevant outcomes in varying sets of circumstances. With greater variety, measurement and assessment become less mechanical. Using one's past experience as a base, and having the imagination and flexibility to do things differently when it is appropriate to do so, may be more important than slavish adherence to corporate standards.

Customers may request those who understand their particular requirements, and with whom they feel a degree of empathy. They may reject the theoretical 'best outcome' selected by a panel for a 'notional consumer' in favour of highly personal responses from those they know and trust. They want to feel special. Hence, people need to be encouraged, rather than coerced, into being sensitive, imaginative and creative when dealing with individual customers.

New Ways of Working

People should be encouraged to adopt whatever patterns of work enable them to give of their best and which add value cost-effectively. 'Teleworking', 'home offices', 'telecottages', 'neighbourhood centres' and other 'new ways of working' are not as novel as is sometimes suggested. Historically, most people have worked at or close to home. Through the centuries, the equivalent of going abroad for many people has been to venture into the next village or hamlet. On occasion, the reception might have been a hostile one.

The notion of leaving home to join significant numbers of other people at an indoor place of work, in order to use tools and an assembly process to produce things, really took off at the time of the Industrial Revolution. The practice of 'going to work' continued with the growth of office work, as early clerical functions took place in rooms and buildings that were added to existing industrial premises. When offices moved to 'central business districts' commuting times increased further.

Certain companies now have extensive experience of various forms of teleworking. Much can be learned from what has happened to initiatives, such as the Rank Xerox 'networking' programme in the middle 1980s. People ceased being full-time employees and established limited liability companies, which then contracted to supply those aspects of their previous roles which could be defined in clear output terms.

The 'networkers' were free to undertake similar work for other non-competing companies, and it was expected that, within a year or so of their establishment, at least a half of the turnover of the new enterprises would derive from non-Rank Xerox sources. The greater independence, which resulted when people took more control over their lives, enabled them to give more objective advice, while the company retained access to the services of those who might otherwise have joined rival companies.

Subsequent experience has shown that situations, circumstances and fashions can change. Alternative means may be found of sourcing a required input. Corporate requirements evolve. Individuals and organizations can grow apart. Non-competing clauses to protect one party might become overly restrictive for another. A single model might not cope with every eventuality.

Today Xerox uses a variety of patterns of work, rather than one approach to teleworking. The pragmatist seeks to create rather than close options and, while committed to a particular course of action, remains open to other opportunities. In the course of a lifetime it may be necessary to become reborn and to change direction more than once.

It is essential that individuals monitor developments and remain realistic in terms of the value of whatever it is they are offering. A degree of adaptation may need to occur over time. This could range from quoting more competitive rates to accepting the need to acquire a range of new skills.

Some individuals come to rue the day they cut themselves adrift from organizations that could have helped them to adjust. Not all companies welcome back those who have previously flown the nest. Others are more tolerant. They recognize the value of a two-way flow of people into and out of varying degrees of corporate embrace and commitment. An introverted culture can benefit from a comparative understanding of how matters are dealt with elsewhere.

Those in exile, the corporate equivalent of the 'stateless person', should seek out new forms of membership organization that could act as support networks. Some relevant services might be provided by professional bodies and trade unions that are responsive to the changing requirements of their individual members. Others are being introduced by entrepreneurs who recognize and react to emerging needs.

Robert Terry set up the Webtrain network to support the training community and treats his 'associates' as longer term collaborative partners. Denis Roberts established The Networking Firm, and a related training programme, to help those who operate through virtual teams. Barry Curnow created courses to meet the distinct development and updating needs of independent consultants, as well as founding the Maresfield Curnow programme of 'Brainstrust' meetings.

New Style Social Contracts

Future mechanisms for securing access to skills will need to take account of the interests and aspirations of the suppliers concerned. Within any particular group requirements may vary. Some individuals may be primarily concerned with finding future opportunities to work upon similar types of problems. Others might be more interested in moving into new fields and developing additional areas of competence.

Relationships should build upon individuality and mutuality. More of a balance needs to be struck between individuals and organizations, if the latter are to retain the services of those they most value. Such an equilibrium needs to be sustainable if arrangements are to last. Many organizations need to establish a new social contract with those upon whom they depend, whether as customers, suppliers or business partners.

A greater willingness of organizations to meet the needs of individuals could lead to a blurring of the distinction between corporate employment and individual operation. It is in the interests of most companies that those supplying them with skills are well-supported in terms of access to information and development resources.

Steve Shirley set up F International as a result of her own experience of wishing to continue working while having a baby. She quickly built up a pool of freelance 'teleworkers' who operated from their homes. Over time, their desire for interaction, collaboration and support, led to the establishment of neighbourhood offices and other responses. The company has grown into FI Group which continues to review and evolve its ways of working to match the changing requirements of its people for flexibility, personal opportunities and social contact.

Employees should think of their employers as clients to whom they supply certain services. They need to understand the nature of what is wanted and which aspects of what they do represent most value. They must also understand how customer requirements are likely to evolve and anticipate the combinations of offerings likely to be demanded at different points in the future.

The more widespread adoption of a virtual form of operation is turning companies into portfolios of contractual relationships with various other individuals and organizations. Each party specializes on the basis of comparative advantage. Protodigm, a subsidiary of the pharmaceutical company Roche operates in this way, and at a particular stage in the supply chain, through a network of legal arrangements and a minuscule support staff.

Disputes can and do arise between the various contracting parties that make up virtual and network organizations. Managing and resolving them makes new demands upon people, both those in the periphery and those forming the core. Empathy and sensitivity are required.

Exercise: Satisfaction Analysis

If organizations are to establish more open and trusting relationships with their people, they need to understand how various aspects of corporate life can have a positive or negative impact upon employee satisfaction.

In relation to your organization, what aspects of corporate culture, processes or practices increase or decrease the degree of satisfaction and enjoyment which you [or your colleagues] derive from your working life? List these in order of priority. What changes need to be introduced to increase the 'positives' and reduce the 'negatives'?

Taking the Initiative

Employees also need to think about the markets for their current and future services, rather than in terms of specific jobs. The latter may bear little relationship to the contributions, which particular individuals do or do not make, and they may be 'here today and gone tomorrow'. In contrast, assuming a customer is likely to survive, it will continue to need certain forms of services.

Market awareness involves understanding the world beyond one's own organization. How is one placed in relation to alternative sources of supply? Who else is out there in terms of possible customers and actual or potential competitors? Is demand from within one's own organization likely to increase or decrease? Do other companies have similar or related needs?

Increases in demand can be met by operating in new ways. This might involve moving up a 'value chain' and deriving a higher income from a more effective use of one's capability. A reduction of internal activity could be balanced by undertaking work for other organizations. The latter could represent an opportunity for an existing customer to establish a cost centre and share overheads or generate incremental income. Alternatively, it could enable someone to reduce their dependence upon a single 'customer' and take the first steps towards an independent and portfolio career.

People who carry out this sort of analysis should be prepared to test the rhetoric of 'greater individual responsibility' by taking the initiative. Those who wait to be asked may be disappointed. An employer might not approach the issue from their particular perspective.

Teleworking initiatives often result from responses to individual circumstances, or a particular situation that affects a group of colleagues, when people themselves develop and champion arguments for change. It should not be assumed that internal suggestions will fall upon deaf ears. In some corporations, managers are actually 'tasked' to listen. They may encourage proposals for alternative ways of operating. Many employees need to become more 'entrepreneurial' when developing, articulating, representing and negotiating their cases.

Certain realities must be recognized and taken to heart. The sustainability of a set of relationships can depend upon clear evidence of advantages for all parties. Immediate and other colleagues may be affected by a suggested change. Hence they may have views which will need to be taken into account. Their support of what is proposed may also depend upon whether they too are likely to benefit. Any formal representation to an existing employer should clearly set out how the organization concerned is likely to gain from the new arrangements.

Premature exposure to independent operation can sometimes lead to a person being burned. Collaboration can ease the transition from one lifestyle to another. It can also reduce the risks. Taking responsibility for one's future may mean saying 'hello' rather than 'goodbye'. Before cutting themselves adrift, people should examine the options that might be available for establishing a different form of relationship with a current employer.

Some individuals cut off their noses to spite their faces when dealing with an existing paymaster. The backing and continuing commitment of an employer can be invaluable during the early stages of a new course of action. The more proposed arrangements will benefit one's present organization, the longer such support is likely to be retained.

Many of those who enjoy the greatest success as independent operators are also the most assiduous at cultivating and retaining corporate relationships, especially with current and former employers and customers. A larger organization might not necessarily have all the skills required to deliver effective responses. However, by virtue of its scale and presence, it may be more likely to face a flow of new business opportunities. Maintaining contact could enable one to share in these.

Enduring relationships between individuals and organizations can benefit both parties. Many people do not find it easy to market themselves as lone practitioners. Hence the value of relationships which may provide a succession of assignments, while for the major corporation they allow flexible access to a pool of trusted associates whose contributions can often be directly charged to particular projects.

Checklist

1.   How much account is taken of individual interests and aspirations when your organization establishes its goals and priorities? Does it consciously set out to improve the quality of working life? Does it invite comment and feedback?

2.   How sensitive and legitimate are its approaches, priorities, processes and practices.

3.   Do you feel there is potential within either yourself or your colleagues that is not being fully recognized, tapped, developed or utilized?

4.   Is there a fair balance between the interests of the organization and those of the individuals who work with it and for it? What more could be done to encourage and support individual interests?

5.   What attempts are made to comprehend the motivations and drives of particular individuals? Are people helped to understand themselves better?

6.   Does whatever emphasis is placed upon teamwork and corporate processes and practices, inhibit and constrain individuality and personal initiative?

7.   Are people enabled to be true to themselves? Are they rewarded or penalized for overtly seeking greater personal self-fulfillment? Does the organization glory in individual success?

8.   Is sufficient effort being devoted to making the culture of your organization more innovative and entrepreneurial? What would liberate people?

9.   What role might greater individual creativity and personal initiative play in this process?

10. How might the organization champion enterprise? What could, and should, be done to help people form and operate teams and networks which could research and establish new ventures?

11. Are new ways of working and learning encouraged? How might these make it easier for people to harness and apply their full potential? What initiatives are you taking in these areas?

12. What sponsorship role should your organization play? What support, or new forms of relationship, might it offer or provide? Should it encourage or create joint venture opportunities?

7

WORKING WITHIN

The worse the weather, the closer the cows.

Life takes root and people settle where the circumstances are the most favourable. Family groups congregate along river valleys with their rich soils, on the shores of natural inlets that provide shelter from the elements and in the shade of oasis palms. All around them may lie less hospitable land: densely forested hills that are difficult to clear and plough, exposed, rocky and barren headlands and burning, endless and featureless sands.

Restless souls part company with friends and the familiar and set off to look for new opportunities. They may have to travel for considerable distances before encountering conditions as favourable as those they once enjoyed. Some experience great privations on the way. Others get lost. Venturing out causes many people to value what they have left behind.

Severing a link with an organization, perhaps to secure a promotion or salary increment elsewhere, can involve sacrifice as well as risk. It may mean turning one's back upon significant emotional and intellectual investment and leaving behind a network of colleagues whom one knows 'warts and all'. Yet it is possible to develop in new directions without junking the past.

Avoiding Burning Boats

The value of what people have to offer is often employer, sector or context specific. It may not be recognized elsewhere. Many of those who resign from companies subsequently rue the day they cut themselves adrift from a corporate cocoon.

They wish, with the benefit of hindsight, that they had established some form of continuing relationship.

A serious attempt should be made to involve an employer
as a business partner in new plans, especially when its current
capabilities and contacts are relevant to one's future intentions.
In California's Silicon Valley, people can move with ease between employers and readily set up in business on their own
account. Hence companies operate a variety of employee share-
ownership, share-option and profit-sharing schemes to entice
new talent and hang on to their existing staff.

Opportunities for capital accumulation, rather than salaries, enable companies to compete for scarce skills. Various
forms of partnership and collaboration are used to sustain relationships. Adobe, a software supplier, and other companies
also attempt to secure a share of new wealth created by former
employees by themselves investing start up capital in their
new ventures.

There may be scope for various forms of co-operation. Perhaps some tailored, or value-added, service for a particular
target market could be based upon a product supplied by a
current employer. There might be the possibility of some form
of part-time or complementary, consultancy role that would
provide a welcome source of income during a start-up phase.

In the last chapter we saw that organizations themselves
are changing the nature of their relationships with interested
parties, with a view to delivering mutual benefits. This ought
to make senior management more open to suggestions from
within. It would be perverse if greater attention were paid to
approaches from those who have hitherto been unconnected
with a company, than to those from individuals who have played
a part in its development.

Images of Conflict

In responding to competitive conditions, and more challenging
threats, management thinkers and corporate strategists have
resorted to a range of military analogies. Markets are portrayed
as jungles. The international marketplace is viewed as an arena
of conflict in which giant corporations are locked head to head
in global battles to the death. They wage economic world wars.
Protagonists are spurred on by the lure of mass markets of
unprecedented scale.

Competitors watch each others every move. They seek to emulate successes and avoid mistakes. They slug it out with competitive advertising and marketing campaigns. Like arms races, these become ever more sophisticated, demanding and consuming of resources.

Strategists aim to outwit opponents. They build up elite project teams and train special forces who parachute into major bid situations. New product groups seek out 'killer applications'. Information is hoarded and knowledge stockpiled, for when it can be used to secure an edge.

Managers focus upon concealment and deception. Weaknesses are covered or disguised to avoid alerting customers or, worse still, the opposition. Some are hidden or denied to such an extent as to become not only out of sight but also not addressed. People who might be able to help cannot step forward with their contributions, if they are not aware that a problem exists.

In relation to deception, the ends are sometimes thought to justify the means. The overriding internal objective might be to score points. Externally, the aim could be to join the winning side. When no stone is left unturned in the search for competitive advantage, regulators need to be alert and on their toes.

Those in positions of authority may become quite ruthless at exploiting situations and sweating resources. On occasion, they will take advantage of customers, perhaps by repackaging a solution developed for one client by using their know-how, and, subsequently, selling it to a direct competitor. They may drive their people into the ground in order to secure a desired objective.

Companies employ 'investigators' to obtain inside knowledge. They poach each other's staff to obtain specialist competencies. Headhunters seek out the potentially mobile. As corporate bounty hunters they are always on the alert for opportunities to sell skills to the highest bidder.

Business activities are viewed in terms of actions, engagements and encounters. There are potential orders and competitive bids to be won or lost. There are targets to be hit or missed. Products which are in demand, wanted by many people, are milked; while the demise is plotted of others that may be well received but by fewer people.

When outcomes are categorized as successes or failures,

there will be winners and losers. These labels become attached to individuals and groups. Not surprisingly, people want to distance themselves from failures and bury them. Successes are celebrated, so that those who become associated with them may benefit. Reporting becomes selective. Bad news is hidden. Lessons are not learned from mistakes. Curriculum vitae tell half a story or less.

From Conflict to Collaboration

Military analogies miss the point. Like the poor, conflicts seem always to be with us. However, for long periods they may be the exception rather than the rule. They happen as a result of breakdowns in normal patterns of political and diplomatic activity. Sometimes they result from mistakes, forcing circumstances that most people would prefer to have avoided.

Conflicts are avoided wherever possible because they are intense and unpredictable. They are disruptive and extremely wasteful of resources. They divert people from a wide range of longer term and more productive activities. Great harm can be done in relatively short periods of time. Many people may become innocent and unintended victims. It might take a long time to recover fully.

Commercial conflicts too can burn energy and neutralize capabilities. The competitive tender process may well result in a lower price for the buyer. The spur of competition might also stimulate more creative responses than would otherwise be the case, just as wars sometimes force feed innovation and scientific advance. However, such gains can be secured at a cost.

In competitive bid situations, what about the resources consumed by those who lose? Who remembers the discarded ideas that are not incorporated into adopted solutions? Corners may have been cut as a result of the tight timescales set for the tender process. Would more have been achieved if the best members of all the short-listed teams had been able to collaborate? What might have emerged if they had been allowed the time to do a 'proper job'?

The consequences of war can be brutal. It is not surprising that people seek to negotiate, bargain and accommodate in order to avoid them. They strive to find common ground, to stress the interests which different parties have in common, as a means of counterbalancing an unhealthy obsession with what divides them. While particular outcomes may not satisfy everyone, and cries of 'sell out' might be heard, on the whole they could be preferable to the alternative of conflict.

Diplomats do not take isolation for granted. They aim to overcome divisions and draw together self-contained islands. They forge alliances and seek to uncover and reinforce whatever might hold them together. They identify and tackle the forces that threaten to tear them apart.

There are those whose business is conflict reduction. They stress the value of networks of co-operative links and mutual inter-dependency. They champion the adoption of new practices. Too often, the traditional practice is to cut off diplomatic links just when the stakes are the highest and the need for communication is the greatest. Instead, they advocate the installation of hot-lines and crisis centres. When the temperature rises it may be better to talk than to plot.

Adjusting to a New Era of Co-operation

After a long period, in which a succession of management practices have appeared to perpetuate and intensify competition, we have entered a new era. Various developments, especially in information and communications technologies, have increased massively the potential for co-operative and collaborative activities.

Traditionally, when wars end, citizens' armies are stood down. People are demobilized. They become free of the constraints and orders of military discipline and are allowed to go their own ways. They take off their uniforms and leave the barracks behind. While they may set off towards a wide diversity of homes and occupations, they are likely to share a common desire to enjoy the peace. They are united by an aspiration for a more balanced life; perhaps less ordered but richer and generally more satisfying.

Those in positions of authority face new challenges. People are no longer mere players who are compelled to subject themselves to the demands of a higher purpose. They themselves are now a target audience. They become the recipients of a range of programmes and services designed to liberate and support them. They may be provided with the skills and given the means of adapting to civilian life.

Whereas it was by joining an army, and through collective

action, that they might have contributed to a footnote in history, the emphasis now switches to personal fulfillment. Each person might pay taxes and/or receive benefits. The well-being of society depends upon how many of them are able to make a successful adjustment. Civilization itself becomes the extent to which the social fabric enables the widespread achievement of individual aims.

Many managers in major companies face a similar challenge as they seek to extricate themselves from competitive races that depress margins and frustrate their people. They need to establish longer term collaborative arrangements that are likely to be both more profitable for the corporation and more satisfying for those involved. Their success depends upon the totality of the responses of individual and involved customers, employees and partners. Corporate performance is both a cause and a consequence of the state of these relationships.

Corporations need to adjust to the requirements for successful collaboration. New support mechanisms have to be put in place. Effort that was once devoted to the corporate win must now be redeployed to supporting and enabling individual initiative. Whereas once the lone entrepreneur might have been viewed as a threat to corporate unity and purpose, enterprise should now become the essence of what a company is all about.

For some organizations, dramatic adjustment is needed. Individuals and teams must be viewed as potential business partners to be backed up with appropriate support, in return for a share of the returns likely to result from their endeavours. The corporation becomes a supplier of venture capital, a source of licensed technology and a provider of a range of specialist business services.

Exercise: Greenhouse Analysis

Organizations should endeavour to create the conditions in which innovation, creativity and enterprise can flourish. Encouragement needs to be given but if a hundred or a thousand flowers are to bloom a company must be equipped and ready to deal with the consequences.

In the corporate greenhouse of your organization, what changes need to be made to the culture and the

environment to enable new ideas to germinate? What support is required to stimulate subsequent growth? Are there sufficient stakes in place to cope with the number of shoots which may emerge? If thinning becomes necessary, who will do this? Will the plants that are produced be sufficiently hardy to survive outside?

From Employer to Corporate Sponsor and Partner

The new corporate investor has privileged 'inside' knowledge of its potential enterprise partners. It knows where they have been and what they have been through.

It is perverse that in recent years so many corporations have devoted so much management time to alienating, de-skilling and eliminating innumerable future business partners. Jim Harding, the Chief Executive at Mouchel, put the emphasis upon capability building and value generation. He used the analogy of turning a flat fish into a friendly and adaptable dolphin to emphasize the nature of the changes required: an intelligent front end of new advisory services and relationship management skills; and a strong tail of support services which include new career and knowledge development mechanisms.

Elsewhere, many of those who have been de-layered might, with proper support and appropriate collaboration, have been capable of generating future opportunities. By focusing more upon helping them, many corporations might have enabled themselves to adjust to new conditions, and create fresh income streams, rather than perpetuate an anorexic decline.

Take the masses of data which large corporations hold. In many cases, much could be learned from these treasure houses of information. A variety of techniques are now available for undertaking analyses, assessing patterns and predicting requirements. However, many of those who could have asked the right questions, and derived benefits from such sources, are no longer employed.

A data store could possibly form the basis of new joint ventures between data owners and bright individuals or creative teams. The latter could offer to find ways of generating value from it in return for a 'share of the cake'. A new breed of 'information entrepreneurs', data mining or knowledge entrepreneurs, is emerging.

Employees, individually and in groups, often spot opportunities that are missed by their employers. Whereas a company might be active across a range of markets they are usually more narrowly focused. They may spot a specific means of going direct to customers with a solution to a particular need which they are known to have, but which existing products and services do not address. As a consequence, they may leave to set up their own enterprises.

They may be in a position to offer in-depth expertise and highly specialist knowledge. They might also have the necessary commitment to establish and retain a pole position in what may come to be recognized as a new market sector. Moreover, it could be one they themselves create. They need only excel where it matters. Any supporting services that are required could be outsourced, bought in, or obtained from partners.

One of Europe's 'hi-tech' success stories, the German company SAP was set up by former employees of IBM. They realized that companies were interested in 'ends', whereas vendors were offering them the 'means'. Customers wanted resource planning and other processes, rather than various technologies and re-engineering projects that might or might not result in an integrated solution. They, therefore, set out to design and produce in software form sets of model processes which people in different sectors could simply load and use.

Staying in the Game in Order to Change it

The process of corporate socialization, with its diet of teamwork and appeals for solidarity, can make a latent or budding entrepreneur appear withdrawn or conspiratorial. They may feel guilty about being self-interested, even though they might well be sowing the seeds of a development that could serve both individual needs and the general good of a parent organization.

People should not assume that a suggested change of role will be met with hostility. Increasingly, forward-looking managers interpret such approaches as evidence of enterprise, rather than of a lack of loyalty. It can all depend upon whom one approaches with new ideas, when, how and for what purpose. Investors in Industry, now 3i, allowed its public relations team to form an independent company, Shandwick, which was able to supply services to both itself and other companies.

Should an existing employer prove unreceptive, it may be necessary to look for another one. Some new business concepts require a level of capability and funding which a new enterprise would find difficult to provide on its own. Hence the need for a corporate patron.

Guy Hands developed the concept of principal finance, or raising money through the issue of bonds to buy cash generating assets. However, he needed the support of a financial institution to implement his ideas. He shopped around for a suitable backer. Eventually, he joined Nomura International as an employee but with a package that reflected his entrepreneurial role. Together, an individual and a company were able to accomplish something which neither could have achieved on their own.

Not all corporations are so receptive. Organizations often delegate selection, assessment and career development responsibilities to specialist personnel and human resources departments. In many companies, particularly larger ones, such professionals apply relatively standard criteria or formulae. This is especially so when survivors in slimmed-down units have further redundancy cases to cope with. Few staff may be judged and rewarded on an individual basis. Most simply belong to one category or another.

Inevitably, many intermediaries act as a distorting screen between those with suggestions for new ways of working and contributing and others who might benefit from their ideas. Individuals who appear 'unusual' or who seem not to 'fit', may be screened out of 'fast track' opportunities and confined to backwaters.

Many people find themselves under pressure to meet the standard criteria for advancement. On occasion, to progress may mean betraying ones principles or at least moving further away from alternative options that would provide greater personal fulfilment.

Others find their particular contributions are either lost or watered down in the context of a group or collective operation. Not everyone necessarily wants to be a team player. Some people derive greater satisfaction from working alone and being themselves. They have their own ideas. Those with itchy feet should not wait for too long before taking the initiative. Leave a fish on deck for a few seconds and it may be taken by a gull.

Identifying Allies and Accumulating Support

Every effort should be made to achieve direct contact with those leading front-line operations. Staff concerned with delivering value and satisfaction to customers face, daily, a reality that others may distort. Approaches should highlight the contributions which suggested changes could make to their responsibilities, objectives and priorities.

The focus should be upon how the organization will benefit from what is being advocated. Many cynical managers no longer give the benefit of the doubt to individuals. Any hint that the main driver of a proposed change is someone's personal desire for a different lifestyle might cause whatever is put forward to be perceived as a ploy or rationalization. As a result of suspicions concerning self-interest, a proposition may not receive the objective evaluation it deserves.

As in politics, a week in business can sometimes be a long time. The fact that a company has always supplied the whole of a particular market requirement by itself need not be taken as immutable or sacrosanct. Once the suggestion is put that members of the sales force could perhaps operate as 'independents', but with corporate support, a company might well see the advantages. In certain sectors or geographic areas, such an arrangement could allow those who remain within the core team to focus upon 'key accounts' or higher margin opportunities. A variety of options could be considered for putting an alternative strategy into effect, ranging from an agency or franchise agreement to joint ventures.

Some companies have established, or encouraged the formation of, mechanisms to help their staff cope with fundamental changes of role that might, or might not, involve a continuing relationship with them. Cable & Wireless established career action centres to help people plan and equip themselves for future moves. The original impetus came from the need to help internationally mobile managers handle the transition between assignments.

Former IBM staff have established Skillbase as a means of securing further opportunities to undertake work for 'big blue'. Skillbase also markets their services to other organizations. It was initially based upon the experience of Xanadu, a support network established by former employees of Xerox who had left the corporation to form their own companies.

Responding to Individual Needs

Increasingly, as has already been pointed out, companies are becoming 'internal markets' within which individuals need to promote themselves to colleagues. Enlightened employers ensure there is sufficient information to allow people to identify the areas of opportunity in which they can make the greatest contribution, while remaining true to themselves.

Companies setting out to replace standard contracts of employment with agreements that are tailored to the particular needs of different individuals and groups, should prepare for a number of issues that are likely to arise. Each pattern of work can present its own particular management problems. A diversity of arrangements can greatly complicate the task of coordinating inputs from people who are working in different ways.

'Contractitus' might be avoided by providing training which covers the negotiation, setting up and management of different forms of relationship. Supporting systems should be capable of recording what has been agreed, monitoring performance and ensuring payment. Care needs to be taken to ensure that coordination, development and support demands are not excessive in comparison with the advantages accruing to the parties concerned.

The benefits of more fulfilled and energized people should be set against the costs of changing to a more flexible model of operation. In market sectors, where the likely customers are known to all suppliers, relevant information is easily accessible, appropriate technology is widely available, people are mobile and quality certification is the norm, the treatment of staff can become a critical 'differentiator'. It might be one of the few areas in which an imaginative provider could secure competitive advantage.

Committed and engaged people, who feel fairly treated, are more likely to become creative, involved and active participants in corporate activities. Those who believe that a company has been receptive and responsive are more likely to reciprocate by opening up and giving more of themselves. Ultimately, such reactions are likely to result in performance improvements.

Companies, which work with their people in the creation of a greater diversity of lifestyles and working patterns, can

also contribute to a range of social goals. Thus fewer journeys to and from a designated city centre place of work could
reduce environmental pollution, transport bills and the disruption of congestion at peak periods, as well as saving office
overhead costs.

Intrapreneurs

Some businesses break down easily into manageable and
family-sized units. These can give people a sense of what it is
to run their own business. Thus each title produced by a
periodical publisher, or a group of titles, could form a distinct
unit with its own editorial team; while a retailer might own
a number of outlets each of which could be run by an accountable manager.

Waterstone's, a bookstore chain, offers its employees an opportunity to acquire a personal portfolio of skills. Decisions
concerning when each training course is taken are left to the
individuals concerned, but working through a series of stages
equips people to manage a branch store. The company attracts
people with an interest in books and enables those who are so
inclined to obtain some of the satisfaction that can result from
running their own business.

The extent to which those managing individual units feel
and behave like entrepreneurs will depend upon how much
local discretion they are given and how many aspects of an
operation are prescribed from the centre. In many sectors, the
extent of what is mandated, or performed centrally, has steadily increased in recent years. Consequently, those in the front-
line, and without direct experience of support facilities located elsewhere, may develop a misleading view of the economics of acting independently. On the other hand, some may
identify local or special needs that are not being met by services determined in a remote head office.

Much will depend upon the nature of the particular business. If an activity requires both collective effort and significant amounts of capital, individuals may not find it so easy to
'do their own thing'. Negotiating a variety of special arrangements with people who supply a relatively standard input might
be regarded as an expensive luxury or 'more trouble than it is
worth'. For those requiring finance, and the inputs of colleagues,
there are also the 'transaction' costs of negotiation with various other parties.

The UK Post Office has created an internal innovation fund to which groups of staff may apply for the resources to develop their ideas for new businesses and services. Priority is given to proposals that could have a significant impact upon particular groups of customers. A number of the organization's early e-business initiatives resulted from backing local enterprise with central corporate support.

Exercise: Visioning

To enter into an effective dialogue and a fruitful discussion with the representatives of an organization, individuals need to understand their own personal drives, be sure of the direction in which they are headed and retain a sharp picture of their intended destination. People require well-defined and unambiguous objectives in order to know when and how to conclude negotiations or whether to break them off in favour of other alternatives.

Do you have an overriding aim or explicit purpose in life? Do you possess a clear vision of where you would like to be? Is it shared by others who are close to you? Is it capable of achievement? How might it form the basis of a new settlement or collaborative arrangement with your current employer?

Identifying Opportunities

Within many companies there are areas of operation which do not realize their full potential and other opportunities which do not receive the care or consideration they deserve. This could be because of their relative importance or the short attention span of senior staff. The concern of top management could be focused upon issues of greater perceived significance from a corporate point of view.

Internally, colleagues and superiors may simply just not see the 'prospects' in a given situation. There may be other more pressing claims upon the resources that are available for investment. In contrast, there might be sources of external funding that would have an interest in the area in question. Establishing the activity as an entity in its own right could be a means of introducing additional funding and an element of separate equity.

Corporate processes and procedures are often a compromise between different requirements. The use of standard approaches may be acceptable where needs are homogeneous. However, in the event of greater diversity, certain areas may receive requests which they cannot handle. Their capability, and how they operate, might not be appropriate for meeting such requirements. Establishing a degree of independence, and treating distinct areas on their own merits, could make it easier for them to respond and adjust.

Opportunities for a 'step change' level of improvement can often be identified by searching for a way of operating without a particular problem. The management of stock presented great difficulties for a Portuguese furniture manufacturer. Uninova devised a means of enabling customized items to be made for individual buyers. Effectively, they can now design their own products, which are made to order, thus doing away with the need for a separate warehousing function.

Management Buyouts

The management buyout has become a popular route to the establishment of a significant business in an area with which those involved are likely to be already familiar. A new entity can 'hit the ground running', with the benefit of existing customers and tested suppliers. Almost any type of business could become the subject of a buyout, although third-party providers of finance may only be interested in entities of a certain size.

Compared with an option, such as franchising, the management buyout route can give an entrepreneurial team greater opportunity to break free from an existing formula. A buyout, unlike many franchise options, is generally a team activity. Most companies and sources of finance would be reluctant to back a project that is largely dependent upon a single individual, even if there were evidence of its acceptability to the other people involved.

The buyout can be an exit strategy, as well as an entry option. A management buyout could be a means of passing management and ownership responsibility from one or more founding entrepreneurs to a successor generation drawn from within. This was the case with the design consultancy Wolff Olins.

So many buyouts have occurred that numerous professional advisers claim to be able to assist the process of bringing interested parties together. An injection of fresh finance may well be required to bridge a gap between available funds and the price which the company selling the enterprise concerned expects to receive. Hence, financial institutions and venture capitalists are generally involved, as few salaried managers are likely to have accumulated enough capital to acquire a significant enterprise from their own resources.

Most 'high street' banks are reluctant to provide all of the finance required by buyout teams. Thus approaches are made to venture capitalists with relevant experience. Unlike bankers, they may wish to play an active role in the management of companies which they support.

Much will depend upon the nature of the individual business, for example whether there are assets against which loans could be secured or significant amounts owed by debtors which could form the basis of a sales-linked funding arrangement. Some teams were lucky enough to conclude arrangements that have become largely self-financing. Of course, attention needs to be paid to such practicalities as the level of fees and the nature of any penalties, for example for early repayment.

The higher the share of finance provided by the buyout team, the larger the proportion of equity which they will own and the greater their prospect of financial gain. However, to raise the money required might require a second mortgage on a house. Such arrangements can increase the personal risk of those involved.

Preparing for a Buyout

The initiative for a buyout usually comes from members of a local or unit management team, who are attracted by the idea of controlling their own independent enterprise and realizing opportunities outside of the constraints of existing corporate ownership. The first step is to prepare a compelling case which can be put to the appropriate 'decision makers', such as the members of a parent company board. The argument should stress the commercial and strategic advantages of a sale to the current 'host' organization. For example, it might free the parent of the need to make incremental investments in an area that is not considered a 'core business'.

Continuing to run an ongoing unit, while at the same time preparing it for independent operation under an arrangement in which one may have a substantial financial interest, raises a host of legal and ethical issues for all concerned. Inevitably there will be difficult trade-offs. For example, should money be saved today for a current employer at the expense of lowering the value of the business tomorrow? Learning how to handle such choices can be a good preparation for the challenges likely to face the board of an independent operation.

Dealing with an existing employer, one that may be known 'warts and all', has its advantages. But there are also dangers. While having honest and realistic counsel is one thing, being typecast is another. Often colleagues just do not see, or accept, that particular individuals might be capable of achieving more under different conditions. Buyout teams also need to remember that those with whom they are negotiating are being paid to act in the best interests of their employer. They should expect discussions to be business-like and must act accordingly.

On occasion, those with a good idea can face a dilemma. To progress matters they may need to table proposals and yet once these are presented they could well be taken advantage of by others. Senior colleagues might 'go off' with an idea. An alternative buyer could be approached. The company itself may consider it has the right to adopt elements of a suggestion where its own property is at stake.

Particular care needs to be taken when the assets of an organization are involved. The directors have a duty to preserve whatever is owned by an organization, whether physical property, finance or intellectual capital. When title is transferred to a new entity, any valuation needs to be fair from the point of view of all the parties involved. Often there is room for considerable debate, and sometimes the potential for fraud and deception.

The question of transferring undertakings from one owner to another can be an emotive one. Good corporate citizens sometimes complain that a company which has funded the know-how underlying a new venture might be denied an element of the future return which it deserves. Notwithstanding the legal protection they may have, many of those who might find themselves working for a new employer worry that their new employment conditions may be less favourable than before.

Others could be more interested in whether there are hidden assets and liabilities.

Employees have a moral duty to declare any conflicts of interest and directors are under a legal obligation to do likewise in the boardroom. One danger of encouraging internal entrepreneurs could be that people may be tempted to conceal areas of opportunity in order that these can be personally exploited. It could incite some to become selfish and deceitful, while a few may descend to fraudulent behaviour.

Both companies, and those with whom they are negotiating, should endeavour to become aware of any divided loyalties. The senior management of organizations which are in receipt of internal proposals for different relationships and arrangements should establish some means of ensuring that they are fully and fairly considered. People should be required to state any interests they may have and refrain from voting on such matters.

Where considerable effort is devoted to the evaluation of proposals, people should avoid trivial applications. When the same individuals appear to submit or table a succession of proposals the corporate patience can become severely strained. The limited time of colleagues should not be needlessly wasted, either on ill-considered initiatives or by encouraging people to put a great deal of effort into developing and presenting a case that may have little chance of success.

Those who are eager to change direction should not focus exclusively upon external market opportunities. There might also be a prospect of working from within. People should not be put off by the enormity of what is at stake. Adversity and challenge can make individuals and organizations more interdependent. The scale and complexity of an undertaking, and the need for mutual support, can bring people together. Some coalesce into tight and winning groups.

Checklist

1. Does your organization have some form of enterprise initiative or incubator unit for developing new businesses?

2. Are suggestions from its people actively stimulated and followed up?

3. Does your organization know who is, or might, become interested in breaking out or changing direction? Are such people encouraged or discouraged? Is a database of budding entrepreneurs maintained?

4. Is it possible for people to become intrapreneurs? Are they helped to locate others who might have an interest in working with them?

5. Is the acquisition and development of relevant entrepreneurial and enterprise development skills encouraged and supported? Is specialist guidance and counselling available?

6. Are staff with intrapreneurial leanings helped to formulate and critique a business plan? What forms of 'start up' and subsequent assistance are provided?

7. What alternatives to 'traditional' employment are offered? How flexible is your organization in responding to the individual and special needs of its people?

8. How receptive is it to proposals from those who would like to operate in a different way?

9. Are management buyouts encouraged? How easy is it for people to identify and create opportunities? What is done to make facilities, time and other resources available to them?

10. Does your organization seek, negotiate and retain a stake in new ventures that are created? Does it become an interested and value-adding partner?

11. Are processes in place to ensure that relevant and legitimate interests are both disclosed and protected?

12. Are negotiations between the representatives of your organization and its people frank and fair? Do they lead to outcomes that are acceptable to all the parties involved?

13. Are there effective arrangements for protecting intellectual property?

14. Is adequate recognition given and compensation provided for the use of both individual competencies and corporate capabilities?

8

BREAKING OUT

Go to sea or go hungry.

From time to time events happen in life which cause us to view ourselves and others differently. Sometimes the unanticipated, such as the shock of dismissal, can result in people losing self-confidence, becoming disoriented or turning in upon themselves. Some do not recover. They remain bitter and twisted, forever after observing life through distorted lenses.

On other occasions the disruptions may be provided by natural forces, when the unexpected can introduce a sense of wonder and a glimpse of magic. The snow falling heavily and quietly at night can blanket the landscape, town and countryside alike, with a soft covering that muffles many of the normal sounds of modern life.

Regular routines are interrupted. People stay at home. Cars remain in garages. Trains do not run. Notorious traffic bottlenecks fall silent. Some communities become isolated. Their members' thoughts quickly turn from the trivialities, distractions and trappings of daily existence to the essentials of life. Will they still be able to get bread and milk?

Looking at the World Differently

For some, the solitude brings time for reflection. The more active venture outside to find that the world, which they thought they knew, has changed. Many traditional points of reference are no longer visible. Much of what has been ignored and taken for granted suddenly become objects of wonder and beauty, so much so that photographs may be taken as a permanent record of one particular day that turned out to be different. While never a substitute for 'being there', such photos can act as reminders long after the snow has melted.

The observant notice signs of activities that may hitherto have been overlooked. There might be footprints and tracks in the snow, contributed by a number of other species. Their patterns may reveal similar preoccupations. Thus there might be heavy concentrations of prints at the edge of those areas of water that remain unfrozen or which have thawed. In normal times, many people remain either unaware of, or not really focused upon, that which is most important to those around them.

And then it begins to fade. White turns to grey. The thaw sets in. People get to work clearing paths with spades and pouring grit onto roads. Runways are swept by snowploughs. Aeroplanes take off. The world returns to normal. Memories of the innocent optimism of childhood are replaced by regular anxieties, preoccupations and frustrations. It is back to the daily grind.

Routines allow people to cope with the mundane. They enable us to put the unimportant in its place. However, some take them too far. When every aspect of the working day is programmed, life is replaced by technical existence.

Some people appear to be natural catalysts or instigators of enterprise. Richard Branson started while still at school. Others delay taking the plunge. Becoming an entrepreneur might not be their first wish. They may want to first discharge prior obligations to members of their family. However, a discontinuity can trigger a revelation or lead to the realization that a change of direction might be needed.

Disruptions to routines and the familiar can have positive results. A sudden illness, or the loss of a loved one, has caused many people to alter course and bring more balance into their lives. Such incidents, rather than market research reports, have provided the inspiration for many of the entrepreneurs who were interviewed during the gestation of this book.

Interruptions and shocks sometimes act as a spur to creativity. People become energized. They suddenly notice links, observe patterns and forge new relationships. This metamorphosis can occur in a traditional businesses, and often does when corporate recoveries and renewals occur. Allied Carpets was turned around in under a year. When it was floated, staff who had previously invested in the company found themselves holding stock worth 75 times their original outlay.

Exercise: The Snowfall and the Thaw

People need to distinguish the priority elements of their lives from the ephemera and trivia and those aspects which are distractions.

If the snow should fall, what are the main features of your life that would remain visible? Would you be able to recognise your world? Could you find your way home? Who would you set out to rescue if they were lost? Who would worry about you if you became trapped in a drift? After the thaw, what and/or who, would you be most pleased to see again? What and whom would you most like to see washed away?

Rediscovering the Magic of Open-minded Innocence

Someone new to a field may question what others take for granted. In areas as diverse as ballistics to the outdoor advertising of Scheffer's Reklame, new entrants have challenged existing assumptions and found new ways of doing things. As they grew older, they retained the natural curiosity of the child. They just 'looked people in the eye' and asked: 'Why?'

For some a glimpse is all they need. A simple sign can set them off in new directions. A mere spark is sufficient to kindle a fire in their imaginations that might rage for days and consume all those barriers which have been standing in their way. Its light may enable them to cut through mists and fogs. It could illuminate unexpected routes to novel destinations.

Others are less lucky. They coexist with the uninspired and remain in darkness. Many corporate cultures and working environments inhibit, rather than encourage, innovation and imagination. They are dull, lifeless and unexciting. Little is done to introduce variety, stimulation and magic into people's lives. No wonder they retreat to their homes, or book themselves into hotels, to perform an occasional creative task.

Individuals establishing new enterprises should begin with an open mind and a blank sheet of paper. They need to become more observant when looking at the world and perceive what is happening around them in new ways. Just as it is with a fall of snow, a freshness of vision can lead to the discovery of additional patterns and relationships.

Many people over-complicate matters. Some do so pur-
posely, in order to foster dependency. Simplification enables
people to assess the salient features of a situation more easily and clearly. Managers should attempt to filter or blanket
the endless trivia, irritations and distractions of corporate
life.

Too many management initiatives create further pressure,
establish new rituals and result in additional reports which
have to be compiled and considered. All of these erode what
little time may remain for the exercise of individual and collective imagination. If a corporate snowfall could be organized,
which programmes and projects would people like to see
blanked out?

Some feel trapped. Pension provision represents an area in
which many people do not begin with a blank sheet of paper.
Few who plan to 'make a move' in their 30s, 40s, or early 50s
will have put enough aside to secure financial independence.
Those, who are able to take 'early retirement' and draw a pension, often find that the amounts they could receive are significantly lower than would be the case if they opted to defer taking advantage of the fund they have built up. Many will wish
to continue contributing. This realization, and normal living
costs, puts them under pressure to retain an income flow or
secure an alternative one.

Assumptions and past practices can limit. Nothing should
be taken for granted, starting with the very existence of a corporation. It should not be assumed that an organization is
needed. What value does it add over and above that which could
be achieved by people themselves, if they were free to associate together as circumstances might dictate? Out of such questions could emerge a new rationale for a company and a different basis for establishing and restructuring relationships
with those who wish to associate with it.

Why not 'go it alone'? Many people with large personal 'turno-
vers' operate as individual practitioners. Because they sell a
personal service they are effectively their own 'products'. Of
course, they may retain some form of secretarial and accounting or 'bookkeeping' support, perhaps on a part-time basis.
Otherwise, they do not establish or own an organization as
such. Nevertheless, some creative individuals have incomes
'running into millions'.

There are as many ways of breaking through the prison walls of a former life as there are of escaping from a jail. Some are dramatic, such as taking dynamite to the bars. Others could be more subtle, such as leaving while concealed in a laundry bag.

A friendly warden can help. Mention was made in the last chapter of IBM's Skillbase. British Airways, Ford and other companies have also created mechanisms to help people leave the corporate embrace and set up in business on their own account. XR Associates was established by former Ford employees who admitted the car company as part-owner of the enterprise in return for the provision of office space and other services. XR Associates markets the skills of those on its books, both within Ford and to other companies.

Creating New Enterprise Concepts

Establishing the essence and rationale of a new venture should be the first priority. What value is it seeking to create and for whom? Is what is being provided or proposed special or distinctive? How will it fit into the overall scheme of things? For example, is it a self-contained product, or consumed in conjunction with other goods and services?

A surprising number of companies, including some well-known names, struggle to survive because there is really nothing unique, special or particular about them. If they folded, their customers would simply go around the corner and buy something similar from another supplier. After a time they would not be missed. 'Me to' enterprises are soon forgotten.

The commercial worlds and lifestyles of many entrepreneurial individuals become integrated. Just as the Chinese language does not distinguish between the heart and the mind, these executives mix the two. Some become passionate and feel the urge to live their business vision and strategy.

The people, buildings and other tangible factors, which traditionally enable us to identify the existence of an operation, can enable a business concept to be put into effect. However, in themselves, they do not constitute an enterprise. For many companies they represent areas of cost, which may or may not be relevant to the process of value creation.

Capabilities represent capacity or potential which, in a particular situation, may or may not be relevant. Various forms of

human and physical resource from skills to equipment all
have a cost, whether they are owned or contracted. However,
they only have a value to the extent that an end customer is
will-ing and able to pay for a product or a service to which
they can make a contribution.

There is no substitute for a winning business concept that
is rooted in the needs, values and requirements of customers. While the garrulous may be too busy talking to notice
what is going on around them, the intending entrepreneur
should listen and watch. Even the polite chit-chat of wine
bar society may be revealing of unfulfilled needs. The effective observer needs to be a detached and reflective partici-
pant.

People make tracks in the snow. They leave other footprints
which reveal what is important to them, from the patterns of
transactions on their credit card statements to the orders for
the 'usual please' which they place. From the habits and preferences revealed through past transactions it is possible to
speculate about what consumers might wish to do, or how they
might respond to new or different product offerings.

The Significance of Relative Scale

Some organizations are able to aggregate and analyze transactions involving a large customer base. They may have an
advantage in relation to forecasting future patterns of consumption and predicting the relative speeds at which different groups might adopt new offerings. They may have the
scale to invest in data-mining services, the resources to establish callcentre front ends, and the product range to support cross-selling initiatives.

As the real costs of particular technologies continue to fall,
what the corporation can afford today could be in the hands of
sole practitioners tomorrow. The packages will come. In the
meantime, although individuals are likely to have experience
of far fewer cases to generalize from, it may be possible for
them to have more intensive relationships with others.
Hence, they may examine many more facets of what consti-
tutes value for a purchaser. In place of 'width' they may have
the advantage of a greater 'depth' of detailed knowledge.

Personal observation can reveal not just what has been
bought, but why and what subsequently happened as a result.

Motivations can be assessed before, during and after different stages of a relationship. Desires, drives, feelings and reactions can be explored.

The mechanical understanding that results from management analysis may not tell the whole story. It might need to be complemented by the instinctive perception that can grow out of direct participation in particular relationships. An effective response to the requirements of an individual customer can require a combination of both corporate analysis and personal involvement and insight.

Mutual awareness of the respective contributions of individual empathy and imagination, and corporate capability and support, can form the basis for establishing new relationships between people and organizations. Each should concentrate upon what the comparative advantage and the principal of subsidiarity suggest they are best equipped to do. Rather than resent their dependence upon other parties, both should view such a situation as a prerequisite of arrangements that have the potential to endure.

Where relationships do not last, and for various reasons individuals and organizations reach an impasse and a parting of the ways occurs, those concerned should recognize that such a break up can be a traumatic experience for many people. An employer should acknowledge its responsibility for helping people to cope with voluntary, or enforced, separation.

The company that both strengthens the distinct advantages of its particular people and partners, and at the same ensures the continuing relevance and value of its own special contribution, binds the members of its network, or value chain, more closely together. Conversely, a jealous 'beggar thy neighbour' strategy can lead to defensiveness, the hoarding rather than the sharing of understanding, and eventual fragmentation.

The Creative Combination Elements

People have an increasing range of choice in terms of when, where and how to consume. Along with a greater capability to tailor to particular requirements, this means that the number of possible permutations and combinations can appear endless. The issue is often not whether new combinations of options can be brought together, but rather who is going to do it.

Employees in larger companies have traditionally been

under tremendous pressure to move cautiously and build upon existing strengths. The widespread adoption of quality has encouraged incremental and gradual evolution rather than discontinuity. Internally, people may run about like headless chickens, but externally the corporation creeps like a snail.

To corporate clones, creative people can appear temperamental, self-centred, insensitive to others and generally difficult to manage. They are driven by their own talents, obsessions, and preoccupations, rather than by the need to 'fit in'. Hence they can become abrasive and outspoken when they feel thwarted, unappreciated or undervalued.

If an organization is struggling to handle a few thinkers and challengers of the status quo, how would its senior management cope with a situation in which creativity needs to become the norm? The experiences of companies such as 3M, suggest that innovation can become institutionalized to form an integral element of corporate culture. However, this process takes time and many contemporary corporate contexts provide little time and scope for reflection. In the meantime, the frustrated may look elsewhere.

Those who 'have a go' tend to be the individuals with a positive and active approach to life. They are confident, persistent yet flexible and willing to take risks. They can visualize success and they rejoice and celebrate it when it comes along. They do not wait passively for opportunities to arise or arrive. They go out and create them.

At the same time, impetuosity should be avoided. Tucked into many a fold, along the most rugged of Cornish cliffs, it is possible to find simple dwellings which were once occupied by those who put their boats out to sea when the conditions were right. They did not expect life to owe them a living, but neither did they take needless risks. They monitored the tides and sea conditions to avoid both rocks and storms. When deciding whether or not to venture forth they took into account all that they knew and could sense and feel.

Advantages and Drawbacks of Specialization

For potential entrepreneurs, specialization is both a blessing and a curse. It may enable them to develop a capability in a particular field and, perhaps, a distinct reputation. However, as a consequence, they may become both less aware of and insensitive to the totality of a situation.

Realization of the limitations of individual operation can give further impetus to a drive for collective action. It also provides criteria for assessing the extent to which a particular form of organization is justified and whether its activities should be extended or reduced. If one could start again, what elements would be networked together and which set free? Which of the elements are likely to be needed on a recurring or continuing basis and which could be contracted in as required? Would a consortium be desirable, or advisable, in order to assemble all of the elements involved in assessing and responding to emerging total requirements?

Most people are concerned with particular elements of a whole. The subdivision of labour in large organizations reinforces this. It encourages them to define 'the whole' in terms of visible production capabilities, rather than the totality of customer requirements. In some situations, no one may have an overview or the 'big picture'. In others, the presence of 'niche suppliers' is evidence that enterprising individuals have spotted particular gaps and have come together to fill them.

Machines can be broken down into components. Data is disaggregated. Professions fragment into specialist interest groups. Consultants form sector teams and academics subject units. Organizations have traditionally accepted and practiced the principal of subdivision. Public bodies and governments have their departments and universities their faculties. Management approaches, such as the identification of core competencies and the search for outsourcing opportunities, encourage people to focus.

Specialization and concentration can be healthy from a corporate perspective. Without them, an organization may spread itself so thinly as to accomplish little. However, there are also dangers. Companies need to understand 'what they are about'. But what they ought to be about should be determined by what needs to be done to create and deliver value for clients, customers or users.

From a customer perspective, what is available from each individual supplier may represent only one element of a total solution to a particular problem. In an attempt to make a sale, each supplier will be tempted to exaggerate the contribution which its particular goods or services can provide. The unscrupulous or unaware, may even claim that what they provide will, in itself, deliver a sufficient or comprehensive response.

All too rarely is the focus upon an emerging issue or a generic problem. Too often it is upon particular products or selective features of an institutional arrangement inherited from the past. As a consequence, areas of considerable opportunity can become hidden, lost between the cracks. Progress is incremental, as a succession of unco-ordinated improvements are made to individual aspects of a concealed whole.

Assembling Winning Formulae

Fundamental breakthroughs often occur when insights from one area are brought to bear upon the problems of another. People suddenly see a pattern or discover a connection. The establishment of new links and relationships between elements of capability, such as people, knowledge, or technology, can be the source of a new business concept.

For example, transactions over the internet can be undertaken at a small fraction of the cost of visits to shops or banks. Thus bringing together software development and Web design skills and specialist knowledge of retailing or banking can create more effective models of operation. Potential 'winners' ought to be collaborations between organizations, such as Intuit or Logica that understand the various combinations of tech-nologies involved, and companies with 'brand awareness', such as American Express.

The individual elements of what might be brought together to provide a new product or service could be known to many people, but few may understand the ways in which they could be combined. Being able to overcome the practical problems involved can be an important source of competitive advantage. Others may understand various components, but not how to assemble them into an acceptable whole.

Winning formulae are often counter-intuitive. Many of them result from people looking in a different direction from the crowd. For example, why do so many companies assume they have to peer into the future to spot opportunities? Edward Lambert and Matthew Norton looked back 100 years when searching for a distinctive role for the bespoke tailor Norton & Townsend. As a consequence, they revived an old practice of visiting people in their own homes for the measurement and fitting of suits.

One entrepreneur noticed that outside broadcast teams going

on location, required a variety of different pieces of equipment of varying sizes. Particular items would be carried by each member of the group. This gave rise to a variety of problems, ranging from frequent searches and delays during security screenings at airports, to the frustration of being unable to operate on arrival at an end destination due to one or more of the components being lost, misplaced or damaged in transit.

The solution, a classic case of bringing all the elements together, was to provide a robust and air-transportable container of standard and acceptable dimensions into which all the equipment required could be quickly and safely packed. This approach maximized the prospect of everything required arriving safely at an end destination. While en route the members of the crew, freed of their 'portering' role, could concentrate upon planning their creative contributions. So convenient was the new system that the entrepreneur's company was able to earn a significant margin upon the various individual components which were bought in from other suppliers.

The seeds of many winning business concepts lie in the gaps between the various elements that constitute 'existing provision'. There are many opportunities in the arena of relationships between organizations that tend to be overlooked. This is because people are focused internally, upon squeezing greater performance out of those within their particular unit, rather than thinking more positively about how it might operate differently with other people and entities. For example, could one cut out those in the middle and achieve a direct contact with end customers?

Exercise: Breakout Analysis

Too many of us are trapped behind prison bars of our own creation. Some people are emotionally, intellectually and entrepreneurially lazy. They are simply too complacent and may need to think in terms of 'breaking out of jail' in order to confront the realities of their plight.

If your current situation represents a prison in which you are incarcerated, what are the main factors that keep you confined? Which are the weakest bars and which are the strongest? Which ones should

you cut first? Do you have what it takes to break out?
What tools would you most like to receive hidden in a
loaf of bread? How astute are your jailers? Could you
talk your way past them? Who on the outside might
help?

Going it Alone or in Collaboration with Others

Should one 'break out' alone, or either join, or enlist, the support of, one or more co-conspirators? In many large companies it has become an article of faith that teamwork is a 'good
thing'. People are structured into teams. Work is given to
teams. Teamwork training becomes mandatory. People are
assessed according to whether or not they are perceived to
be 'team players'. There are awards for 'teamwork'.

The author recalls joining one corporate group at the end of
a day-long review meeting and just as the delegates were com-
pleting their 'assessment' of the session. Corporate forms had
been provided for this purpose. Those present gave themselves
high scores for 'involvement' and 'participation'. The senior
director present congratulated these 'team players'. However,
when their visitor asked them about what they had achieved,
in relation to the tasks they were supposed to have been working upon, there was an uncomfortable silence. The feedback
form had not mentioned 'outputs'. It had only asked about various indicators of teamwork.

Too many groups spend so much time struggling to be effective as a team that they overlook the reasons for their establishment. Some completely lose sight of their original purpose.

Other groups are given vague objectives or tasks that should
really have been passed to an appropriately qualified individual
with relevant experience and knowledge. On many occasions,
teamwork is not necessarily the most effective way of working,
or the quickest. It all depends upon the task, the circumstances,
desired outcomes and the nature of those involved. One should
strive to avoid a conscious, or an unconscious, bias for or against
any particular way of working.

People can hide in teams or use them to avoid the assumption of personal accountability. Some freeload. They will sit
back and let others do the work. The amount of effort put in by
many individuals may actually be inversely related to the

number of people in the team. What emerges might be a compromise, the minimum that is acceptable to all, rather than a combination of the best which each person could contribute on the element for which their individual skills and experience would be most appropriate.

Not surprisingly, many highly qualified professionals prefer to work alone on specific projects. They like to take personal responsibility for particular tasks and will only approach colleagues when they require specific and specialist advice, or feel a collective input would be helpful at particular stages, for example where idea generation would be appropriate. Some appear difficult to work with because they insist upon a clear brief, in order that their expertise is focused upon areas where they feel they could make a distinctive contribution.

Selecting Colleagues

With traditional employment, individuals often have little choice concerning those with whom they work. Colleagues were either there first or, if they have subsequently been brought in, their selection may well have been undertaken by other people. As a consequence, many people have to work with others whom they neither like nor respect. Not so in the case of the entrepreneur. Starting again, creates an opportunity to select one's own personal 'gang' made up of people with whom one feels comfortable.

Compatibility is important when collaborative partners are selected. Effective entrepreneurs acknowledge the interests and drives of others and, moreover, seek to understand them. They take the time and the trouble to find out what makes them tick and they endeavour to position what needs to be done in terms of the agendas of other people.

Those who are inclined to put off wielding the axe should be especially wary when hiring others. Avoid those who seem more interested in the nature of the 'package', benefits and facilities, than in identifying the contribution they could make or discussing the value they might be able to add. Also, give those who are unrealistic, or over eager to please, a wide berth. People with 'big company' backgrounds can find it difficult to adjust to smaller organizations in which they are expected to do more for themselves.

First priority should be given to those with a drive for individual achievement and fulfilment, yet who have complementary qualities, competencies, expectations and perspectives. 'Compatible' and 'complementary' are key words. It really helps if people instinctively 'get on'. However, those who are too similar may merely duplicate rather than 'add value' to each other. A degree of diversity can produce a rich mixture.

Unity and Diversity

Opposites can, and do, attract. Talent scouts and venture capitalists sometimes endeavour to bring quite different people together. It takes two pieces of flint clashing against each other to produce a spark. Companies, such as Nissan Design International, recognize that abrasion, even conflict, can result in a creative struggle that yields beneficial outcomes.

At the same time, several of those encountered had subjected themselves, and their fellow directors or business partners, to various psychological tests. Some found that their scores, and those of colleagues, were closer than expected. Those administering the tests had warned them of the dangers of surrounding oneself with similar people and yet the businesses run by these homogenous groups were growing rapidly.

Many tightly knit and effective teams are made up of people with similar ages and motivations. While diversity may be a spur to creativity within a research context, the building of a successful core management group is often based upon bringing together 'birds of a feather' with compatible personalities rather than those which are divergent and potentially divisive.

It helps if there are obvious and natural roles into which particular people can slot themselves, or be placed. With many groups, especially those composed of employees in larger organizations, too much time and energy is spent upon internal rivalries and attempts to exaggerate or play down individual contributions. At its worst, continual sniping and activities that undermine can neutralize considerable talents.

Those, whose personalities are too similar, can sometimes tread on each others toes. When everybody present sees things the same way, or has a strong desire to reach agreement, there may be a dearth of the critical but constructive discussions which can move understanding and business development forward. Many enterprises have come unstuck as a result of a lack of challenge rather than excessive debate.

Today's ally may become tomorrow's rival. The partnerships which last are often those between people who are deficient in some respects. Individually they may not have what it takes to succeed. However, collectively they may embrace what is required. The whole is clearly more than the parts and the benefits of collaboration outweigh the costs.

When in doubt stay out. There are no laws which state that one must have a certain number of business collaborators. Many people live to regret forming relationships which they entered into hastily. Differences of interest and emphasis do arise, especially during the early phases of an enterprise when those involved may go through a steep learning curve. Various partners sometimes react quite differently to particular demands that are made upon them.

A united and cohesive team can greatly increase the chances of success. However, once the numbers increase beyond four or five people unity and synergy may become more difficult to achieve. The core team should be kept as small as possible. Each new person added to the group compounds the problems of keeping in touch and reaching agreement. It also increases the risk of fragmentation into factions and the emergence of a caucus of 'insiders'.

The Extent of Relative Contributions

When several partners are involved, the assessment of relative inputs and contributions becomes more difficult. During discussions individuals may emphasize the time they have committed rather than focus upon the value which this has generated. As a business expands, some partners may also find it more difficult to allocate incremental time than others.

Portfolio workers can face a particular challenge. Individuals, who become accustomed to the variety and greater security that results from not having all one's eggs in one basket, can suddenly face growing claims upon their time from an enterprise that starts to take off. To match the inputs required, and the contributions of colleagues, it may be necessary to drop certain other activities. Ultimately, one may be drawn back into an unwelcome dependency upon a single source of income, the very situation from which escape was previously sought.

One area in which others can sometimes help is with initial research and investigation. It is often surprising how much information is available for little more than the cost of the time devoted to active search. However, it may still need to be assembled, brought together into a form that can be used. The key is to ask the right questions. People should be encouraged by any difficulties that are encountered. They could suggest that others have not pursued similar lines of enquiry. They might inhibit those that follow.

Flexible use can be made of portfolio workers to keep down costs. Undertaking on-line searches for others is itself an activity which some people are able to undertake from home.

Many business schools seek short duration projects for students on MBA and other courses. Funding a market research study, or the preparation of a business plan, can be a cost effective alternative to employing similar people via the consulting firm, which they join after graduation. Many such exercises can also benefit from the inputs of supervising members of staff.

Ultimately, the rewards which people take out of enterprises tend to reflect what they put in. No one should be naïve enough to aspire to disproportionately high returns for minimal effort. When the boats lie on the quay side, or are at anchor, their operators should not expect to catch fish. Those who do not take the initiative or commit have only themselves to blame.

Checklist

1. Would you like to change direction and establish your own enterprise?

2. If so, what steps are you taking? What, or who, is holding you back?

3. Are you inwardly directed and self-motivated? Do others regard you as self-contained?

4. Have you identified a potential business opportunity? What elements might be combined to create one?

5. Is there a formula which you could follow or a model which you might be able to adapt?

6. Are your ideas primarily rooted in a customer need or requirement or your own desire for a particular form of lifestyle?

7. How serious are you about 'breaking out'? Do you really want to do it? Who might help?

8. Have you thought of 'all the angles' and undertaken a risk analysis?

9. Are there those whom you trust and who might be able and willing to critique your plans and provide an honest opinion about the merits of your ideas?

10. Do you have all the elements that it might take to succeed? What is missing?

11. Are there particular qualities or capabilities that you lack? Do those close to you feel that you have what it takes to make it on your own?

12.   Do you want to 'paddle your own canoe' or work with others? Would you benefit from the support of compatible collaborators? Who would complement your own skills and experience?

9

BUILDING THE ENTERPRISE

Take a bath, wear a belt and look interested.

Put up a new wooden fence in an urban area and observe what happens. A few neighbours may notice it and pass an initial comment. For a short period it could become the subject of polite tea-time conversation. The observations made might be pleasant and favourable.

Invariably, the fence will also attract the unwelcome attentions of other groups. Nocturnal predators such as vandals who break bits off and spray-painters who deface it. The well-meaning attempt of a individual citizen to make something better, an initiative to improve the look of a property is en route to becoming yet another eye sore.

Contending Forces

Life is a continual struggle between progressive and reactionary forces, between those who give and those who take and between those who create and those who destroy. Some fight a losing battle and give up. Others persist. Through sheer will-power and endeavour they make progress, if only of the 'two steps forward and one step backwards' variety.

Many people live uncertain and inhibited lives. They feel as though suspended between conflicting and counterbalancing forces. They do not fall onto the ground and yet they are still constrained. Considerable momentum may be needed to break free from the gravitational pull of a combination of negative forces. Achieving this may require collective effort.

Early associates and initial customers should be chosen with care. While it may be possible to correct some mistakes over time, those who are in on the ground floor, for good or ill, can have a disproportionate influence upon the future development of an enterprise.

Some people bring out the best in us and others the worst. Some inspire, others deflate. Some encourage, others undermine. Some raise our ambitions, others cause us to lower our expectations. Some are complacent and easily satisfied, while others are demanding and push us to ever higher levels of performance. We find some people easy to work with and others a pain.

Children are often portrayed as naïve. They are also well-informed. Their worlds, from the stories they read to the games they play, are peopled with 'goodies' and 'baddies'. This fundamental distinction, between those who help and those who harm, is evident in computer games, the cartoon films they watch and the wisdom of past generations captured in fairy tales and perpetuated across the centuries through the core stories of many faiths.

In later life, particularly in sophisticated societies, simple messages are invariably qualified. We are told to avoid simplistic generalisations or invidious caricatures. Such views are portrayed as unbalanced, even though the term 'balance' suggests contending forces. Clear examples of black and white thinking are replaced by the featureless grey of the sophists.

Sometimes caution is thrown to the wind. Thus management writers advocate trust and empowerment with little hint of the possibility that some might take advantage of both of them. When they are exploited the consequences can be lethal. Prudent people confront the essence of the human condition. They address both the positive and the negative aspects.

Leeches and Parasites

If a business is to become more than a device for managing the affairs of a single person, a surplus, margin, or return upon the work of other people will need to be achieved. The entrepreneur should never lose sight of this reality which is recognized by most employees.

A combination of people with different experiences, personalities and skills can compensate for the deficiencies of particular individuals. There is a potential for the whole to be more than the sum of the parts. However, there are people who for one reason or another do harm rather than good. Their negative impacts can range from 'freeloading', through bothering and undermining the morale of others, to criminal damage.

Over the years, international investigators Kroll have found many examples of corporate theft and sabotage from self-interested, disgruntled, greedy and malevolent employees. Those involved range from junior staff to trusted senior managers and directors. Make no mistake, these people are out there – beguiling and plausible – and always on the look out for a soft target. Moreover, the most poisonous snakes sometimes have the shiniest coats.

Some imbue and instill, whereas others drain and suck. Some people create value while others consume it. When the latter are customers, the enterprise has the prospect of gain. When there are too many of them among those who should be producing value for others, it will suffer.

There are a large number of people who can spot an opportunity to feed upon the imagination and drive of others a mile away. They line up to encourage the entrepreneur to take risks. If a venture fails they will have lost only the time of day. If it succeeds, they will be eager to secure a share of the action.

It is far easier to climb aboard a bandwagon that is already rolling than to design and construct one from scratch. Many experts are full of advice for others but lack the ability to take the initiative themselves. A new business needs people to create opportunities as well as solve problems.

Judgement is needed to separate the time-wasters, margin chisellors and bloodsuckers from those with the interest and ability to add value. The former group are legion and will not wait to be asked. They are attracted to entrepreneurial innocence as mosquitoes are to exposed flesh.

People with desirable qualities might need to be sought out and coaxed. They can be cautious and may have to be persuaded to attend an initial meeting. They guard their time, saving it for the opportunities which offer them the greatest potential to make a positive contribution. Those who already know individuals who add value start the enterprise game with the equivalent of an extra couple of throws.

Values

The subject of values may seem woolly to a hard-nosed entrepreneur. Yet they can highlight obligations, accountability and responsibility for 'adding value'. Also many businesses that have had a sense of purpose, beyond financial returns, have prospered, while more narrowly focused competitors have stumbled or failed. People should listen to their hearts as well as their heads.

Explicit values covering such matters as improving the quality of life for customers, creating opportunities for employees or making a contribution to society enable those who associate with companies, such as General Electric or Hewlett-Packard, to feel they are doing something worthwhile as well as making money. Increasingly, those who have a choice opt to join networks and communities that treat them fairly and with respect, and whose values they share.

At an early stage, the people forming the core team of an enterprise should identify, articulate and agree the values that are important to them. These will determine how they believe they should treat each other and what they look for in others. Matching people to values, reduces the risk of exploitation and increases the prospects of sustained contributions and mutual benefits.

Ben Cohen and Jerry Greenfield might not have appeared to be the best equipped people to set up their Ben & Jerry's ice cream business. Their previous backgrounds lacked many of the elements that venture capitalists look for in prospective entrepreneurs. However they had, and still have, a strong sense of values. Thus they site factories according to potential for significant social impact rather than use a distribution model to select locations that would minimise transport costs.

The founders of Ben & Jerry's played to their strengths and took steps to compensate for any deficiencies in their personal experience. Their explicit beliefs have attracted loyal customers, committed employees and supportive media. They have also been smart enough to bring professional managers with the skills which they lack into their enterprise.

Values are assuming ever greater significance. Shared values are not just a 'nice to have'. They can be essential for survival. Thus without proper attribution people may be reluctant to share their knowledge. Without a common commitment to learning, particular individuals may fall behind and, as a consequence, might no longer pull their weight.

Written value statements are not enough. Marks & Spencer has a reputation for quality and excellence because its essential values are internalized and practiced. People live them. During his last three years as chief executive at the US telephone company Ameritech, Bill Weiss established and supported a leadership development programme to build the values, strategies and leaders he believed were crucial to the future development of the business.

Networks and Relationships

When money, information and knowledge are available to all, collaborative networks are differentiated from each other by their values, codes and rationale. People prefer to associate with those whose values they share. Without empathy, compatible attitudes and acceptable behaviour, disintegration and break up may occur.

Increasingly, corporations operate as networks of relationships which must be held together and sustained. A common purpose, or a set of core values, such as Johnson & Johnson's credo, represents vital social cement that can bind the dispersed members of distributed organizations to each other.

Similar to churches, companies can fragment when central beliefs are no longer shared and visibly practiced.

Governments of countries with ageing populations are seeking to reduce their commitments to their citizens in order to balance their budgets. With many larger companies also seeking to reduce the 'social costs' of employment, the world could become a colder place. Individuals are having to assume greater responsibility for their own welfare and future well being. Many feel uncomfortable, insecure and alone. New support mechanisms are needed.

The massive expansion in the number of different sources of information and channels of communication which has occurred can also lead to fragmentation and isolation. The universe of possibilities has greatly expanded. Because there are so many other options, particular individuals may feel less significant. Given the range of choice, why should anyone want them?

In the electronic age and knowledge society, people need to

develop a sense of self-worth. It is difficult for those who do not love and respect themselves to be fair and warm towards others. Petty and selfish actions that diminish self-respect should be avoided in favour of acting with courtesy, dignity, integrity and humanity; behaviours that build self-esteem and encourage appreciation, consideration and admiration in others.

Those who do not belong to clubs, or mutual support networks that recognize their individuality, may come to feel that no one cares. The human being behind the e-mail address is lost. The phrase 'computer to computer communication' is too often used to refer to the potential of technology rather than its use for human purposes. People are living organisms not extensions of machines.

Membership of collaborative networks can give individuals a new sense of purpose and meaning. Transactional efficiency and relevant, but impersonal, support services, while highly desirable, may not be enough. The network that cares about its members, and shows that it is concerned, may command greater allegiance. People yearn for identity and warmth. They want to feel special and they need to thaw out.

The establishment of sensitive and responsive support networks represents an epic business opportunity for entrepreneurs. It also suggests a model to which larger organizations might aspire. Thus the corporation could exploit the potential of its infrastructure and capabilities to transform itself into a provider of a range of services that would support not just one vision in the boardroom, but the entrepreneurial visions of a multitude of venture teams.

Innovation and Understanding Essential Requirements

Management commentators and government programmes stress the need for innovation and creativity. They advocate and champion the adoption of the latest management techniques. Literature, history and folklore are replete with examples of innovators who have made major contributions to the advance of human civilization.

Yet building a business need not involve or require novelty per se. Discoveries and pioneering breakthroughs are only relevant insofar as they relate to those needs and requirements upon which the entrepreneur is focused. Innovation for the sake of it can prove a costly indulgence and a distraction.

Many of those interviewed have built rapidly growing businesses by introducing tried and tested products to those unfamiliar with them, bringing existing, but hitherto separate, and unrelated elements of a solution, together or helping people to make better use of overlooked capabilities. Some people successfully employ the same basic formula, albeit in different contexts, for most of their business careers.

The focus of others was upon innovation, but from a customer rather than a product or technology viewpoint. What would significantly increase 'value', 'satisfaction' or 'enjoyment' from a user perspective? Could the lives of consumers be made less complex, happier or more rewarding? How might the accessibility of existing provision be revolutionized?

Timing might be more important than genuine innovation. The best surfers are prepared to wait when selecting which wave to ride. Capitalizing upon trends in the marketplace, and moving in quickly when particular products and services become fashionable or reach a take off point, may make sense in certain markets. However, those who are first can incur all the costs of creating initial awareness. Catching the tide is often cheaper and easier than inventing a new means of water-borne transport.

The intending entrepreneur should ask basic, even simple, questions in order to grasp the fundamentals. Does an idea form the basis for developing a business? Are all the building blocks available? Many enterprises fail because all the various elements needed for success are not in place.

People should stand back from their proposed businesses and consider questions which a potential investor might ask: Is there a clear demand? Have possible customers been identified? Are objectives clear and sales and financial forecasts realistic? Have 'what if' questions been addressed, for example, what if sales grow more slowly than expected? Do the members of the venture team have the complementary capabilities, experience and drive to make a go of it?

Exercise: Winner or Loser Analysis

To build a business people need to be effective at winning new customers and securing additional contracts. In terms of how they go about doing this, they need to recognize whether they are displaying the characteristics of losers or developing the mind-sets of winners.

Scale and the Virtue and Vanity of Size

In some sectors, the means of production may set a minimum threshold of scale for economic viability. In others, there are options, choices of channel and technology. Enterprises differing widely in size may operate effectively. It is positively helpful if those who are co-operating to establish a new business share similar expectations about how big it ought to grow.

The experience of Barbour, which makes waxed jackets, illustrates the principle of compounding. Such companies grow steadily like rolling snowballs because in their formative years, or periods of great opportunity, profits and cash are reinvested in future development. To sustain momentum entrepreneurs may need to 'raise the bar' and establish new challenges.

The desire for financial success and greed, which, leads many people to establish businesses, often becomes self-defeating. Some companies stubbornly refuse to grow because any surplus cash is taken out by the initial entrepreneurs in the form of salaries, pension contributions or dividends. The founders are then surprised when later they seek to 'sell out' and find that potential buyers are not prepared to pay as much as was expected for a hollowed out shell.

There is no law which requires people to carry on building a business beyond those stages that bring an entrepreneurial group the most satisfaction and make the best use of their particular skills. People who 'realize a capital gain' and retire to prop up the bar of the clubhouse at the local golf course are sometimes criticized for not further developing the enterprises they have established. It is surely up to each owner of a company to determine the point at which all or part of their share holding should be disposed of.

In reality, certain people are more effective at some stages in the development of a business than at others. Thus, a person who is highly motivated and gifted during the concept form-ulation and formation period, might be less able to delegate or cope with the management aspects of subsequent growth. It is surely better for such an individual to concentrate upon establishing a succession of ventures and to subsequently relin-quish control to others who, while not so creative at the start-up phase, may be better able to handle later challenges.

Individuals and management teams need to be sufficiently self-aware to assess the value which they can add at each step in the evolution of an enterprise. This will determine the point at which it might be advisable to hand over certain responsi-bilities to professional managers, or to sell all, or part, of a business. Much will depend upon the contributions which other people are likely to make in relation to their cost, and the extent to which the worth of an enterprise is likely to rise or fall over a further period of time.

Realism is a valuable and rare quality, and it should not be confused with cynicism. People sometimes overlook the cycli-cal nature of many businesses, or do not detect the point at which an undertaking reaches a point of highest value. Thus they sell before or after the peak.

Others fail to appreciate that their enterprise could be split into distinct units, with different aspects forming stand alone ventures. Doing so might allow them to retain activities with growth prospects, and to which they could make a significant contribution, while disposing of other elements that might rep-resent a closer fit with the ambitions of another entrepre-neur.

Owner/managers do not necessarily have to wrestle with challenges that are beyond them. Maybe there are other peo-ple who have the skills and experience to tackle them. Per-haps they would provide what is required for further expan-sion in return for an equity stake. Going to someone, whose experience and capabilities are more relevant, could be seen as a sign of pragmatic good sense rather than as an indica-tion of weakness. Such a step also gives someone else an op-portunity to be true to themselves.

A growing, evolving and changing enterprise can provide opportunities for a great many people to become involved in ways that are appropriate to their interests, inclinations and capacities. Each enterprise could evolve into a market of its own, providing a framework, within which various contractual arrangements are employed, to allow a succession of different combinations of people to provide the specific inputs that will allow it to grow and develop.

Winning New Business

A new enterprise could be launched with a bang. Press releases and media events could tell the world about a new offering or one could slowly creep up on selected prospects. Some people begin quietly. They put out feelers, seek appointments and keep their brochure budget for when they have achieved a critical mass. It all depends upon the nature of the business, for example whether relatively large numbers of customers are being sought for a packaged product or whether one is seeking an initial client for a more complex offering.

For those launching a new businesses, who are in the latter position, getting a first purchase can appear the toughest challenge of all. Everyone seems to want details of previous work done and existing and satisfied customers to talk to. Recent employers sometimes provide support of inestimable value simply by becoming an early user of a service being offered by one or more former employees. The corporate midwife brings the new venture into the world. Marketing and business plans give way to an actual assignment.

Many people are naïve when it comes to winning business. They imagine target decision makers will read their mail shots rather than throw them into a rubbish bin. They underestimate the time it takes to turn interest into an order. Even when positive reactions are shown, a purchase may not occur until the following year's budget becomes available. Indeed, funds for the current financial year may be largely committed across a whole sector, a factor to bear in mind when recruiting new staff or committing to overhead costs.

Many individuals and start-up enterprises face the dilemma of whether or not to submit competitive proposals. How effective are you at securing business in such situations? Could you be more successful at landing contracts or retaining customers? Many big name corporations are surprisingly ineffective. The great majority of companies win less than a half of the competitive races they enter. Failure is the norm.

The approach to winning business, which adopted by many people, condemns them to defeat and disappointment. Because of how they operate, some bid teams appear doomed to fail from the moment they decide to respond to an invitation to tender. The occasional success may mean only that competitors have been more inept.

Winners and Losers

Losers are undisciplined and reactive. They pursue far too many opportunities. Because of the sheer volume of work and tight deadlines, bid team members have little time to think. They react mechanically to invitations to tender that cross their desks, treating them as 'in-tray' items. They cope by adopting and operating corporate rules and procedures, which are rarely questioned. Success is viewed narrowly, in terms of the number of proposals submitted.

The focus of losers is internal. They concentrate upon the practical problems of producing proposal documents, such as ensuring all curriculum vitae are in a standard format or making arrangements to get an authorizing signature in time. They describe their jobs in terms of 'writing proposals'.

Members of losing teams tend to be preoccupied with the immediate needs of their employers. Each group works alone, making little effort to learn from either their own experience or that of others. Senior managers are rarely involved, even though individual contracts may be of strategic significance. When major bids are a matter of corporate life or death and the top people are nowhere to be seen, one wonders what it is that has a higher claim upon their time.

Winners are selective. They ruthlessly prioritize their prospects. They are not afraid to turn down invitations to bid. The construction company Henry Boot suffered a drop in turnover as a result of being more discriminating, but the company's profitability improved. Letting some opportunities go allows more attention to be devoted to those that are retained.

Many winners do not wait to be asked. They take the initiative, proactively setting out to build relationships with those organizations with which they would most like to do business. When they do respond, it is with commitment. They allocate sufficient resources early on to build up an unassailable lead. Bid teams contain an appropriate mix of skills and have clear objectives.

Winners are externally focused. They monitor what is happening in the business environment and how this is likely to impact upon potential customers. They analyze the particular requirements of each prospect. They also devote much effort to understanding how buying decisions are made and who is involved.

Throughout each stage of the purchasing process winners remain sensitive to the changing concerns of buyers. They are flexible during negotiations. At the same time, they are also prepared to walk away from an opportunity should it become apparent that concluding an agreement on the terms offered would not satisfy their own commercial objectives.

The communications and proposals of winners address the perceived requirements of the potential customer. They target those who can influence the purchase decision and stress the relevance of their corporate capability and the value they could add as a business partner. They look smart and keen and they exude a strong desire to do the work.

Winners define their roles in terms of establishing and building new relationships. They consciously set out to relate to, and match, the culture of the buyer. Wang became a supplier of support services to Dell by demonstrating empathy, shared objectives and 'cultural fit'.

The visible and active support of senior management can be decisive in close contests. Redwood Publishing wrote senior staff, including the Managing Director, into a proposal submitted to BT and won the business.

Winners are active learners, open to ideas and eager to build new capabilities. Win or lose, they reflect upon outcomes and search for better ways of doing things. They subject their processes and practices to a continuous cycle of refinement and review. They invite outside experts to identify areas for improvement. Lessons, hints and tips are shared with colleagues.

Requests for a list of past clients may seem designed to exclude the recent 'start-up'. At the same time, the availability of opportunities could allow a new player to break in. Simply entering a race might help to establish a reputation. Ultimately, the best competitive tender strategy is to avoid them by becoming a preferred inside supplier, whose quality of past work and understanding of the client, secures a regular flow of commissions.

Strategic partnering and relationship marketing are the

favoured strategies of many suppliers. Longer term partnerships allow companies to work with customers in defining
their requirements, thus avoiding the low margin 'commodity
traps' that can result from waiting for a requirement to be
determined by the buyer and then put out to competitive
tender.

Ambitious companies should monitor trends and developments relating to purchasing and partnering practice and assess their likely impacts. For example, is the proportion of
business opportunities being put out to competitive tender
likely to increase or decrease?

Those who recognize their limitations should explore the
possibilities for linking up with enterprises that have greater
marketing muscle. Many corporations such as BT, IBM and
Xerox have partnership and other schemes for providing marketing support to former employees and other collaborators
who sell 'solutions' that incorporate their own products.

Network partners and supportive larger organizations can
help new businesses to respond effectively to tender opportunities. Central bid teams and proposal preparation units could
be among the services provided by a corporation to its partnerships and internal venture teams.

Exercise: Vulnerability Analysis

When building a business you need to keep an eye
upon areas of vulnerability. In competitive situations,
you should ask colleagues to play the part of the opposition. Ask them what they would do to wipe you
out.

If you were a saboteur what would you do to inflict
the greatest harm upon the business? How could you
kill it? What could be done to prevent this from happening?

What elements of your business plan are most at
risk? What news do you most dread? If it happened,
how would you cope? Are you keeping an eye upon
your key customers and the cash coming into and
going out of the business? What about the situation a
few months ahead?

Avoiding the Tender Trap

Buyers are ever more demanding in their requirements. Standards expected of responses are rising. Pressure upon the margins of suppliers is intense. Performance guarantees are increasingly sought. The costs of preparing proposals, which do not succeed, may be irrecoverable.

Competitive tendering presents a dilemma for many businesses, particularly newly established ones. It may consume a larger proportion of resources during the start-up phase when time is at a premium. The opportunity cost of preparing a proposal may be enormous. In some cases only larger enterprises may be eligible or the risks of failure may be too high. A degree of pragmatism and balance is required when deciding which opportunities to pursue.

Leveraging Insight, Imagination and Initiative

Entrepreneurial vision and imaginative applications of emerging technologies can create 'new games' in the marketplace. Why should established players be any better at them than new entrants? Frontiers of opportunity may be equally available to all. The smaller company that is better able to design a website, rather than the established multinational, may be the one that attracts attention and interest.

Cakes and fresh fish are ordered electronically and dispatched to customers at home and abroad. Complex services are provided for corporate clients that may never meet face to face. Internet businesses exist that are run from attics and yet outsell high street stores.

Some e-business entrepreneurs have enjoyed almost instant success, while more substantial organizations have struggled to make a mark. Visitors enticed to a site cannot be coerced to remain. When not interested and engaged, they move on.

Various social, political and technological trends favour the small business. For example, a growing number of talented people have 'had enough' of working for larger organizations. They prefer the freedom to pick and choose where, when and with whom to make a contribution. As people seek lifestyle changes in mid-career, so expertise and experience that was once only available to major corporations become available for hire to smaller enterprises.

In certain countries small businesses are 'in'. Government procurement policies may specify that a certain proportion of particular types of contract should 'go' to small companies. They create subcontract opportunities for small and medium-sized enterprises (SMEs) as the 'big players' endeavour to include them within their consortia in order to satisfy public procurement guidelines. Even where SME participation is not compulsory, the 'raters guidelines' that are issued may allocate points for the inclusion of them in a proposal.

The spread of personal computers and presentational software has levelled the playing field in terms of the 'look and feel' and physical quality of proposals. It is no longer so immediately apparent whether a report is from a small partnership or a major international company. Both may have been produced using the same packages on similar equipment. Individuals can submit documentation that is as smart as that sent in by large corporations.

In relation to what differentiates one proposal from another, again the smaller enterprise may score. The SME may have fewer specialist resources to call upon, but greater flexibility due to avoiding the delays which securing permissions and approvals can involve. A small tight group may find it easier to reach agreement on the essentials of a proposal. Without the many distractions of corporate life, they may also have much more time to think about them.

Urgency and stringency can stimulate creativity. Developing businesses require revolutionaries rather than mercenaries. The entrepreneur should cultivate realism but avoid defeatism. While self-delusion can be fatal, self-confidence may be justified. Being small, focused, flexible and fresh has its advantages. The small company only competes with the relatively few people in larger competitors who actually have the time and inclination to reflect and who are working upon rival bids.

Many small companies successfully win business against larger competitors. Simons Palmer Clemmow Johnson beat the much larger Saatchi & Saatchi to win a major contract from British Gas by putting in a proposal which significantly developed the concept in the brief accompanying the invitation to tender. They simply out-thought the competition.

Giants with Clay Feet

Many new market entrants almost paralyze themselves by exaggerating their competition. Large corporations can, and do, benefit from established images and strong brands. People feel safe in dealing with them. They may be reluctant to take risks or to court challenge in relation to their choice of supplier. Hence, a preference for working with companies that are known. The conservatism of many customers can act against the young enterprise.

However, in many cases 'big company' puffery, trappings and arrogance are intended to conceal a lack of real substance. Synergy may be more talked about than achieved. Within many larger enterprises, there are few if any economies of scale. Groups finish one project or task and move onto the next, generally without reflecting or sharing what they have learned with others. The tyranny of time sheets and pressure to increase the proportion of hours charged to clients may cause such activities to be regarded as 'down time'.

Various contractual commitments entered into on differing timescales can limit flexibility. The 'crawl out' costs from a particular market or arrangement may be considerable. Managers under pressure to reduce operating costs often compound such problems by concluding longer term agreements in return for price reductions. Some companies lose opportunities as a result of being unable to extract themselves from prior legal obligations.

Many of those employed by large organizations, or providing services to them, are mainly concerned with supporting the corporate machine. Put a few fee earners into a building and it is surprising how many other people may be required to support them, from switchboard operators and cleaners to personnel and accounts departments. The major office block becomes a community in its own right, a latter day equivalent of the medieval village.

Organizational politics are rife within many larger organizations. Internal preoccupations, such as turf wars, neutralize key members of staff for long periods. They lead to introversion and self-absorption. When the rot really sets in, the impressive corporate edifice can quickly crumble. Scale can also lead to complacency. People assume that challenging and changing are someone else's responsibility. Such activities may even be regarded as evidence of disloyalty.

Many large companies are reluctant to admit that they have run out of good new business development ideas. Rather than return capital to shareholders, they hang on to it through participation in marginal incremental activities, or by remaining in declining markets. Paying out cash to shareholders, through special dividends or share buy backs, would allow each of them to select investment opportunities that match their personal objectives and complement the other investments within their portfolios.

When confronted with bragging about corporate scale the response should be "so what"? The resources described may, or may not, be relevant to future opportunities. Assets can quickly become liabilities when they are no longer required. Redundant people become termination payments. Surplus offices become penalties on unexpired leases. Unused factory sites become environmental clean-up costs.

There will, of course, be occasions when sheer scale, reach and reputation are advantageous. In publishing, Random House can secure top authors by paying them advances that smaller players simply cannot match. Lazy corporate purchasers may contract with easy to find 'big name' suppliers rather than 'shop around' for more relevant offerings.

Rather than struggle to establish a new enterprise, an entrepreneur could gain leverage by coming to some form of collaborative agreement with a larger corporation. Picture Vision, a start-up company, created a means of storing images on the World Wide Web and printing them out on a range of products from greetings cards to mugs. When Kodak emerged as a competitor, it was invited to take an equity stake in the company. The founder partners retained ownership of a significant share holding, but gained the advantage of Kodak's greater international marketing muscle.

Supplementing the Team

Builders of businesses should keep their feet upon the ground and remember 'the basics'. Each time salaries are increased, or new equipment is purchased, the level of sales at which sufficient of a margin can be generated to cover operating costs will also rise. Rapid growth can lead to over-trading and pressure upon cash. A close eye needs to be kept upon debtors. The entrepreneur should be prudent rather than naïve, and pay attention to detail when model contracts are drawn up.

It is so easy for those building new enterprises not to see the wood for the trees. Activity may generate turnover rather than profit and cash flow. A company may become dependent upon one or two major customers. Those with their 'noses to the grindstone' may fail to line up replacement business for when a major project is delivered. Over-eager recruitment may result in excessively high overheads. Risks may be overlooked. Values may be ill-defined. These are all areas in which a balanced and effective board can make a major contribution.

Additional inputs need to be secured at an acceptable cost. While the fees of non-executive directors may represent a much higher proportion of turnover than would be the case with a longer established and larger business, they may still be worth their weight in gold to an emerging enterprise. The interviewees with independent directors were more likely to have a longer term strategy and more ambitious aspirations.

For companies considering a flotation, an appropriate board is 'an essential' rather than a 'nice to have'. Potential investors are much more likely to part with their money if an effective team of competent directors is in place. Individuals holding current and senior appointments should be sought rather than the 'semi-retired' brigade of spongers in search of 'incremental income'.

The corporate governance debate has largely focused upon 'negative' aspects, such as monitoring the activities of executive directors to ensure they do not pay themselves excessive salaries. A visitor from Mars might be pardoned for assuming that all directors of public companies are out to 'feather their nests'. Far too little attention is paid to the significant and positive contribution which the right non-executive director can make to the development of a business.

The biotechnology company Molecules to Market keeps its overheads low by outsourcing as many support and operating activities as it can. Nevertheless, it has recruited a high calibre board which includes six non-executive directors with international business experience who have been selected to contribute to corporate growth in particular parts of the world.

No one should feel compelled to appoint particular types of director just because other companies have them. People should have the imagination to do what is right for their particular enterprise. What about a director of relationships, thinking, learning or creativity?

Those in central roles within collaborative and support networks may find themselves acting as guardians of visions and values and trustees of the best interests of the membership as a whole. Just as the competent director puts corporate concerns ahead of personal and sectional interests, so those elected to governing roles within networks should display impartiality between individual members and promote the 'collective good'.

The developing enterprise frequently requires skills for defined periods, rather than on a continuing basis, as a succession of building blocks need to be put in place. With the growth in the interim executive marketplace many individuals display a professional approach to fixed-term assignments.

Interim managers can be used for particular projects. They can bring relevant experience and skills to bear upon a task and they tend to get on with the work rather than become distracted by political rivalries. Much will depend upon the qualities of the individuals concerned in relation to what needs to be done. The right help can be a godsend. But those who are 'over-qualified' or who 'ruffle feathers' may need to be handled sensitively. Existing members of a team may regard the bringing in of a 'newcomer' as a criticism of their performance.

Although the 'daily rate' of an interim executive may appear high in relation to the cost of a permanent employee, there need not be a continuing commitment beyond the end of a contract period. From the interim manager's perspective short-term assignments may not appear as secure as full-time employment. However, intervals between them provide opportunities for reflection, family and friends, personal development and the recharging of batteries.

The interim executive marketplace has given many people the freedom to work upon projects of their choice. Those who concentrate upon what they most enjoy doing and do best are often surprised by the extent to which they are in demand. They become personal entrepreneurs and fulfill both themselves and those they serve.

Checklist

1. Would you like to focus upon selling your own time or is it your intention to form a business that will also offer the services of other people?

2. Can you distinguish contributors from 'wasters', leeches and 'hangers on'? Do you 'smell a rat'? Who among your friends has 'a good nose'?

3. Why should a customer be interested in you or your business? If you dropped dead, or your business folded, would anyone be seriously inconvenienced?

4. What is special or distinctive about what you are suggesting, proposing or intending to do? It is rooted in an actual need?

5. How will potential customers get to know about you and your offering? What can you provide that is different?

6. Are there alternative sources of supply? How will your offering stack up against them?

7. Will you face competitors with greater experience and more relevant capabilities? Could their advantages be neutralized and the focus of competition shifted onto ground of your choosing?

8. How do you intend to win business in competitive situations and hold on to your customers? How will you respond to invitations to tender?

9. What are your main sources of competitive advantage?

10. Should you incorporate a company in order to secure the privilege of limited liability?

11. How might an effective board of competent directors add value? When and how are you going to set about forming one?

12. How might others help you? Have you identified potential collaborators, investors or partners?

13. Are you willing to share part of your opportunity with the right people in order to bring them on board?

10

DOING IT MY WAY

*You cannot hook a fish that
keeps its mouth shut.*

For a lucky child 'ask and it shall be given' works at least some of the time, and particularly in late-December. Requests to Father Christmas are met, in part if not in whole.

Young children may have a limited awareness of the full range of possibilities. However, even at a tender age, they are subject to fashions and fads. Hence certain items may feature upon many lists. 'Authority figures' close to them, and with a 'pass grade' knowledge of the local shopping centre, are likely to know where and how to buy them. Parents and relations can and do make certain wishes come true.

With the passing of years, innocence gives way to the realization that so much of what was unquestionably believed represents aspects of myths and deceptions. As one gets older, many desires die. Enterprising spirits are dampened. Flames of creativity are extinguished. Expectations are described as unobtainable. Aspirations are mocked as fantasies. The ambitious are portrayed as dreamers.

Some individuals experience a degree of confusion. Advertisements entice, while moralists warn of greed. However, others dream on. Entrepreneurs seek fulfilment through satisfying both their own dreams and those of others. They 'make things happen' all year round for people beyond their own families.

In relation to Christmas, we ourselves perpetuate the myth for subsequent generations. Anyone who sets out to assemble a list of requests and determine which of these to fulfill, taking into account what is known about the children concerned, what they already have, and practical considerations, such as storage space, is already thinking through the initial elements of the entrepreneurial process.

New Ways of Working and Learning

Aspiring entrepreneurs need to get into the habit of dreaming again. The essence of success in business is to expand the universe of what is possible. Rather than assume limitations and accept constraints, one should imagine the activities that could occur, and the operations that might become feasible, if there were no boundaries.

Such musings should not be regarded as idle distractions but practical speculation. Just as the Father Christmas' sleigh of our childhood fantasy was able to overcome the laws of gravity and aerodynamics, so accessible and affordable modern technologies are allowing us to transcend barriers of distance and time, obstacles to thinking and limits to learning.

The world of work is undergoing a profound transformation. People are entering the full-time labour market later and leaving earlier. While 'in the game', continuous change is assumed, lifelong learning is expected and progressive renewal is required. More women are employed and proportionally fewer men. The growth areas are contract and part-time working and self-employment.

As existing jobs are automated out of existence, new activities need to be found to keep people occupied. Some suggest that available work will need to be more equitably shared. Others believe an expansion of personal services, in such areas as leisure, learning, health and lifestyle, could create further waves of employment opportunity. The sense of self-worth of many people will depend upon the extent to which they can value themselves independently of their jobs.

Service employment has steadily grown at the expense of manufacturing. 'Know-how' is accounting for an increasing proportion of 'added value'. Opportunities are opening up, as people seek help in accessing, selecting, presenting, capturing, sharing, and applying information, knowledge and understanding that is relevant to their particular requirements and the value they are seeking to create.

Increasingly, 'knowledge work', which does not require any form of direct physical contact, can be undertaken almost anywhere. Information-based entrepreneurs can operate from barns and boats. They can work at multiple locations or on the move. They can serve one or several clients, alone or in coll-aboration with others, as a contractor or an employee and on an ad hoc or permanent basis. Barriers to entry may be, largely, in the mind.

The growing availability of portable technologies is freeing us from dependence upon particular sites. The most remote points on earth can be reached virtually instantaneously by satellite signals. There is now no hiding from opportunity. Let on that you know something and the e-mails arrive. People seek you out.

Of course there are practical issues to address, such as health and safety requirements, labour law, planning regulations, tax status and social security considerations. Each pattern of work presents its own distinct challenges, but the benefits which companies from Barclay's Bank to British Gas are securing, in terms of greater flexibility and productivity, suggest that the effort spent addressing them could be time well spent.

Progress is not a one way street. A move to individual contracts in place of standard agreements, as has happened at DEC, can add to the cost of establishing new relationships. The benefits of extra flexibility may need to be weighed against any additional requirements and also the advantages of simplicity and predictability which might be lost.

The adoption of distance education technologies, materials and channels can allow learning to be undertaken almost anywhere. Companies, such as British Aerospace, Cable & Wireless and ICI, are developing support networks based upon intranet and other technologies to make learning available to their people on demand, whether at a place of work or at home, throughout the world. Exclusion can be from choice rather than a consequence of location.

The Information Society

Where there is accessibility, it may also be difficult to escape. Personal time and space can be intruded upon and violated. People can find themselves at the beck and call of pestering managers or demanding clients. Some contacts may be welcomed, others dreaded.

The number of messages being sent across a network can increase exponentially as new members join. People who seek the benefits of interacting with others often overlook the costs. Within Sun Microsystems each employee receives, on average, a communication by e-mail every few minutes of every day. Given the time it takes to open and read a message, looking at and digesting all of the incoming mail would not allow some to have any time for work.

Traditionally, relative power determines who demands and who defers. 'Taking control of one's life' is partly about establishing accepted ground rules concerning which calls to accept and which to either record or screen out. Members of entrepreneurial and venture teams should agree among themselves who may call whom, under what circumstances, and in relation to which type of issue. It helps if there is a common understanding regarding these areas, but there should also be mutual respect for the distinct preferences of different members of a network.

Within Policy Publications the time of one's peers is regarded as a precious commodity. Members of the team try not to interrupt each other's thoughts and efforts. E-mail communication is limited to matters that clearly relate to the projects and priorities of the colleagues concerned. Channels of communication are used sparingly and with consideration.

Information is all around us, like the air we breathe. For many people, handling incoming communications has become a race against the clock. Junk mail is binned. E-mails, other than those from a boss, or select colleagues, are deleted unread. Sometimes it is only when people lose their jobs that they discover how long it would really take to go through every item received.

Those who have left companies, such as IBM, ICL and Xerox to set up their own businesses to provide services, to both their former employers and others, often feel disadvantaged. They fear that by being 'out of sight' they are 'out of mind'. This may be so, but they may also escape an enormous amount of time-wasting activity. And besides, how open are major companies about forthcoming strategic changes and restructuring? These are the areas that impact upon the chief concerns of many managers, namely their future financial security and employability.

While some are freed from their dependence upon particular locations by the emergence of virtual and network organizations, and the growing range of activities such as tele-shopping and telebanking that begin with the prefix 'tele-', others find themselves enslaved by contemporary trends. The 'callcentres' that handle a growing proportion of incoming telephone traffic are becoming the sweatshops of the information age. First Direct's unit in Leeds has 3,000 staff. People are herded together and much 'call centre' work is boring and repetitive.

Challenges and opportunities often come together. Information and communications technologies enable and support a whole range of new lifestyle and business options, but in themselves they are dead. When switched on they may operate but they feel neither anguish nor pain. It is our use and application of them that determines whether they help or hinder us.

We decide the extent to which we will be liberated or constrained by new developments and changing circumstances. Or, if we do not take the initiative, such decisions are taken for us by others, and we become either victims or beneficiaries. One person's poison can represent another person's meat. Thus entrepreneurs step in to access, assemble and present packages of information for those too busy to undertake these activities for themselves.

Exercise: Asking Father Christmas

Many people settle for too little, too late. They lack the courage to take the initiative and really reach out towards their dreams.

If Father Christmas could fulfil any wish, what would you most like to do? Who would you want to become? Where and with whom would you prefer to be? Which additional qualities, capabilities or attributes would you seek to obtain? What else would you ask for?

Conformists and Rebels

Traditionally, larger organizations have imposed standard ways of operating, working and learning upon those whom they employ, or are otherwise engaged in activities with and for them. Induction has largely been a matter of acquainting new entrants and suppliers with what is required, knocking off their rough edges and encouraging them to fit in.

In return for an income and prospects of incremental advancement or business, varying degrees of individuality have often been lost. At the same time, self-perpetuating cabals of corporate clones have emerged, consisting of those who make the greatest effort to demonstrate accommodation. The most socialized are seen to be the most successful. They visibly reap sought-after rewards. They become 'role models' for the socially ambitious.

Yet we are all different. For some to be 'upwardly mobile' is to be carried closer to the fires that consume identities and personalities.

Diversity is natural. Biologically it is essential. It is also evident within the various groups that are all around us. The genes are similar, and the environment may be largely the same, yet each new child that joins a family is distinctive in so many ways.

Office architecture, furnishings, piped music and selected smells have all been used to impose the aesthetics of a few upon others. Such practices deny the reality that we differ. We do not all have the same requirements. Some of us are gregarious, while others like to be in their own space. The Rastafarian chant might be an ideal choice for one individual and a string quartet the preferred selection for another.

Rebels are at risk in conformist cultures, because, instinctively, they actively challenge rather than passively adopt. They are sometimes careless with conventions and a few might be portrayed as boorish because their obsessions may drive out common pleasantries. Their focus could be upon a cause, a better tomorrow, rather than the pettiness of the here and now. They may have a mission beyond merely securing acceptance as one of the group. They are driven. There is heat and heart at their core.

Radicals, and those who are simply different, need to be accommodated rather than excluded if an organization genuinely believes in the value of diversity. Companies, such as Silicon Graphics, adopt a virtual model of operation, and provide a variety of non-traditional work environments, in order to meet the differing requirements of individual members of a highly talented and creative workforce.

Work does not need to be soulless and boring. B&Q introduced aerobics and other forms of exercise to energize its

workforce. As a consequence, its staff are fitter and its customers happier. Visitors can pick up a positive buzz at a place
of work.

An office need not resemble a chapel of rest. ASK, the learning company, encourages informality and fun. Its people have
responded with commitment and enthusiasm. Draw back the
curtains and open the window. Let some light and fresh air
into the room.

Active accommodation of diversity requires more than
grudging tolerance. Thus advantage could be taken of open
plan areas to create a variety of different working, thinking
and meeting spaces that address a wider range of requirements. Corning and Tandem Computers have introduced programmes that allow individual employees to change their
patterns of work to match evolving family commitments, particular contingencies and the unexpected.

Recognizing Individuality

It is easy to get lost in philosophical discussions concerning
the relative merits of placing differing degrees of emphasis upon
individuals and communities. The two can be reconciled and
need to be if relationships are to benefit all of the parties involved.

It is becoming ever more difficult to defend communities
that do not allow individuals to be true to themselves. If organizations and networks cannot respond to fundamental human needs, what is their purpose? Why should anyone work
for them, if there are other, and better, ways of fostering self-
fulfilment? In competitive situations, groups that do not enable and support individuality are likely to be out-performed
by alternative suppliers that are better able to harness the
commitment and capabilities of their people. Ultimately, the
unresponsive will fail.

Much corporate behaviour that is regarded as 'anti-social' is
a direct result of individuals being expected to subordinate important aspects of their personalities in order to fit in with
corporate cultures and norms. In an effort to avoid such sub-
mission, people get together and seek ways of protecting and
safe-guarding their views and preferences, and imposing them
upon others. In the resulting battle for power within the corporate hierarchy, some groups win and others lose. While the

tussle ensues, attention is focused within, rather than on the external customer.

Tolerant communities, which can accept, and even encourage, diversity, have less need of power struggles. One group's progression need not result in reversals elsewhere. Freedom becomes indivisible. Different groups can do their own thing to a greater degree. Energy is not expended on internal conflicts, but is focused upon the purposes of the organization.

Corporate career structures impose a perverse conformity upon the lives of millions. They are rarely subjected to fundamental questioning. Does it make sense for young people to be put under pressure when they may have had little opportunity for reflection and integrating what they have learned? Why are individuals expected to assume heavy work responsibilities at a stage in their lives when their children would most benefit from their time? Why not wait until they have greater experience, and more of a sense of who they are and the distractions of raising children and paying off mortgages are behind them? Why are people 'got rid off' just when many are best equipped to make a thoughtful contribution?

Management, and network co-ordination, should focus more upon ends and be less concerned about means. The relevance and quality of thought, and the extent to which value is created, are what is important – not where, when or how the work was done. The latter areas are matters which should be left to those directly concerned to decide for themselves.

The manager should merely ensure that, when decisions about individual patterns of work are made, the views of all those affected are taken into account and the preferences of some do not secure an unfair advantage over the interests of others. Square pegs should not be put into round holes. The extent to which different people are able to cope needs to be matched with the particular demands of each way of working.

Temperament and personality are important. Many time management experts seem to forget this. Thus those who advocate prioritization, and getting down each morning to the most important things first, should not impose such an approach upon everyone. It might, of course, be appropriate for ditherers and procrastinators, who might otherwise put off the more demanding and unpleasant tasks.

However, there are generally alternative means of coping with a portfolio of tasks. There may be some people for whom a more appropriate strategy would be to clear the desks of the less essential items in order to concentrate upon those matters that require serious attention at a time of the day when they know they are likely to be at their best. Being prescriptive can result in the adoption, or even the imposition, of ways of working that are not right for certain individuals.

Too many people have had to constrain, or adjust, the way they naturally work, or think, to fit in with the requirements of this or that procedure or technology. While shopping at the weekend, and 'voting with their money', they sense and enjoy their power as consumers. However, when at the office, they may feel they have little control over their own destinies. The important decisions affecting the quality of their working lives are taken by others. They are simply balls with which others play. If they get scratched, they find themselves thrown into the bushes.

People and Technology

Where people are not important they should, whenever possible, be replaced by machines. This spares them the indignity of being regarded merely as extensions of whatever technology is used. Human accessories can become bored and dissatisfied by routine and repetitive tasks.

From an aeroplane, it appears that machines are in charge. The roads which they travel along appear to take precedence over so many other considerations. The humans who can be seen, as one approaches the ground, appear as a species of benevolent parasite, whose primary purpose is to keep vehicles fueled and oiled, and other manifestations of the physical infrastructure from houses to factories in a reasonably good working order. Sometimes, the machines abuse the little parasites by running over them, or attacking their respiratory systems with pollutants.

The pendulum has swung too far in one direction. Invariably, people are the ultimate consumers, beneficiaries or victims at the end of supply chains. Relevant technologies should be viewed as instruments and enablers, and not as gods to be meekly worshipped for hours on end.

Increasingly, individual customers are becoming more demanding. As they come to expect personal attention, and recognition of their particular requirements, so greater thought is required and human intervention can become more important.

Too often technology is regarded as a constraint rather than as an energizer or liberator. The views of many people have become coloured by their experiences of past projects and information technology (IT) investments that failed to deliver the hoped for benefits. However, more recently there has been a steady improvement in the capability that is available for a given cost. Conversely, the price of a particular level of functionality has steadily fallen in real terms.

As a result of these trends, the IT, which is needed to support the various functions of a modern business, has been put into the hands of quite small ventures. IT has become an ally rather than an oppressor. Individuals working at home can now afford the technology needed to launch their own enterprises.

The performance of modems has dramatically improved, to the point that an individual's capacity to enjoy the full benefits of the information superhighway can match that of much larger competitors. People can even gain the edge over big organizations by taking quicker buying decisions to up-grade. Once large and complex documents, including voice and video elements, can be transmitted, many technical objections to remote working fall away.

Humanity and individuality need to be recognized. Less prescriptive and mechanical management approaches are required, with more discretion given to individual business units, as happens in ABB. In particular, performance measurement and management need to become more flexible and related to both business priorities and individual aspirations.

Organizations are communities of human beings. People are the principal players, not pusillanimous parasites. Under the right conditions, particular individuals are capable of performing heroic deeds. Given some space, and, when allowed to breath and to select their own colleagues and collaborators, many of them can make a profound impact upon corporations, their customers and the marketplace.

Exercise: Gain and Loss Analysis

Some people find it difficult to decide between different ways of working and alternative lifestyles. One method of comparison is to examine what would be gained or lost by selecting each possible course of action.

Set out the main options facing you in terms of lifestyle or how you could work. What would be gained or lost if each were adopted? Weight the gains and the losses – say from 1 to 5 – in terms of how important they are to you. Adding up the scores for each alternative, allows you to rank them on a spectrum from the greatest net gain to the largest net loss.

The Importance of Reflection

Machines operate. People think and feel. Questioning minds need opportunities to reflect and time to collect their thoughts. It is surely no accident that the science of genetics originated in a tranquil monastery garden. It was an Italian Friar, Luca Pacioli, and not a market trader, who wrote the first manual of double-entry bookkeeping.

The hectic day of the modern employee offers little scope for consideration. Companies as varied as Eagle Star and Xerox have recognized that, if people are to be creative, they must be given time to think. Employees are entitled to periods that are free of interruptions, and in which they can sustain a chain of thought. Meetings should be special and productive occasions, rather than regular and time-wasting rituals.

Too often, creativity is driven from the workplace by the relentless pace of events. Leyland Trucks periodically shuts down its production line for a couple of hours to allow collective reflection. When the machines fall silent ideas venture out, mingle and cross-fertilize.

Some people work better in the peaceful setting of the countryside, while others prefer the raw stimulus of an urban environment. The birth of a new dawn, as the first rays of light challenge the darkness, might be the most inspiring time for 'early birds' to concentrate upon more demanding tasks. Others may prefer to 'get down to it' during the cool of the late afternoon and after they have dealt with the distractions of the day's correspondence.

Much depends upon one's mood, or the task in hand. There is no reason why people shouldn't 'get away from it all' in order to undertake reflective activities, while returning to the 'buzz' of an office when tackling work that benefits from social interaction and the stimulus of others.

Those who do not feel responsible for themselves, may not even try to influence their destiny. This is the downside of allocating particular roles and responsibilities without consultation. Create a quality or a research department and other people may think that these activities are for specialists. Companies that are visibly dependent upon creativity, such as the advertising agency Howell Henry Chaldecott Lury, ensure that all members of the team feel accountable for producing good ideas. Everyone should have a licence to think.

Many corporations have placed too much emphasis upon teamwork, role model behaviour and standard competencies. The key to harnessing more of the potential of individual people is to encourage them to be themselves and to work and learn in ways that enable them to give of their best.

Divergence of imagination rather than convergence of appearance may be required. Organizations should work with the grain. They must become less like houses of correction and more like centres of learning.

Flexible Access to Skills

Companies need flexible access to particular skills for various reasons. External inputs may provide a quicker and cheaper alternative to the internal development of specialist expertise. Requirements come and go. There are peaks and troughs of workload to contend with. Some businesses are highly seasonal. A major tourist attraction, such as Alton Towers, and a small seaside hotel, may both want extra staff during the summer months.

Flexible work is not a recent innovation. From time immemorial farmers have needed additional help at harvest time. For centuries craftsmen have moved from one major building project to another. Nomadic herdsmen, knife grinders, travelling entertainers and proselytizing missionaries have all been mobile workers.

New ways of working concern both individuals and organizations. There is no escape from their impacts. Even 'traditional' professions, such as accountancy and the law, are affected. The widespread availability of new technologies, and the changing nature of client operations and problems, are transforming established methods of practice. Practitioners are increasingly having to work collaboratively with colleagues and customers in a variety of locations.

Instead of providing a series of standard and self-contained 'boxes' for lone individuals to operate in, today's professional firm needs to create a very different form of infrastructure. A variety of working spaces with different supporting systems are required, within which groups of experts can come together to work as teams on complex projects. The changes are reaching those at the top. At Arthur Andersen, partners have given up their own personal offices.

Groupings of various forms still exist, but they are largely of choice rather than imposed. Individual members are given greater freedom to determine themselves with whom they will communicate and associate. Those who work electronically may feel sufficiently confident to allow non-members of a particular sub-group to view what is taking place. Such openness can help to break down barriers, remove suspicions and encourage learning across projects and teams.

A degree of accommodation and reconciliation is still required. However, in comparison with past models of operation, it is more likely to be mutual and the requirements of individuals are assuming a more explicit priority.

Where the colleagues with whom one works, and the tasks upon which they are engaged, are continually changing flexibility should be maintained. Alternatives should be kept open. Solutions may have a temporary air about them. A pattern of work, which is appropriate for one team, time or project, may not suit another.

Rather than put all of one's eggs into one basket, and adopt a particular way of working, it might be advisable to experiment with, and support, various options. Groups could be allowed to select whatever process, technology and mode of work is most appropriate in relation to their particular responsibilities and requirements.

A corporation could maintain a pool of working environments, available technologies and facilitating processes and tools. Advice concerning their selection, combination and use could be among the support services provided to work groups. In effect, organizations could become laboratories for creative knowledge workers.

Such assistance could be of considerable value to individuals with entrepreneurial ambitions and groups that may not themselves have the time to assess all of the options. People often have difficulty in fully appreciating how different combinations of components might best be brought together, because suppliers of each element of the whole may exaggerate the importance of its potential contribution. A central support unit can spread its costs over many user departments, each of which might be unable by itself to fund a satisfactory level of support.

Insiders and Outsiders

Those selecting which patterns of work to adopt should remember that relationships involve at least two people. In the case of network communities, there may be considerably more viewpoints to accommodate. Arrangements should be negotiated. Some degree of give and take is likely to be required. Vigilance may be needed to ensure that members with certain lifestyle preferences and particular nationalities are not excluded from participation.

One person may have a preference for early morning telephone conversations, while certain colleagues within the work group may be 'late starters'. Time-zone differences can cause further complications. When live conferencing is required, particular infrastructures and environments may be needed. These should be negotiated among those involved rather than imposed.

When workgroups are dispersed across national borders, other issues are likely to arise. These will need to be addressed. Thus attitudes to 'teleworking' can vary greatly between countries. In one society, spending some time working at home may be accepted as fairly normal. Elsewhere such a practice may rarely happen.

The nature of family life, and the layout of residential accommodation, may make it difficult for those in certain communities to work from home. The 'teleworker' in a private study in a detached 'executive home' in the UK, US or Scandinavia may need to be reminded that colleagues elsewhere might have to house an extended family within the confines of a flat without a garden. Colleagues in India could share a residence with three or four generations, while partners in Japan, where space is at a premium, may find their prospects for growth as constrained as that of a goldfish in a bowl.

Within any form of organization, some will find it easier to play a prominent role than others. A careful watch should be kept to ensure that marginalized groups of 'outsiders' do not emerge. Thus members of an elite team of computer buffs may need to be reminded that others, who are different from themselves, may have the potential to make a significant contribution, for example by thinking through 'next steps' while the 'techies' surf the net in search of the latest cyber-gossip.

Certain 'insiders', including owner/managers or 'relations' in the case of family companies, may not be held to account, as others would be, for inadequate performance. Owner directors might escape peer scrutiny. The progress of a company could depend upon the extent to which they are self-critical and invite challenge. The family-owned furniture company Ercol takes active steps to avoid inertia and stagnation by, for example, learning from outside experience and attracting people from different sectors.

The diversity of circumstances can be such that many network communities require some form of arbitration process to handle the failure of certain partners to reach agreement. Reconciliation should not be obtained at the cost of leveling down to lowest common denominator solutions. Instead, the aim should be to squeeze and secure as much potential as possible out of each situation.

Ideally, each case should be judged on its own merits by a process that is seen to be fair. Members of the community could take turns, just as citizens feel obliged to serve upon a jury, at helping colleagues to resolve disputes.

Involving those Likely to be Affected

People who establish new patterns of work may find that members of their families or neighbours have strong views. Much will depend upon what has gone before. Relationships that are already strained can sometimes fall apart. Someone who is tolerated when rarely about, might irritate when around most of the time. However, the positions of those who are on firmer foundations may be further strengthened.

Changes of lifestyle can have a very significant impact upon a person's immediate family. To begin with, and until people adapt and a balance is achieved, certain problems, distractions and difficult choices may be encountered. Thus a child may wish to play with a parent who is suddenly 'available' more often at home. After some tears, it may be accepted that not all of this time is available for fun and games.

All those concerned should understand that a period of adjustment might be necessary. There will be new roles and responsibilities to establish. Ways of working and living together will have to be adopted that meet the distinct needs of all those concerned.

Each way of working, learning or consuming is likely to have its own particular advantages and disadvantages. These will alter as people, tasks and circumstances change. Managers need to be aware of the various options, and their differing characteristics and requirements, in order to assess when each might be appropriate on a 'horses for courses' basis.

A sense of proportion is needed. Every pattern of work can have its own ardent advocates and determined detractors. Each approach may benefit some more than others. There might also be ways in which the unscrupulous could exploit many of the options.

When faced with change, some people may raise the spectre of all sorts of drawbacks with what is being proposed while eulogizing the current situation. Thus much may be made of the problems of communicating with 'teleworkers'. In reality, many traditional offices do little to encourage effective interaction. People can be physically close and yet isolated within their individual workspaces. When they do get together, for example for meals, the conversation might be banal in the extreme as people endeavour to conceal their true interests or feelings.

Sometimes, it is those who work apart who are most concerned with establishing deeper relationships. When they are able to be together, they may invest significant time and emotional effort in really getting to know each other. Understanding people's varying motivations, and how important a certain project, and its related income stream, is to them, can be

invaluable when deciding whom to allocate to particular packages of work.

Management and the co-ordination of a diversity of dispersed
working arrangements requires great sensitivity. The separation of 'work' and 'home', and the distinction between an employee or contractor and his or her family, may be less clear-
cut. Assessment and evaluation without intrusion and inter-
ference is required.

When selecting an appropriate combination of people and
patterns of work, many companies appear to opt for the maximum of pain and minimal gain. Single or partial solutions are
unlikely to work. The keys to success are to be aware of the full
range of options, while remaining sensitive to the particular
context and focused upon priority objectives. When adopting
new management approaches, the entrepreneur should always
concentrate upon the most promising opportunities.

Along with greater freedom comes corresponding responsibilities. Individuals should no longer hide behind rules or blame
their employers. Increasingly, they have to negotiate with colleagues, families and other communities and are required to
justify their decisions to interested parties. Inevitably, relationships with these groups will change.

Where others are involved, their understanding and support should be worked for rather than assumed. If commercial
rivals, such as BUPA and PPP, can co-operate where they have
common interests and develop a joint electronic commerce solution, greater collaboration within the family ought to be possible.

People should enter into discussions and negotiations with
a clear understanding of their preferences and requirements.
No one should feel compelled to compromise upon or abandon cherished positions. Abdication can lead to alienation.
Freedom results from staying in one's own natural environment and not playing other people's games.

Checklist

1. How might an alternative way of working make it easier for you to secure flexible access to the skills, resources and other capabilities which you require?

2. Could it enable you to deliver greater value to customers and operate and compete more effectively?

3. Are there alternative ways of learning that would allow you to better acquire and build the knowledge and expertise that you need?

4. How could you learn more effectively than your competitors?

5. Have you thought through the practical, operational and management implications of adopting a different approach to working and learning? Who might be excluded?

6. Do the people, with whom you associate, have what it takes to work and learn effectively in the ways that you are proposing?

7. Have they been consulted? Are they supportive? Who is likely to lodge an objection?

8. Would your current organization be open to suggestions concerning how it might secure more flexible access to your own skills and those of colleagues?

9. Do those to whom you are accountable know that you would like to change direction, and are considering the options? Are you working up a proposal?

10. Would they allow you to provide similar and related services to non-competing organizations?

11. Where is resistance to change most likely to arise from
     within your current organization? How might this be over-
     come? Who could help you?

12. Are your family and friends supportive of your aspira-
     tions and intentions? Have they thought through the im-
     plications and possible consequences?

TURNING DREAMS INTO REALITIES

Take your pasty with you.

All forms of life go through a sequence of identifiable stages, whether the tree that endures for many hundreds of years or the insect that completes its whole cycle of existence within the confines of a single day. At certain periods during the journey through life there may be moments of particular vulnerability or instances of great opportunity.

Most human beings are likely to experience a succession of transitions as they age. Each one of these could provide a turning point. Some largely ignore the signs and press on, although they may encounter occasional periods of angst and doubt along the way. Others recognize that nature is taking its course, and use natural clearings, forks and interludes to pause and ponder. They take stock of what is happening, reassess and adjust.

Seizing the Moment

A mid-life crisis can provide an opportunity to free oneself of limiting drives, such as conforming and 'fitting in', and focus more upon self-fulfilment. Those, who reflect upon their experience of life in terms of better understanding and developing the person within, generally find they are working with the grain of nature in seeking to determine their own paths.

Balanced and integrated people recognize that there are both positive and negative forces in life. They are able to reconcile their involvement with organizations, and their relationships with others, with the establishment of a separate inner existence and distinct personal agenda. While they might be influenced by the decisions of other people, individuals may also have considerable discretion to respond and to determine their own futures.

Starting the process, by thinking about what one knows and does not know, need not be expensive. It may only require a quiet corner or a long walk. If companies, such as Dow Chemical and Monsanto, can take steps to turn tacit understanding into explicit knowledge, so can individuals. Drawing up an inventory of personal 'know-how' enables people to put a value upon themselves and perhaps identify the basis for a chargeable service.

Reflection is one thing, action is another. Many people are deterred from making the first moves towards the realization of their dreams by a fear of failure. They come to appreciate what they have when there is a prospect that it might be lost or taken away.

Yet the soft option of staying put and expectations of continuity are fast disappearing. Revitalization, innovation, chaos, the need for constant change – these are the phrases on the lips of today's managers. Rather than 'sticking around' and becoming a target, many people are deciding to fight on ground of their own choosing.

Taking control, moving in a new direction, launching out on one's own and founding a business all involve risks. Some of these are merely inconvenient, like the prospect of less time for favourite pastimes during the demanding early stages of a venture. Others can be more serious, such as conceding a second mortgage on one's house as a condition of start-up funding.

Life can be taken for granted. It is never so sweet as when its hold appears most tenuous. These are the times when it may seem better to live as a mouse than to die as a lion. Others take the opposite view. Sherrie Charlton used her experience of overcoming adversity to set up The Spiral Consultancy which helps people to cope with difficult challenges. Andy Grove of Intel developed a similarly robust reaction to bad news. Receiving the sort of medical report we all dread, gave him a new determination to use his time to the full. He continued working, while, at the same time, taking active steps to learn as much as possible about his condition and how best to manage it.

Luckily most business ventures are not life-threatening. Money, pride and reputation may be at stake, but failure, even total defeat in the marketplace, can represent a learning and character building experience. The rubber ball bounces back.

Early set backs, and painful reverses, deter some from further adventures. They retreat into themselves or seek the solace and security of a previous existence. They settle back into old routines, albeit perhaps with less self-confidence than before. Others find that having tasted the fruit, they want more.

Facing up to Failure

In some parts of the world, people are more tolerant of failure than in others. The Californian venture capitalist would most likely be suspicious of someone who has not already 'had a go'. To be taken seriously it helps to have an enterprise 'history'. Ventures that did not work out quite as planned are discussed, rather than concealed.

Failure is natural. From an early age we fear the loss of whatever we value, whether parental attention, a treasured possession, such as leaving our most loved teddy bear on the beach, or a new found sense of balance. We endure many bumps and bangs while learning to walk.

Thomas Edison was described as retarded at school, but this did not prevent him from being alert to requirements and opportunities. While employed in a lowly capacity on a railroad he noticed that many people on his train did not have anything to read. He brought a printing press on board and ran off a news-sheet. His subsequent career would result in an almost unending stream of discoveries and innovations.

Crippled by an attack of smallpox, Josiah Wedgwood was unable to carry out the normal physical work of a potter within the family business. Instead, he turned to research and started a lifelong commitment to investigation and experimentation which led to greatly improved processes and glazes. Setting up in business on his own account, he introduced superior forms of earthenware, such as 'creamware' and 'jasperware', and became both a successful entrepreneur and a leading scientist of his age.

Edison and Wedgwood started young. Ray Kroc was over 50 when he visited a McDonald's restaurant in California and got the idea of franchising fast food under the McDonald's banner. He negotiated the rights to do this and started on the road to building a global chain of outlets.

Many people are frozen into inaction by the fear of failure or loss. The areas considered at risk, whether a job, status, a relatively certain income flow, prospects of career progression, belonging to something, having an identity or power over others, can sometimes appear more significant or threatened than they actually are. At a point of decision, they may also seem more tangible than 'extra freedom' or 'greater self-fulfillment'.

Whatever might be lost needs to be seen in perspective. What is thought to be real, and at stake, may actually be imagined or mere baggage. A change may result in a different form of standing, and more power over oneself. There could be the prospect of many gains, from new opportunities, having additional time for thinking, playing, and working on more enjoyable activities, greater lifestyle flexibility, being able to determine one's own priorities and associate with people of choice, to the greater self-respect that comes from 'having a go'.

Resistance, and a reluctance to adjust, are sometimes the consequence of a failure to understand either the reasons for change or the benefits that are expected to be achieved. Both the London Borough of Hackney and Bass Brewers undertook extensive internal communications programmes ahead of introducing initiatives to change their corporate culture.

Gerhard Schulmeyer, the Chief Executive of Siemens-Nixdorf, ensured the company's staff understood not only why a major restructuring and staff reductions had to occur, but also the implications for themselves. He explained the situation in face to face meetings with as many people as possible. Human beings should not be expected to commit to courses of action which they do not understand. The 'small print' should be explained.

Fear of mistakes, or unexpected outcomes, inhibits personal and collective advancement. The development of many of the fundamental building blocks of civilization has been based upon trial and error. Certain failures persisted for generations before success was finally achieved.

Few inventors or scientists would expect a first experiment to succeed. The essence of the scientific process is experimentation and analysis, trying again and again, varying this and that, performing a succession of trials under a variety of circumstances. Many of the world's great discoveries were born after years of experimentation. In some cases, innovation and progress have been the result of a lifetime's quest.

The Edison, Wedgwood or Marconi simply keeps on trying. Why should business success be judged on a different basis? Why do we expect people to hit upon a winning formula at the first attempt? Eliminating possibilities should be regarded as an intrinsic aspect of developing a better appreciation of a situation.

Exercise: Gap or Hole Analysis

Companies undertake gap analyses in order to prepare future projections and assess where they are likely to be in relation to where they would like to be. This can lead on to an analysis of the actions which need to be taken to bridge any gaps that emerge between expectations and intentions and outcomes and achievements.

Individuals often lack carefully thought-out plans. Some find it easier to focus upon what exists than to identify what is missing. Are there holes in what you are setting out to achieve? Do you have all that you need to fill them or are certain building blocks missing? What cement do you need to hold the blocks together? What new elements need to be put in place?

Having a Go

At some point individuals have to decide whether or not to take the plunge and, if the former applies, when to make their move. While impetuosity can be dangerous, excessive procrastination may entail for ever waiting in the wings. In an uncertain world, the moment might never be right. In the meantime, possible windows of opportunity can come and go.

Some people do not like to commit until they feel confident that every eventuality has been thought through. Like chess players, they do not want to reveal their hand until they have pondered all the likely outcomes and reactions. Those, who wait for every building block to be in place, may end up being too late. The business equivalent of 'time up' on the chess clock is the missed opportunity.

Individual temperament is a major determinant of a person's willingness to 'have a go'. Thus natural loners may act more quickly than those who feel insecure unless they have the right team around them or the full support of family and friends. Those, who lack confidence in their own judgement, will want to ask everyone else what they think.

Selfish and mercenary people may be less willing to share an opportunity with collaborators than those whose focus is more upon delivering a service to identified prospects. Hence, they may fail to assemble a balanced team with the capabilities to 'accomplish the task'. They may become more concerned with their personal status and prospects, than with the value they are, or could be, creating.

Some like to take out rather than put in. They may have the ability and potential to succeed, but not the drive or motivation. They look for easy wins, opportunities to pick up fruits, without having to climb trees to get at them. Others are more adventurous and energetic. For them the 'doing' may be as enjoyable and rewarding as the outcome.

Those who succeed tend to be the more self-confident and flexible individuals who confront challenges and are willing and able to use a variety of different means to accomplish their ends. They welcome choice. Their instinct is to look for options in order that the best course of action can be identified.

They are prepared to roll up their sleeves and become personally involved in whatever needs to be done. They can influence without alienating. They inspire others, engender trust and are willing to delegate. They are also prepared to acknowledge and address deficiencies. Most have the capacity to focus upon what is most important at any one time. Almost all are passionate about their businesses.

Failures are less demanding and more easily satisfied. They often 'hope for the best', or opt for the first available option that will 'do the job'. They are more likely to put their faith in single solutions. They tend to avoid issues and confrontations. They like to be told good news and look for explanations rather than solutions. They may be clever, but they also tend to be anaemic and easily distracted by the inessential. They also lack resilience.

Any business venture involves a degree of risk. Every effort should be made to identify potential obstacles and barriers and other threats to success. Without such risks, it would not be possible to achieve higher rates of return than could be obtained by simply leaving any investment involved in a bank or building society. But a new venture involves more than just parting with money. It also normally requires a commitment of time, particularly during the early stages, when the cash flow may not be strong enough to cover the costs of obtaining input from others.

People can reduce their exposure to risk by being true to themselves and by endeavouring to do what comes most naturally to them. Listening to your inner voices can help you to determine whether a course of action is appropriate or misguided.

Desirable Qualities

It is possible to learn from others without slavishly following them. There may be several sources of information and understanding about various aspects of what a person is setting out to do. Each may be able to provide individual building blocks, while those involved with them remain unaware of the whole. The entrepreneur may need to envisage what might be achieved through the selection and combination of different elements.

Thus Nicholas Hayek, on becoming chairman of the Swiss watchmaker SMH, virtually reinvented one of his country's traditional industries, which had declined to the point of extinction, by embracing quartz technology. Existing watchmakers learned new skills. Conventional assumptions were challenged. For example, why should people only have one watch? Watches were marketed as fashion accessories and collectors' items.

People should plough their own furrows and not be distracted by seeking to emulate others. Your neighbour may be intending to grow a different crop. Entrepreneurs should be driven from within. The ambitious set their own standards and aim to become their own role models.

Sufficient commitment should be made to create a realistic chance of success. There is always a temptation, particularly on the part of those with a portfolio lifestyle, to hedge bets. A strategy of not putting all of one's eggs into the same basket may result in a new venture being starved of the attention needed to achieve a breakthrough.

A sense of balance is required. Safeguarding resources, holding back reserves, may enable one to fight another day. However, in the meantime, the effort devoted may be insufficient to win the contract. People should aim to commit not too little, nor so much as to be wasteful, but just enough to achieve their objectives.

No amount of preparation can substitute for resilience and flexibility in the face of changing circumstances and fresh challenges. Each day can bring new surprises, some welcome, others less so. Simply 'going automatic', and mechanically implementing a business plan, can be a recipe for disaster. People need to know when and how to adjust and adapt.

Some entrepreneurs have the instincts of the hunter. They equip themselves for the trail or chase before they set out. Everything from waterproofs to weapons is ready to be accessed as, and when, required. They track and stalk opportunities until they are in a good position to strike and the conditions most favour success. Then they pounce. Missing the moment, or withholding commitment, allows the quarry to slip away.

However, prudence is a virtue. It is important on day one to have a realistic understanding of what can be risked. Too many people just 'press on' regardless. They keep throwing good money after bad, until their resources are entirely depleted. It may be wise to withdraw tactically and re-group, rather than forge ahead into unknown territory. Having skirmished, learned some lessons and whetted one's appetite, tomorrow is another day.

Exploration and Discovery

Establishing a new enterprise is tantamount to undertaking a voyage of exploration. Throughout the ages, great discoveries have resulted not from prior knowledge so much as venturing forth and asking the right questions. The journey itself can present rich learning opportunities. Issues that appeared overwhelming at the beginning may turn out to be of little importance, while other areas, which perhaps no one could have foreseen, become of major significance.

Successful entrepreneurs and creative scientists often exhibit a paradoxical combination of dogged inflexibility concerning ends and supple and subtle flexibility in relation to means. They persist in returning time and time again to the central questions that preoccupy and drive them. Like their forebears, these modern knights remain true to their quest, but they respect enterprise rather than magic.

They may also be promiscuous in their search for insights, roaming the highways of many subjects and sectors for sources of inspiration. Their leads may take them to both unfrequented alleys and well-trodden thoroughfares. Whilst it may be said that city streets are paved with gold, the strike or find that first locates the yellow ore may occur in distant foothills where the earliest to arrive have the greatest chance of securing the best claims.

Too many corporate practices appear to deny the realities of the entrepreneurial process. Regardless of circumstances, opportunities to initiate new lines of enquiry may arise only once a year, when competing claims are submitted for budget review. Departures from the plan are often viewed with concern. Thus, unexpectedly bumper sales may give rise to investigations of 'forecasting errors', not celebration.

Boards can face a dilemma. They may desire both creative exploration and the maintenance of prudent control. They have a legal duty to safeguard the assets of a company, which requires them to be cautious in respect of new commitments. Many investigations turn out to have been 'wild goose chases'. At the same time, to be trusted one needs to learn who, when, where and how to trust. Also, risk and return are related.

Growth and development often depend upon the ability to generate a flow of innovations that will add incremental and profitable income streams. Without these, a company may stagnate and atrophy, therefore, a balance has to be struck. Caution often wins over enterprise. To turn a company into a seed bed of new ideas and discoveries might require a process of transformation. The funding of a portfolio of venture teams may demand different attitudes to risk and more flexible resource allocation mechanisms.

The re-engineering of many work processes has reduced discretion and created a feeling that 'big brother' is watching. The consequence is a lack of intellectual challenge. Rather than discuss and debate, bored operatives peer at monitors all day. People are switching stations. To tune them in again may require the introduction of smaller workgroups within which each member can experience a greater variety of more rewarding work and greater social interaction. People will be alone in their coffins for all eternity. While they are alive let them communicate with each other.

Undergoing and Enabling Individual Transformation

Individual and corporate transformation are interrelated. Uncertainty and complexity, whether internal or external, can stress people and their employers. Both are complex adaptive systems. They are also interdependent. When the health of one suffers, the quality of life of the other is adversely affected. The ability of an organization to cope can very much depend upon the extent to which its people are able to handle the pressures they are under.

Most people are facing a need to change. Like it our not, whether in relation to the world of work, ageing populations or claims upon the environment, things cannot continue unchanged. The dilemma for many is to distinguish between what needs to go and that which is of lasting value. There are invariably principles and standards that are worth preserving. In every generation, there are those who are prepared to die for certain cherished beliefs.

Values, principles of conduct and beliefs can provide a moral underpinning. They help us to identify which questions to ask. Archimedes' screw advanced civilization because of the use to which it was put, namely the raising of water to enable wider irrigation in Egypt. Too many people have access to an abundance of money, technology, tools and techniques, but lack a compelling purpose.

We need to understand how we can liberate ourselves by serving others. Directors and corporate decision makers should endeavour to create institutions and adopt processes that make it easier for people to be true to themselves. More natural ways of operating could be introduced, in which communication, adaptation, learning, innovation and change are integral elements of normal work.

Helping people to use emerging technologies, to overcome barriers of geography and time can also lead to less isolation, division and distrust. Henry Trengrouse's rocket apparatus bridged distance – from ship to shore – and enabled lives to be saved. Group promotion rather than self-protection should be the aim.

Few people go to bed in one life and wake up the next morning effortlessly adjusted to another. They encounter surprises and experience shocks. Initial anticipation and euphoria can give way to periods of depression and despair. It is common to harbour regrets and to seek to cling on to aspects of an old life that may not have a place in the new. Individuals are likely to be tested, confronted by uncertainties and plagued by doubts, before they finally accommodate to, cope with and, ultimately, master a new situation.

Those, long subjected to high levels of corporate caution and constraint, may need to undergo a personal metamorphosis. This may require more than a new suit of clothes and a different diet. People may need to uncover additional facets of their persona and discover new ways of understanding themselves. This may require looking beyond what can be seen in the mirror.

Exercise: Personal Development Plan

Identifying development needs is one thing, taking steps to acquire new competencies and experiences is another.

What new competencies, qualities and experiences do you need in order to achieve your personal and business visions? How and where might these be obtained?

Assessment and Reassessment of Self

For some, the change of approach needed may be rather like forsaking films in favour of reading novels. In films, events and developments tend to be recorded, portrayed or suggested through what can be seen or heard, namely physical appearance and the accompanying musical score. The novelist lacks these elements. More attention has to be given to descriptions and intimations of attitudes and feelings. People's motivations are explored and their souls are bared. The central players are characters rather than actors.

Letting go of the baggage of unquestioned assumptions, ingrained habits and unrealistic past expectations is important for individuals and for communities. Advanced societies have a greater range of options than many realise. Much depends upon what people take for granted, and the extent to which they reflect upon what is really important to them.

A process of reassessment can enable people to identify, and choose between, aspects which should be changed and areas which ought to be preserved and cherished. People tend to dwell upon what they do not have, rather than reflect upon their good fortune. How often do people consider how lucky they are to be, in effect, standing upon the shoulders of previous generations?

Would resources be available for foreign holidays if each generation had to excavate cuttings and lay its own railway tracks, build road networks and lay runways, recreate the housing stock, sink mine shafts afresh, put in water, electricity, gas and cable networks or undertake a great many other activities to create the capital that has been inherited from the past? Each day, and in a variety of different ways, people benefit from the creative efforts of those who have gone before.

One generation would not be sufficient to recreate much of what can be freely, or widely, enjoyed. Thus many centuries of toil might have contributed to a rural landscape. Today we can view the results of plantings undertaken by past horticulturists who themselves never saw the full fruits of their endeavours. Majestic avenues of trees fulfill the dreams of those long deceased. They are whispering witnesses of past visions.

There is no need for people to be petty or greedy. At the margin, how important is an extra this or that to people who, in historical terms, already have so much? Why is the comparison so often with the neighbour, rather than with people in other societies or at other times in history?

Those who do take the time to reflect upon what they have in relation to their absolute requirements for a healthy and balanced life, frequently find that in some areas they have achieved beyond what is necessary. Such a realization is important if people are to escape from the traps they have imported into their minds, the treadmills to which they have shackled themselves and the collective prisons in which they have chosen to be confined.

Making Lifestyle Choices

Many people feel unable to break free from a current pattern of work because they seek, consciously or unconsciously, the continuance of the totality of a previous lifestyle. They are reluctant to give in order to gain. When the gap between earnings and expenditure is a narrow one, they are disinclined to prejudice what is perceived as a relatively secure income stream.

A reassessment of what is important in life often results in the identification of areas in which savings could be made and indulgences which could be given up. Not everything is crucial or critical. What would be forgone if this subscription were not renewed? Would a day's life be lost if that expenditure were discontinued?

Could interest costs be reduced by borrowing from another source? Might something be secured more cheaply from another supplier? Would bulk buying or agreeing to pay by direct debit, result in lower prices or tariffs? These are the sorts of questions which the budding entrepreneur should ask.

There may also be ways in which income could be increased. Would a higher return be obtained if funds were switched to a different type of account? Could an unused room be rented out? Relatively small increases in earnings, and modest reductions in expenditure, can give people some headroom. A margin for saving can reduce the pressure and allow them to breath.

And then there are future plans. Returning to the foreign holiday, why not break with convention and write a business plan instead? Becoming absorbed in 'something different' can often be the best means of recharging batteries and securing a fresh sense of purpose in life. It may also prove more enjoyable than breathing fumes in traffic jams and enduring delays at airports.

A good business opportunity is sometimes easier to find than the space to park a quarrelling family on a crowded beach. If working out the numbers is a hassle, then so is packing for the annual holiday. The difference concerns the purpose. The choice is between preparing for the rest of one's life and planning to get through the next two weeks.

On reflection, what has hitherto been accepted as reality may turn out to have either been a dream or someone else's view of what existence ought to be. The pressures of life may simply be social conventions that are uncritically followed. Under closer scrutiny, customary practices are often revealed as compromises that cannot satisfy the differing requirements of distinct groups.

Searching for Soul Mates

Those who feel trapped by the expectations, assumptions and norms of those around them should endeavour to seek out others who are like themselves. The chances are that they are out there. More encouragingly, they have never been so easy to locate.

Developments, ranging from the construction of secure housing estates to the formation of internet discussion groups, are allowing people to identify and associate with others who are more likely to be compatible in terms of interests, requirements and aspirations. Increasingly, societies, communities and organizations can support greater variety. They no longer need to opt for lowest common denominator solutions that satisfy no one.

Individuals can take the initiative and seek out the companionship of like-minded fellow travellers. They can join the networks, associations, clubs and societies that attract those with whom they would like to associate or coexist. Corporations, which are intent upon transforming themselves into enterprise support networks, should make it easier for people with similar interests, compatible personalities and complementary skills to come together and form effective venture teams.

Shoes that no longer fit should be thrown away. Otherwise they will constrict and may distort. Relationships need not be for life. People should not be condemned from birth to remain constrained by arrangements that do not suit them. They should be allowed to move between groups, retaining some memberships while both discarding and adding others as their interests change. The growing desire of people to be true to themselves creates a host of opportunities for those with the inclination to be proactive in the formation of interest and other groupings.

Once people have decided what it is they wish to do, and have assessed the skills, capabilities and resources they are likely to require, they may identify the need for personal development. Setting up in business can make a variety of new demands upon an individual. The magnitude of the challenge will depend upon the scale of adjustment required.

The lucky ones are those who focus upon what they enjoy doing and do best to such an extent that they turn a hobby or pastime into a business. In such cases, the development needed may be indistinguishable from leisure activity.

Individual or Collective Endeavour

The formation of a new enterprise, or assumption of responsibility for an existing one, may require a new approach to relationships. In the past, the astute operator may have treated colleagues warily or attempted to undermine them. In a new context, success might be dependent upon whether colleagues hold together and support each other. Breaking out is often a collective activity.

Appearances may have been important in the past. Rather than avoid effort, while seeking to maximize individual credit, the emphasis may need to change to getting on with the work in the interests of a whole venture. Tasks that are evaded, and duties shunned within a smaller group, may end up not being done. The reality of individual contribution towards collective achievement may need to replace the personal posturing associated with creating the impression of being a team player.

One person's dream can become another individual's nightmare. People should not compare themselves with others. Nor should they cultivate or retain stereotyped ideas of what a business venture ought to be. However, there may be advantages in seeking to share in the potential created by others, where and when a relevant contribution can be made.

Those who fancy the entrepreneurial lifestyle, but who lack a business concept, could consider a franchising option. There are generally a variety of them available at any one time. While the package offered will not be unique, it may be a new development and might offer exclusivity within a particular area. Its introduction may also benefit from advertising and other forms of support that are provided in return for a franchising fee.

The rapid expansion of certain franchise chains is evidence of the power of combining central and shared support with the drive of individual entrepreneurs. Many corporations could emulate this model as a mechanism for bringing new products and services to market. Committed partners take the place of disinterested investors and dependent employees.

Authors share their insights with others in return for royalties. Inventors provide opportunities for others by licensing

222 INDIVIDUALS AND ENTERPRISES

exploitation rights. One route to securing leverage on a good idea, is to package the main ingredients for success and offer it off the shelf to those who have the finance to replicate it, in return for a share of any resulting income.

Growth and Dependency

Many entrepreneurs are under tremendous external pressure to grow and develop their businesses. Their dreams are hijacked. They lurch from one treadmill to another. Greedy financial institutions, eager to obtain 'margins', encourage them to borrow for expansion. Avaricious professionals push for acquisitions or a flotation in order to secure further fees.

Expert guidance can open people's eyes to new possibilities. However, these may, or may not, be appropriate. Some of those lured into the water, enticed by the light twinkling upon its surface, quickly find themselves out of their depth and are swept away by hidden currents. The invoices of the smartly attired advisers who attend the funerals of those drowned are satisfied from the estates of the deceased.

Reactions to suggestions and sirens, and whether to resist or bow to them, should depend upon the rationale and purpose of a venture and the goals and ambitions of those concerned. A balanced and realistic assessment should be made of whether a proposed rate of development or possible expansion is a natural one or artificial. Forced growth brings its own problems.

The optimum size and shape for one business may be quite different to that of another. The fish and chip shop might be smaller than the department store and yet it may bring its owner greater satisfaction and provide less anguish. Many people stretch a concept too far and become overextended. What was once a joy becomes a burden.

A business may not need to expand or diversify. It might not face a choice between growth and death. There could be other options, for example improving quality, becoming more distinctive or discerning, striving for better margins or enhancing reputation. By some criteria, the smallest could be the best. A business of any size could be a source of pride and satisfaction.

Smaller enterprises can bring their own rewards. It may be easier for people to see a direct link between their own efforts and collective outputs. Individual contributions are more likely to be apparent. In the past people were invariably told how important they were, even when they featured among the statistics of head count reduction plans. In the smaller enterprise every person may actually be important, in that in the absence of any one of them certain things might not get done.

It is possible for a business to expand beyond its natural size. People overreach themselves and overtrade. Founders can become remote from their colleagues and customers. Those who join later may not share the commitment of those who experienced the formative stage. External investors, or professional advisers, could usurp control. Striving for ratios could strain relationships. A family feeling, the intimacy of a natural community, might be lost.

Sometimes those involved with entrepreneurial ventures have a strong desire for identity and visibility. Such a need could be accommodated by splitting, or hiving off, family-sized units. Each entity could be given a distinct 'personality' and an appropriate degree of autonomy.

In the big corporation multi-skilling may be a fad. In the smaller enterprise it can be essential. People just have to get down to a whole range of activities that may have previously been done by others. By way of compensation, they may also shed a great many of the tasks that were previously undertaken to serve the corporate machine rather than benefit end customers.

Large organizations can breed dependency cultures. Over time, people become conditioned and desensitized. They react to corporate stimuli, the annual assessment exercise or the presence or absence of a boss, rather than listen to 'inner voices'.

Within smaller groups there are fewer places to hide, whether from others or from oneself. Psychologically, people have to grow up. Assuming responsibility for an enterprise, and working autonomously, can both require a higher degree of self motivation. Successful people tend to be 'inwardly directed' self-starters. At the same time, individuals must avoid becoming obsessively self-absorbed. They need to recognize that it may be necessary to give something of value to others, in order to receive back their commitment and support.

They may also have to face up to certain accountabilities and realities that were previously avoided. There may be particular activities that people would prefer not to perform. A

common example is personal selling. In the smaller enterprise one is closer both to customers and to prospects. Without specialist sales teams, it may be necessary for people to
assume responsibility for both making initial contact calls
and concluding sales negotiations.

Independence can be bracing and demanding. Withstand-
ing the forces of competition requires sure foundations and
strong welds. When setting out on an enterprise journey, people should take their visions and values with them. Like Cornish pasties, they can provide vital sustenance.

Checklist

1.   What would you lose as a result of changing direction? What might you gain?

2.   Are you willing to 'have a go'? Is the timing right? Are those close to you supportive?

3.   How committed are you? How strongly do you feel about what you are setting out to do?

4.   Have you assessed your personal strengths and weaknesses in relation to the opportunities which you have identified? Will you be able to handle the challenges and the pressures?

5.   Have your responses to such questions surprised you, or are they confirmed by other evidence?

6.   In what areas are you deficient? Are these peripheral or are they at the heart of what you are seeking to achieve?

7.   What could, and should, be done about the deficiencies you have identified?

8.   What is the nature and scale of the transformation which you need to undertake? Is there time? Are you sufficiently determined to succeed?

9.   How might you prepare for the role in life which you are seeking? Can you afford it?

10. Are there opportunities for you to 'try out' or 'dry run'? Could you take on an interim role which would enable you to secure relevant knowledge and experience?

11. Will others among those around you also need to change? Are they willing to do so? Have they got what it takes?

12. How will what you are proposing to do develop you? Will it close other options or open up new ones? Will it increase or decrease your market value?

12

WHO ELSE IS OUT THERE?

Dropped crumbs attract birds, mice and rats.

Throughout the ages people in isolated settlements have looked up into starry night skies and wondered who else might be out there. On this earth, when highways were muddy tracks, it could take weeks or months for a letter to reach its destination. Today we have quicker ways of reaching out to others who may share our dreams and who might also have an interest in helping us to realize them. Messages start to arrive from almost the moment they are sent.

Deviants can become prophets once they begin to attract disciples. Distracted day dreamers become revolutionaries from the moment they enlist the support of agitators and fellow conspirators. Followers allow social isolates to become leaders.

Collective Endeavour

Collective effort can have an extraordinary impact. It may take an exceptional individual to out-perform a motivated team composed of complementary talents. Many games and sports can only be played by groups of people. The loner may be able to watch, but not participate.

Travellers in unfamiliar territory seek out guides. Where danger lurks, a party needs to be large enough to allow some to sleep while others stay awake. Caravans and wagon trains offer mutual support. Life on the frontier was possible because people helped their neighbours.

Sturdy and independent pioneers have to be multi-skilled in order to cope. However, as small settlements are established, they quickly learn the value of a degree of specialization based upon comparative advantage. A division of labour is natural. Some animals take turns at looking out for predators. In an age when the pendulum of opinion, in certain large corporations, appears to have swung against them, the value of specialist roles may need to be relearned.

Without a combination of skills a venture may not succeed. The strategy of companies, such as General Electric, is to become, and remain, a leading player in every market in which they operate. In service sectors that attract new entrants, talented people may significantly improve their prospects of becoming 'leading players' by joining forces to offer a joint capability.

A degree of specialization can make it easier for individuals to be true to themselves. Because a range of skills is needed to run a business, the involvement of others can increase the chances of each member of a core team being able to adopt a role that is to their liking.

The enterprise journey need not be made alone. When crossing the frontier that divides known business practices from the uncertain wilderness of new possibilities, support and cooperation can be invaluable. To succeed in certain situations, it may be essential.

Collaboration enables people to complement their own strengths and weaknesses. Once a gap has been identified it can be filled. For example, those lacking in imagination, or the ability, to develop a new business concept, could simply buy into a franchise arrangement. The intending entrepreneur acquires a complete package with an established brand reputation, appropriate training and technical support, ongoing marketing and, in many cases, territorial exclusivity.

Voyages of discovery invariably require a crew. The more ambitious the venture, the larger the team that may need to be involved, both in preparing for the journey and undertaking it. Most of those who provide supplies may have to be left behind. With space on a vessel at a premium, only the most resilient and versatile should be taken on board.

Selecting Colleagues

When sailing into uncharted waters, more care needs to be devoted to the selection process. Mutinies occur when the sea is rough, provisions run low and scurvy sets in. Taking someone along for the ride may not be doing them a favour. Volunteers who understand the risks involved, as well as the potential rewards, are preferable to mercenaries or the press-ganged.

When choosing business partners, objectivity is required. Account needs to be taken of the likely term of a venture. Thus, quick wits may be needed in dealing environments, while level heads and tenacity may be more important over a longer haul.

Priority should be given to forming a core team. Its size will depend upon the opportunity. In general, the ideal core team is relatively tight. It should cover essential requirements, but need not embrace the qualities to cope with every eventuality. Situations and circumstances can change and particular inputs of skill can always be contracted as, and when, required.

Existing organizations, which are striving to build more entrepreneurial cultures, may need to recreate aspects of the frontier spirit. Empowerment should encourage self-reliance and co-operation based upon mutual interest, rather than new forms of dependence and superficial teamwork. Too many companies lazily adopt new rituals and slogans, rather than actively engage in substantial collaboration rooted in comparative advantage.

In many larger corporations, employees can develop a range of general team working skills without having to pay too much attention to what is really motivating close colleagues. Personal associations tend to be temporary as people move up, around or out of the organization. Hence few managers may acquire the skills to build longer term relationships.

Many of those, with whom most people work, will have been selected by others. Some may be modern mercenaries who sell their services to the highest bidder. Economic necessity intrudes. Free association with those of one's own choosing is often limited to 'out of office' hours.

Few people are surrounded by volunteers. The press-gang principle still applies. Individuals are allocated to roles. As soon as one project is completed they are assigned to another, preferably with as little time as possible in between. This minimizes the opportunity to learn the lessons of whatever may have made a venture a success and to share with others how any difficulties encountered were overcome.

Information, Knowledge and Opportunity Sharing

Within hierarchical and competitive companies, people used to be reluctant to share, help out or do favours for others. Even information directly relevant to colleagues might be hoarded in order to boost position power. Individuals would strive to deny their potential rivals knowledge, which might enable the rivals to get ahead at their own expense.

The degree to which people need to associate with others, may depend upon many factors, one of which is the extent to which knowledge is explicit or tacit. They may, or may not, know what they and others know and do not know.

In individualistic corporate cultures, new knowledge is deemed to have been created when it becomes explicit and can be captured or 'badged'. Particular individuals may be keen to put their personal stamp upon it. Know-how may not be shared until it has been sufficiently packaged to allow certain people, who have made a distinct contribution, to be credited as 'authors'. Intellectual property can be valued and bought, licensed and sold.

More information has been produced in the last 30 years than was created in the previous five millennia. Accessing, synthesizing, communicating, deploying and applying relevant and appropriate information, knowledge and understanding is becoming a major challenge.

Increasingly, companies are having to become knowledge building and exchanging communities. Glaxo Wellcome uses its corporate intranet to enable over 10,000 researchers at a variety of locations to tap into research data. ANS Communications allows its clients to share much of its corporate information from remote access points. Cybersource Corporation can deliver its software products to customers via its network, while Great Food Online, as the name suggests, offers a similar service involving speciality foods.

In some sectors, people would find it difficult to develop better ways of doing things without close and continuing interaction with colleagues. Companies, such as Honda and Matsushita, recognize that those who work together and observe each other can evolve and share tacit knowledge. While they might find it difficult to articulate and explain what they have learned, it is incorporated into improved ways of working. Such learning can be difficult to replicate outside of the group.

Because it is not explicit and captured it cannot be copied or bought.

When people are forced to move on to new tasks as soon as others are completed, they may be denied an opportunity to periodically savour whatever success they may have achieved. Remaining 'on charge' as an 'income earning unit' allows little time for reflection. There are no sabbaticals for recharging batteries and recording what was done and experienced for the benefit of others. Opportunities for individual consolidation and corporate learning are lost.

If a corporation is to become an incubator of enterprise these practices must change. People need to be helped to better understand themselves and each other. They should be allowed to create roles for themselves that tap their inherent strengths and natural capabilities.

Venture teams should be encouraged and enabled to 'self-select' their members. They should be allowed to run for the duration of an opportunity, in order that those involved might secure the fulfillment that comes from staying with a project from concept to profitable realization.

Companies need to devote more effort to stimulating and accommodating the entrepreneurial drives of individuals. There are alternatives to traditional models of ownership. Thus the Scott Bader Company, a manufacturer of resins, is owned by The Scott Bader Commonwealth, a charitable trust of which only employees can become members.

Staff share-holding schemes can allow traditional employment to become a route to the achievement of the financial rewards associated with successful entreprenuership. The flotation of 'hi-tech', 'service' and 'buy out' companies, and the growth in the scale of professional partnerships, has significantly expanded the ranks of the seriously wealthy. The number of employees of Microsoft, who have become dollar millionaires as a result of their holdings of company stock, is now measured in thousands.

Compatibility and Diversity

Those, who are forming a core team to venture into the unknown, will need to take more care over deciding with whom to associate. The nature of the relationship is more demanding, and the consequences of picking the wrong people can be more traumatic. The relative importance of the various factors that will need to be taken into account are likely to be quite different.

For example, while diversity can broaden a collective perspective, too wide a range of personal circumstances may give rise to future disagreements and ultimate fragmentation. Someone who is in need of a relatively quick payback of cash, and further returns at regular intervals thereafter, may not be an ideal partner of an individual who is comfortable for the present but is seeking a larger reward at some point in the distant future.

It helps if core colleagues share a common time-scale. Over what time period are they expecting what sort of return? Where expectations and assumptions differ or diverge problems can result. Thus, one individual may be seeking a capital gain over five to ten years, while another may be looking for a longer term commitment and involvement in an enterprise.

At certain stages of life people may experience many claims upon their time. Disruptions, discontinuities and developments, such as moving house or location, marriage or having children, can result in significant changes of view and perspective. While they are young, people may move into and out of relationships and situations, as they sample a succession of options and assess different possibilities. As people get older, they may settle down and come to understand better what they want and their lifestyle preferences.

The business partnerships that survive are often those between people of a similar age: that between Lords Hanson and White is an example. Many successful venture teams are composed of individuals who have known each other for many years and their acquaintances. Some may have lost touch, but on setting out to establish an enterprise they combed through their memories in search of compatible souls and one or more kindred spirits came to mind.

Shared assumptions and compatible values can aid collaboration. But excessive homogeneity can be counter-productive. At its extreme, it can lead to bigotry. In chaotic and confused circumstances, diversity can increase the prospects of successful adaptation. Too narrow a skill and experience base can inhibit development and, by trapping an enterprise in a particular area of work, might increase the risk of business failure.

When selecting business colleagues and partners, a good

rule is: if you are in doubt walk away. People need instinctively to 'feel' that it is right. Ask basic questions. For example, if you were never to see certain individuals again how would you be affected? Also, could risks be reduced by entering into an arrangement for a trial period, perhaps while market testing a new concept? Such an approach might be prudent for all concerned.

There are various tests, which can be taken, that generate personal profiles on dimensions such as how individuals relate to others, how decisive or flexible they are and whether their focus is upon the team, agreed outcomes or themselves. The use of diagnostics can add to, and complement, other sources of information about people. However, they can be harmful when they are the sole basis upon which decisions are taken.

Exercise: Allies and Enemies

Companies undertake 'helps' and 'hinders' analyses to identify the forces that are assisting them and those which are inhibiting them from moving in desired directions. They can then take steps to capitalize upon and support favourable factors and tackle or avoid any obstacles, barriers or pitfalls. Individuals can do likewise, but at the earlier stages in the development of an enterprise, they may find it easier to focus upon who could help or harm them.

In relation to what you are setting out to achieve, who is in a position to help or harm you? Which of these people are neutral and who is actively for or against you?

Where do each of your allies and enemies stand on a spectrum from indifference to commitment? What could, and should, you do to secure more positive and practical support from your allies and to neutralize the negative impact, influence or potential of your enemies.

Networking and Relationship Building

As people travel through life, they should take note of others
with particular skills, whose paths they cross. Company
apparatchiki who fit in and play the game may not register,
but certain individuals and personalities may stand out because they are distinctive.

Those to register are people who can do things rather than
those who have responsibility for things. The former could well
make a useful contribution where an appropriate slot exists.
The latter group might hold impressive job titles, but they may
have little to offer because it is others, rather than themselves,
who actually do the work within the units concerned.

Some individuals find that others come to them with ideas
and opportunities for collaboration. Such approaches should
be treated courteously. Listen to what is being said and reflect
before making a considered response. When proceeding, do so
with due diligence and an eye open for hidden risks and liabilities. Those who are dismissed out of hand may not call again.
When declining an offer, people should indicate the areas of
activity and forms of participation in which they could be interested, provided of course they wish to continue the relationship.

Suppliers or services are finding that success today is increasingly dependent upon actively re-establishing past relationships and developing new ones. People circulate and build
up networks of contacts with people who respect them and know
'what they are about'. At business and social events, they listen to others, and discover their interests and priorities, before talking about and selling themselves. A relationship that
might yield a flow of contacts and leads over many years could
be at stake.

Those with country gardens who share their surplus vegetables with neighbours may find that, later in the season, the
grateful recipients return the favour. New potatoes freely given,
rather than disposed of, in early summer may yield rosy and
crisp apples in the autumn. Like the inhabitants of a medieval
or frontier village, confident networkers willingly help others,
sharing information and opportunities, in the knowledge that
a kind deed may well be reciprocated.

For relationships to last, the reason why something is being done can be as important as what is being done. Members

of a core team should have a common understanding of the rationale and purpose of an enterprise. They should be made explicit and tested from time to time to ensure they remain relevant and still have the same meaning for all those involved.

Good prospects for collaboration are those with similar amounts to invest, compatible attitudes to risk and consistent views on such questions as the likely scale of an enterprise, who are able to provide the commitment required of their particular role. The likely timetable for development, and the expected demands of a growing enterprise, should also match the lifestyle plans and preferences of both themselves and their families.

Collaborators should not become too complacent, or comfortable in their relationships. On occasion, a degree of tension and vigorous debate can be healthy. When it is absent, an enterprise might stagnate. Incisive and open questioning should be encouraged. However, nettles need to be grasped. Differences should not be allowed to widen and become disputes.

Ending Relationships

While preparing for independent operation, it may be helpful to reflect on both the advantages and the disadvantages of teamwork, and the factors that lead some teams to be more successful than others. Thought should also be given to the likely dynamics of relationships within groups of different sizes. For example, within a small board, an even number of members could be evenly split. An odd number of directors might find it easier to secure majority votes.

Cracks have a inexorable tendency to widen as pressure builds. When individuals take up sides and assume entrenched positions, the gulf between them may become difficult to bridge. While a fundamental difference of opinion festers unresolved, momentum may be lost. Hence, while every effort should be made to achieve a resolution, matters should not be allowed to drift.

It is naïve to expect that there will be absolute agreement on all points and at every stage in the development of an enterprise. Relationships can reach a point at which they have served their purpose. People can, and do, grow apart. An initial set of assumptions and expectations may no longer apply. Some individuals are more flexible than others. For very good reasons, there may need to be an agreed 'departure' or split.

Relationships do not necessarily need to last forever. There may be a certain inner momentum and logic to the development of an enterprise that is independent of those who have created it. People also change, and their interests, priorities and paths can diverge. They cannot be expected to run, forever, in parallel. If a collaborative arrangement becomes a straight-jacket, individuals will find it difficult to be true to themselves.

The self-aware, who draw a distinction between their personal interests and those of enterprises with which they associate, are more likely to be alert to any mismatch between people and organizations. They may also sense a possible parting of the ways. Many businesses fail to reach their full potential because members of a founding group do not recognize the need to change how they operate or when to let go. They plough on oblivious and regardless.

Ending an arrangement generally requires careful handling. Sensitive individuals initiate action before a collaboration has outlived its usefulness and while goodwill still exists. Situations where one party seeks to conclude a relationship, which another wishes to continue, can be particularly fraught. Problems can also arise when two partners with equal shares in a business decide to go their own ways. In such a case, a dispute could lead to deadlock.

Eventually, even the most lasting of relationships are terminated by the death of one or more of the parties. At some point, most people experience a desire to slow down in order to enjoy an easier lifestyle. Income streams from previous periods of pensionable employment might also reduce the imperative to earn. The focus of interest may shift to preparation for retirement.

Much will depend upon the personal circumstances of the individual. Thus, a younger person might adopt an independent lifestyle in order to maintain a previous level of earnings, at least until major items of expenditure, such as mortgage payments and the costs of children's education, are complete. Thereafter, the emphasis could shift to the securing of a more balanced life. Certain income generating activities may be dropped to release time for voluntary or charitable commitments that bring greater satisfaction.

The Companionship of Others

Self-assured people with drive, who offer a highly personal service, may be able to operate as sole practitioners. Lone rangers require a strong will, and need to be self contained and inwardly directed in order to sustain their motivation. They only have one pair of eyes and ears. They lack colleagues who can question and draw various matters to their attention.

Certain personalities are inclined to drift when they are not under the spotlight. They need to be chivvied along. Collaborators can help and encourage each other. They feel under mutual obligation to perform. Regular meetings provide opportunities to discuss, progress, chase and identify any gaps that might have emerged. Cover can also be provided during periods of holidays or when there are other distractions.

The involvement of others can result in the pooling of resources and the sharing of risks. An individual could be reluctant to tie up a significant proportion of family capital in a single venture. Another might not be able to raise, from personal resources, the capital required to establish a business. One or more colleagues chipping in may make the burden bearable.

Bringing in other people might also enable someone to maintain a portfolio lifestyle. While operating alone, the time required to launch and establish an enterprise may preclude other activities. With colleagues sharing a workload, it may be possible to assume, or continue with, other roles. These might provide a welcome source of income, during a start-up phase.

A degree of specialization might allow an individual to simultaneously participate in more than one venture, particularly where certain roles could be performed on a part-time basis. This further reduces risk, while also allowing a person to acquire a comparative understanding and build a broader base of experience.

Throughout history some of the most successful individuals have also been egotistical, ruthless and plain repellent. Being loathsome does not make an individual ineligible for entrepreneurial roles. However, times are changing. Where people have a choice, as they increasingly do, between broadly similar alternatives, they may opt to buy from those who are more straightforward and considerate and join networks composed of those whose values they share.

We are entering an era in which it may actually help to be considered a fair, thoughtful and balanced individual. Those who think of others and are concerned about the 'general good' are more likely to be elected to leadership roles within virtual organizations composed of collaborating peers, than those perceived to be self-seeking. In a connected world of electronic markets that are based upon mutual trust, business ethics becomes a 'key success factor' that is actively sought rather than a peripheral 'nice to have'. Charlatans, rogues and exploiters beware.

Some criminal gangs appear adept at using emerging technologies to support networks of interdependencies. The scale and complexity of their operations can represent an alternative, or parallel, economy. It should also be possible for good citizens to collaborate in the building of sets of relationships to support and further legitimate business interests.

Family Enterprises

Certain relatives might wish to become involved with a new enterprise. Should one entice and encourage or deter and dissuade? An approach should not be dismissed out of hand. The right relationships and compatible roles can bring individuals and generations closer together. The mix of opportunities provided by a business might create a more integrated family unit.

In many countries, especially in sectors such as agriculture, a significant proportion of total turnover and production is generated by family businesses of one form or another. A start-up venture, particularly one operating at or near to home, may provide opportunities to involve different members of the family. The range of work, from 'stuffing envelopes' and 'cleaning up' to 'keeping the books', could offer possibilities for several people to contribute.

Much will depend upon the circumstances, the type of business and the attitudes and temperaments of those concerned. When everyone is involved, it may become more difficult to switch off in the evenings. Close proximity for long periods could result in tension and stress. Minor irritations may lead to friction. Also, family members might be less inclined to question than other colleagues. Performance issues may become more difficult to resolve.

Some owners of family companies actively prepare selected relatives for particular roles. Children and siblings may be required to obtain relevant experience elsewhere prior to being brought on board. Others rule them out, avoid making the choice themselves or decide each case on its own merits. Taking steps to include certain individuals may result in others feeling excluded.

The nature and extent of the involvement of relatives in an enterprise should depend upon the situation and context. Too much time together can lead to people getting on each others nerves and might inhibit personal development. It could also result in too many eggs being carried in one basket. A less risky option would be for each adult member of a family unit to develop his or her own portfolio of activities. Where these are complementary, mutual support could be provided to enable individuals to cope with peaks and troughs of workload.

The recruitment of younger relations could allow for a dynastic succession. Some find the prospect of an enterprise, which they have founded, continuing for a further generation especially rewarding. At the same time, libertarians who believe that people should be encouraged to be true to themselves would not wish to compel the involvement of someone whose real interests might lie elsewhere. Each individual should be free to choose the form and degree of their participation.

Familial feuds should not be brought into the boardroom. This can be unsettling for non-family members, as can the prospect of certain relatives receiving promotions that are not justified on the grounds of personal merit or the quality of their contributions. Individuals should be valued according to their inputs and the complementary qualities which they bring to the table.

One needs to be sensitive to the likely reactions of colleagues when considering whether or not to introduce family members into a jointly owned business. Finding a role for someone, who in other circumstances, would not be in the frame, might set a dangerous precedent. It could lead to allegations of nepotism or favouritism and may cause future resentment.

Within family enterprises, friends and relations should be

objective when viewing their own qualities in relation to what it takes to succeed. A reluctance to involve 'outsiders' could stunt the growth of a company. At the same time, people need to remember why they established a business in the first place. The primary motivation may have been to do with life-style rather than economics. If this is the case, it might be perfectly valid for investors to accept a lower financial return in order to maintain family control and retain the satis-faction this provides.

Mere devices, such as 'putting a spouse on the payroll' to save tax, should also be avoided. However, genuine contribu-tions to the development of a business should be encouraged. The 'pros' and 'cons' of each situation should be carefully ex-amined and account should always be taken of the possible implications for other valued relationships.

Exercise: Team Assessment

The involvement of others is invariably needed to im-plement a business vision. An assessment should be undertaken of the extent to which those who have been brought together form an effective team. Until this is done, deficiencies cannot be identified and addressed.

How effective are your board and your core man-agement team? Could they add more value? Is indi-vidual and group performance measured? Do you and your enterprise colleagues work well together as a team?

What are the main barriers to, and inhibitors of, a more effective contribution? What needs to be done in terms of both individual and group development to create a more united and productive team?

Information and Support Services

Increasingly, companies are recognizing the importance of knowledge transfer and shared learning. Consulting firms, such as Arthur Andersen, Ernst & Young, McKinsey and Price Waterhouse, have developed information services and networks to support their consultants. Individuals can plug into simi-lar services through associate relationships with larger firms.

Some companies, such as Attitudes Skills and Knowledge, offer shared earnings opportunities to those with distinct skills and intellectual capital.

It may be necessary to share information with supply chain partners in order to get the best out of them. Tesco, the supermarket chain, has found that allowing selected suppliers to access stock and promotional data enables them to co-ordinate their own activities better. The various parties are able to track each others responses and anticipate decision points.

Networking allows people to learn from others about what to do in particular circumstances, and also discover lessons concerning what not to do. It is perverse that so many slots on conference agendas, journal articles and management books are devoted to sanitized 'success story' case studies, when there is such a demand for insights and advice on obstacles and pit-falls. The same anaemic examples crop up on platform after platform and in title after title.

People contemplating risky courses of action should have a healthy desire to learn from others about the most likely causes of failure. When talking with entrepreneurs, many themes crop up repeatedly in conversations. Perfecting the product, get-ting and managing the right people, attracting customers and relationship building, all tend to take longer than expected or planned.

Disappointments happen. The unexpected occurs. Forecasts prove inadequate. The consequences of wrong decisions some-times appear to be attached to elastic. They keep coming back, like unwelcome ghosts to haunt the remains of a business. Most entrepreneurs experience sleepless nights. Families may need to be prepared for grouchy days.

Finding, renting, leasing or buying premises turns out to be a nightmare for many companies. Start-up enterprises find it difficult to anticipate accurately their requirements. Obtain-ing money from certain customers can be like getting blood out of a stone. Some of the largest companies are among the slowest of payers. In all these areas and others, forewarned is forearmed. When planning the voyage, it helps to talk with someone who has experienced the squalls and currents. Sup-port networks can provide pools of expertise that can be dipped into.

Assistance needs to be balanced and appropriate to what

people are endeavouring to do. For example, just sending e-mail to each other may not be enough. Gazing at a monitor all day can be a poor substitute for direct contact with people, whether end customers or immediate colleagues. A peer, mentor or counsellor, with whom sensitive and difficult matters can be discussed, can be invaluable. Ambitious people create personal networks composed of those who they trust and to whom they can turn.

An increasing range of services are designed to help the aspiring entrepreneur establish presence in the marketplace and create an appropriate form of organization. World Wide Web hosting services, many of which are linked with website building tools, can assist in the creation of a distinct Web presence. Collaborative networks can share the costs of marketing. There are 'virtual office' services that can provide 24-hour cover.

Corporate Services

Rank Xerox provided a range of support services to help its 'networkers'. These included the use of psychological tests as part of the selection process; discussion with other teleworkers, the formal critique of a business plan and practical advice on such matters as filling in a VAT return. The company believed it was in its own best interests for those intent upon setting up their own businesses to have the best possible preparation for independent operation.

Oxfordshire County Council has introduced new support arrangements for those taking advantage of its 'flexiplace initiative'. Means had to be found of providing feedback for staff who miss opportunities for informal contacts as a result of being separated from those responsible for supervising the outputs of their work, for example people working from home.

DEC has had to establish new ways of, physically, bringing people together at the start of projects in order that geographically scattered team members can get to know each other. Because a wide variety of working patterns are now possible, individual contracts are issued. The company recognizes that particular arrangements are increasingly likely to be unique.

There are a growing number of support services that can be bought in from various consultants. Such inputs can be costly. They should only be sought in relation to important objectives, when internal alternatives have been exhausted, outputs can be clearly defined, and are likely to be used, and a relationship can be effectively managed. The end result should be an increased capability rather than greater dependence. People should not be allowed to seek external advice simply as a means of avoiding personal responsibility or tough decisions.

Major companies, such as Shell and London Electricity, and many government departments, have central units to advise on the procurement of external services and the achievement of value for money. While seeking to avoid bureaucracy and the growth of central overheads, the board of an entrepreneurial company should keep a careful watch over the extent and nature of bought in services. Information and assistance comes at a price.

Professions and Professionalism

Professional organizations and practices should not be viewed merely as providers of support services. They can also represent a way of operating which should perhaps be emulated. For certain businesses, the professional model might be more relevant than a managerial approach.

A true professional puts service to the customer before considerations of efficiency. The focus of professional effort is the resolution of the problems of individual clients. Integrity and quality of work are important to professionals, as is the accumulation of competencies, knowledge and experience. Individual practitioners may well aspire to expert standing among their peers. Such recognition may be more significant to them than financial rewards per se.

An enterprise could adopt professional values without necessarily taking on board other attributes of professionalism, such as operation through a partnership structure rather than as a limited liability company. Much will depend upon the aspirations of a founding group.

In the case of the smaller enterprise, professional and managerial approaches can lead people in different directions. Managerial growth may require a greater emphasis upon packaging, and the definition and marketing of standard products and services. A professional orientation may result in more of a focus upon discretion, personal service, client-led growth and the development of individual skills and interpersonal relationships.

In reality, most enterprises require elements of both professional and managerial approaches. As customers demand and expect more individualized services, and as employees take further responsibility for their own development, the balance may shift towards professional attitudes and values. Satisfactory solutions, rather than the economical use of inputs, may become the 'driver'. Instead of trying to 'squeeze a margin', individuals will expect to be fairly paid for achieving successful outcomes for their clients.

Some entrepreneurs set up ventures rationale and purpose of which is to provide certain forms of specific assistance on particular contractual terms to other businesses. The growth of more enterprise-oriented cultures, and of entrepreneurship, creates many opportunities for people to provide a whole range of specialist services that growing firms require.

Increasingly, smaller enterprises are likely to resemble larger corporations in the extent to which they outsource, or buy in from specialist contractors, the particular services which they need. Given the great diversity of requirements, which a growing business can have, such a trend creates opportunities for a great many people to develop portfolio lifestyles in areas that are close to their natural strengths and inclinations.

Checklist

1.   Are you setting out to form your own enterprise team or are you looking for opportunities to join venture teams which have been established, or are being assembled, by others?

2.   Are you clear about the nature of the contribution which you could provide and the form of commitment that you would like to make?

3.   Have you assessed your strengths and weaknesses frankly and identified the areas in which you will need to supplement your own competencies, experience and qualities with those of others?

4.   Are you looking positively for opportunities to collaborate with others for mutual benefit or are you reluctantly seeking help on account of your own inadequacies?

5.   By nature, would you prefer to hoard and protect or to be open and to share with others?

6.   What other forms of support will be required? Have you prioritized your requirements and distinguished between the essential and the 'nice to have'?

7.   Have you established a timetable which indicates when certain forms of support will need to be in place? Have you discussed this with your family and the other people who are likely to be affected?

8.   Who and what will be needed on a continuing basis, as opposed to being contracted in as and when required?

9.   Have you profiled the roles and the characteristics of those who would form a 'dream team'? What is the minimum core group which would ensure 'lift off'?

10.   Have you thought about the longer term? Who needs to be signed up now and who could be brought on board at a later date?

11.   Who might help you to form a core team? Who could advise you on the identification of possible providers of specialist expertise? Your current employer? A potential source of venture capital? A professional body?

12.   Do those who might be interested in helping know that you are looking for support?

13.   Which networks, programmes or initiatives might enable you to 'spread the word' and make contact with like minded people?

14.   Are there services which you yourself could provide to others who are seeking to break free and take greater control of their lives?

13

WHERE DO I TURN FOR HELP?

There is only air and space in
a shaft for so many.

A spider, setting out to build a web, makes a careful choice of location. Preferred sites offer anchor points, whether the corners of a room or twigs that are relatively close together. The decision is not rushed. The effort to produce a complete web is such that the spider must not waste time and opportunity by starting in the wrong place.

Once the main strands of a web are attached, the spaces between them are quickly filled in with a network of other threads. Without firm anchor points, the cobweb might collapse or be blown away in a breeze. With them it may endure long enough to catch some prey.

The versatility of the spider's web gives it an ability to survive out of all proportion to what one might expect given the minute size of the threads. When the wind rages and blasts, its flexibility allows it to cope with the movement in different directions of the various twigs to which it is attached.

Threatening gusts pass through a web like so much unwanted junk e-mail, while the prize that is sought – the fly – is caught and held fast until it can be fully digested. So long as the main lines hold, any other threads that are broken can be repaired and the trap can continue to be used. What survives today can capture tomorrow.

Creating a Web of Support

Start-up businesses require secure foundations in the form of distinct opportunities to deliver value and an effective core team. A network of flexible support provides the main strands of business development with the additional capabilities needed to succeed. Without them, a venture may be incomplete. The resulting web should be able to catch and hold on to prospects and withstand market forces and competitor attack.

Many new ventures operate as flexible networks. Patterns of electronic communications act as the links which hold together the separate strands of independent contributions. Unlike the spider's threads, the electronic network can support a variety of different patterns of operation. Established organizations aspire to network form because of the flexibility, the enhanced responsiveness in the face of opportunities and the greater resilience to external threats.

Dissimilar approaches and structures can require diverse support services on different terms than conventional organizations offer. Some of these, for example a call forwarding or conferencing system, may relate to the model of operation which has been adopted. Webs vary according to the conditions and circumstances.

Secure and self-confident individuals are quite prepared to turn to others for help. They do not regard this as a sign of weakness. They look for anchor points. They seek out integrating links. They spin and weave.

They also actively build the core relationships that can create firm foundations for the building of an enterprise. While cherishing their individuality, they recognize the contributions which other people can make. Indeed, the support of others with complementary capabilities can make it easier for them to be true to themselves. It can enable them to play to their particular strengths.

At the same time, they are realistic in terms of what can reasonably be expected from others. Some enterprises are intensely personal. Involving additional people and personalities could require a degree of accommodation and compromise that might change the nature of what is being undertaken and sought.

There may be core responsibilities which should not, or cannot, be abdicated. Someone has to hold an enterprise together, provide a sense of purpose and direction, and ensure it remains true to its vision and values. Someone has to take ultimate legal and moral responsibility for its activities and undertakings. At the end of the day, someone may also need to grasp the difficult nettles, and confront the awkward choices that others may prefer to avoid.

In the fullness of time, a board may assume the mantle. In the meantime, a founding entrepreneur may need to bear the burden.

Much will depend upon the extent to which a single person is the 'keeper of the vision'. The contributions of others are more likely to be fundamental and long-lasting where they understand the rationale, purpose and design of an enterprise, either because they have 'internalized' a founder's vision or because they may have played a part in its formation.

Confident entrepreneurs are able to communicate their drives and visions to others. Sharing a vision is different from giving it away. In the latter case, its exploitation value may have fallen, but in the former it could well be enhanced as a result of the extra capability and commitment that may now be put behind it. One extra pair of hands and the log may begin to role.

Looking Close to Home

One's immediate family should not be overlooked as anchor points. Without their full emotional support, an entrepreneur may build upon foundations of sand, and at some future date may come to face a difficult choice between business commitments and familial obligations. Close relatives may not tolerate the competing demands of activities, in which they do not believe.

Psychological support from relations and friends is one thing, their active involvement is another. We saw in the last chapter that their participation in a venture may require sensitive handling. Much will depend upon what is proposed. An injection of finance into the business, in the form of additional share capital, might be more welcome than a salaried role. Some may fear the latter will reduce the resources available for other priorities, including themselves.

Some members of business families prefer to keep their distance. They may already have quite enough on their plate. In some instances, they might have their own ventures to establish. Becoming involved could be viewed as being drawn, or dragged, into shouldering an additional burden. In another case, someone who is not involved may feel excluded or not wanted and might be hurt as a result. Entrepreneurs should be sensitive and 'read the signs'.

The balance of advantage and disadvantage will reflect such factors as the nature and scale of what is being undertaken. Integration of a micro-enterprise into a family might help to avoid isolation and division, so long as other desirable activities are not compromised.

As an enterprise grows, and when external staff are involved, the introduction of 'friends' and 'relations' into a business needs to be handled with care. Loyal employees may feel sidelined or threatened and might become concerned, rightly or wrongly, about the implications for their future prospects. Allegations might arise that jobs are being found, or created, for 'passengers' who will not pull their weight.

People are not fools. An arrangement that is a contrivance, for example to spread income for tax purposes, is likely to be seen as such. Some entrepreneurs become too clever for their own good. The signals that certain proposed actions might send out should be borne in mind.

Many people find questions of non-performance more difficult to resolve when their relatives are personally involved. In general, where a situation is likely to continue or become worse, it is better to take action sooner rather than later. Any individual, whether a family member or not, deserves to be treated fairly and honorably, but also firmly and appropriately.

Exercise: Cobweb Analysis

People need to understand the nature of the support that is available to them. Thinking in terms of a cobweb can help individuals to assess the nature and strength of their personal networks.

What are the main strands in your web? Are they firmly anchored? Which are the weakest and the strongest relationships? What additional links are needed to hold or bind the various threads together? Does your web have the strength and flexibility to withstand whatever challenges it faces? Is it in the right place to catch those opportunities on which you have your eye?

Securing the Fundamentals

Where a business has been incorporated with limited liability, company assets, rather than personal possessions, need to be protected. In cases of fraudulent trading, both could be at stake. Directors have particular, numerous and onerous duties and responsibilities. Hence boardroom colleagues need to be chosen with special care.

A limited liability company exists as a distinct entity in law. It can have obligations, both legal and moral, to a variety of parties. An owner-director must remember that he or she has certain duties of care to the company itself. Thus, a director undertaking a transaction, perhaps out of an act of kindness but without declaring an interest, could become subject to legal penalties.

Many people devote so much attention to securing financial backing and technical skills that they overlook other forms of support. Over the longer term, these may be equally important, if not more so. For example, to whom does one turn when legal issues arise? What about emotional, moral and intellectual support? Who might act as a confidential sounding board? Is personal coaching, or the perspective of a director, rather than a manager, required?

The strongest anchor point which a business can have is an absolute commitment to the highest moral principles and observing the law. Integrity is one quality which should be sought in all members of the core team. Directors, and other key players, should be sensitive to ethical issues and have an innate sense, an instinct, for what is right and what is wrong.

Shady operators who sail close to the wind should be avoided like the plague. Sophists who are full of mitigating arguments about bribes being commonplace or tax deductible in other countries should be shown the door. Relationships can depend upon honesty and fair dealing. One slip, and the reputation of an enterprise may be forever compromised among those that know, just as a single defective strand can result in the whole of a web being blown away.

People can pay a high price in both personal and business terms for lowering their moral guard. Those who set out on a course of personal growth and fulfillment, sometimes end up with lower self-esteem as a result of cutting corners. The external world might be impressed by their arrival, but they know what they have done, and have not done, along the way.

The moral stature of some people diminishes in inverse proportion to their material gain. They find it impossible to escape from a spiral of further concealment and compromise, because they end up confining themselves to a sub-world inhabited by flawed people like themselves.

Also, word gets out. Certain beetles are attracted by the smell of dung. The business that was once sought out may find itself shunned and excluded from contract opportunities.

Governments that wish their countries to undertake higher value activities are likely to assume a more resolute stand towards corruption in its various forms. Blue-chip organizations are reluctant to form partnerships, especially those involving valuable know-how, with those whom they do not trust.

Support networks must recognize that entrepreneurial activity involves ethical dilemmas. Simply drafting a moral code might not be enough. Training may need to be provided. Perhaps there should be a helpline to which people could refer for guidance. When does an acceptable 'thank you' become a compromising bribe? At what level does a 'finder's fee', which reflects effort put in, become an unreasonable exploitation of a position of influence?

Arranging Flexible Support

A growing business may require a succession of very different forms of external assistance. Support organizations and units need to determine which services should be provided internally and which should be contracted out. In some areas, a network or central resource could limit its role to providing guidance on how to select appropriate contractors. In certain cases it might maintain a recommended list of suppliers.

At each stage in the development of an enterprise, decisions need to be made about the most appropriate means of securing flexible access to required capabilities. Much will depend upon the strategic importance of what is needed, relative costs, the pattern of demand and future expectations. It may be advisable to retain direct control of areas that are sensitive or that could provide a basis for new rivals to enter a marketplace.

Beyond a certain level of usage, the balance of economic advantage may tip in favour of maintaining an internal capability rather than buying in. However, the experience of virtual companies suggests the extent of the core should not be exaggerated.

If the requirements for implementing a business concept are carefully thought out, it may be possible for many of the elements that are traditionally found in companies to be contracted out to specialist suppliers. Support functions, ranging from accounting to marketing, can be successfully outsourced. Core activities might be limited to such tasks as liaison with selected investors, maintaining vision and values and the protection of brand identities and intellectual property.

Some very successful companies have outsourced virtually all aspects of their operations, save the legal duties and responsibilities of the board, and the monitoring of such matters as image and reputation. Other companies have become unstuck, or have limited their scope for manoeuvre, as a result of entering into inflexible arrangements. The risk of being constrained, rather than liberated, increases the more rapidly the situation and context are changing.

Certain people have a natural preference for more rather than less control. They are not comfortable when they are unable to see and direct those around them, or where resources and relationships which they consider vital to corporate operations are not directly owned. Such individuals may need to be put under greater pressure from colleagues to relax and trust than those whose natural inclination is to simplify and operate as leanly as possible.

Avoiding Loss of Control

The early days of an enterprise can represent a period of high risk. The nature of arrangements entered into, and their terms, may be more important than their subject matter. When people are learning quickly, and having to react to the reality of many things not going according to plan, the consequences of an agreement concluded in haste can return to haunt a management team for a long time thereafter.

Perhaps the greatest caution should be reserved for various suppliers of financial services. In general, relationships with them should be entered into at a time of relative strength, rather than during a era of weakness. Too many management teams postpone necessary action for too long in the naïve hope that 'things will turn out all right'. At a moment of vulnerability, greater security may be demanded and reluctantly provided. When under duress, a larger equity stake might have to be given away to obtain much needed support.

Having escaped from the control of an employer, many entrepreneurs discover their freedom is short-lived. They quickly become subject to the continuing and rising demands of equity partners or find that their livelihood, along with their mortgaged homes, are at the mercy of a bank manager. Many people spend their waking hours struggling to extricate themselves from a deep pit which they alone have dug. Like a butterfly with treacle on its wings, they thrash about but cannot lift off.

Every effort should be made to avoid slipping into debt during a start-up phase. An overdraft should represent temporary accommodation. Many people become dependent upon such funding just as their bankers decide to 'pull the plug'. Are resources really needed 'up front' or so early? Could an asset be rented or leased for the duration of its use, rather than purchased outright? Should one endeavour to 'get the business' first and staff up for it afterwards?

An utterly realistic assessment of commercial prospects should be made before adding to overhead costs, such as accommodation charges or making employment commitments. This is particularly important when a founding group has limited resources in relation to the start-up or entry investment required. Without some return, such money can only be spent once.

Although not always possible, in start-up and growth situations, ongoing commitments should only be entered into to the extent that a profit margin on contracted income will allow. When staff and accommodation costs are added to other formation fees, a negative balance can quickly build up unless these are covered by profitable business. A deficit can be very difficult to claw back out of future margins during a period when there is future growth to fund.

On some occasions, the pattern of anticipated cash flows might be such that some temporary accommodation may be needed. Relationships with bankers should be based upon accurate forecasts and early notification of any departures from budget. At the same time, a business team should be prepared to negotiate hard on whatever terms are offered. Certain banks 'try it on'.

One should not expect too much from a local relationship.

Increasingly, branch managers are subjected to central guidelines, rules and practices which determine whether or not loans
can be made. A financially dependent business may find that
critical decisions concerning whether it will be allowed to live
or die are reliant upon the runs of a distant computer programme. In such cases, a high priority should be put upon securing and preserving the scope for independent operation.

Financial Partners

One alternative to an overdraft or loan support is to consider
some form of venture capital. While the principle of 'better 20
per cent of something than 100 per cent of nothing' is valid,
there is little point giving away a high or disproportionate stake
in an enterprise in return for a supply of finance that may only
be temporary.

Within one or two years of set up, many entrepreneurs rue
the price they paid to secure initial funding. The proportion of
the equity in an enterprise that was given away is no longer
available for other actual or potential partners whose contribution might be more significant and long lasting. Key members of staff may be lost to competitors because a prior allocation of shares provides little scope for further participation.

Other things being equal, every effort should be made to
achieve self-financing growth. Are there potential customers
who could pay for much needed areas of capability through
their purchases? Are objectives too ambitious? Would it be better to grow more slowly rather than cede a significant degree
of control?

The ideal situation is to find some means by which early
customers fund the development of an initial capability and
new products and services which can subsequently be sold in
modified form to further clients. Many entrepreneurs use an
initial order to launch their businesses. Many bankrupts spend
significant sums before they set about eliciting purchaser interest.

For some, the ideal may not be possible. Target customers
may be unwilling to buy from an organization that does not
have a minimum level of capability. They may want to visit a
new operation's site to verify that it has the capacity to 'do the
job'. The involvement of significant numbers of contractors in
a project, particularly when an enterprise has not been in

business for long, may positively deter prospectors from buying. They may lack confidence that such arrangements will be successfully managed for their own benefit.

A proportion of available funding should be held back for the unexpected. When operating in unknown territory, 'success' is usually more costly, and takes longer to achieve, than is first thought. Invariably, the unexpected involves extra expenditure in the short-term, whether to take advantage of a sudden opportunity, or to overcome an unanticipated obstacle. Some slack should be built into timetables and a margin of security incorporated into financial plans.

A counsel of caution can sometimes appear a trifle boring and unimaginative to a born risk taker. However, those who are seeking the greater freedom of independent operation for lifestyle reasons need to remember the consequences of failure. Going to bed every night worrying about whether their house will be repossessed the following morning may not be what they are seeking.

Exercise: Overlapping Circles

Before a stage show can be seen, all the areas in which action is to occur must be lit. Various circles of light from different sources need to come together to illuminate the whole. People should adopt a similar approach when ensuring that all 'success requirements' are covered. Particular attention needs to be paid to the stars of the show, especially when it is their production.

Set out the requirements of your prospective customers in terms of what they want or need. This could be done by arranging post-it notes in a circular pattern on a wall. Priority desires could be positioned centrally and less essential 'interests' towards the periphery.

Now write down what you feel you can do and would like to do, distinguishing the 'can' from the 'would like' responses if post-it notes are involved. These could be assembled into two further circular groupings.

How much overlap is there between the three circles, namely the requirements of customers, what you can do and would like to do? Are the central desires of your prospects covered? As the area of overlap increases, so will the probability of personal and business interests coinciding, and the less dependent you are likely to be upon external support. When and where customer requirements are not covered, additional help might be required.

Support Networks

Ambitious individuals assemble personal support networks composed of those who can provide them with specific advice and counsel. In a hi-tech environment, such as that at Sun Microsystems, an open and creative culture is essential. Those who are talented, yet abrasive or not supportive of colleagues, can be helped by personal counsellors. The Lancashire Constabulary brings in external mentors to equip people with the skills they need.

It is not a sign of weakness, or of lack of fibre, to seek help. A problem shared may indeed be one that is halved. Even competitors sometimes collaborate to mutual advantage when they face the same challenge.

BUPA and PPP are arch rivals in the private medical insurance market. Yet they worked together to develop an EDI system which both use for dealing with claims from hospitals. Similarly, Braun, Moulinex/Swan, Philips, Tefal and Rowenta, all suppliers of electrical goods, co-operated to develop a common framework for working with independent service agents, many of whom handle the products of two or more manufacturers.

Support networks come in many different forms. Companies, such as Leyland Trucks and Xyratex, actively encourage their employees to suggest and develop better ways of doing things. A natural next step is to support them in the formulation and exploitation of new business concepts.

ASK Europe has a mechanism for creating and marketing new products and services and sharing the resulting incremental income streams with those who have contributed the know-how required. The company has itself become an entrepreneurial support network.

The extent to which a particular company should allocate resources to the support of entrepreneurs will depend upon the proportion of future revenues which is likely to be derived from the resulting ventures. Corporations, such as Xerox that have operated programmes to help employees leave and establish new ventures, have found that those who, for one reason or another, are not able to take advantage of them can become envious of the favourable treatment received by a few.

People do tend to watch each other. The provision of a facility as innocuous as a crèche could cause childless employees to feel that they are in some way cross-subsidizing colleagues who have children. Staff in roles that are unlikely to become a springboard to a different life may begrudge the time that is given to other employees to develop a business plan. The resentment can become all the more intense when those who are helped are seen to reap substantial financial rewards as a result of the success of new ventures.

Producer and marketing co-operatives are widespread in many parts of the world. Small farmers share the costs of storing produce or engaging in marketing activity. Their pooled budgets enable common activities and initiatives which would be difficult to fund on an individual basis.

Collaborative marketing can make it easier for a group of suppliers to offer one-stop shop contact, assistance and provision. The purchaser has access, via a single source, to related goods and services. Such arrangements work best when providers of complementary items and lines get together.

Franchise arrangements can cover virtually all the elements needed to create a viable business. Complete packages are assembled and offered which can be implemented in a local context. As the number of establishments and outlets increase, greater economies of bulk purchasing are secured.

Other types of support network include different forms of on-line services. Neighbourhood business centres can provide various facilities, including a range of equipment to supplement that which is available at home or in small offices. On a larger scale, there are science parks and premises that are split into incubator units to meet the needs of businesses at an early stage of development.

Corporate and Public Services

Since time immemorial, wealthy patrons and ambitious monarchs have supported enterprise. Leading and prosperous citizens, and impecunious royal patrons, have backed the voyages of explorers and privateers in the hope of securing a share of the spoils. The practice continues. For a corporation, the rewards can range from incremental income and profit, to opportunities for trying out new ideas. For governments, there is the prospect of additional revenue from taxation and, when new jobs are created, lower claims upon welfare budgets.

Major companies should not be overlooked as sources of relevant support. IBM and Hewlett-Packard are increasingly targeting micro-enterprises and home office applications. IBM offers services to help small businesses create and manage a presence on the World Wide Web.

Both BT and Cable & Wireless have run programmes aimed at the 'small office home office' or SOHO market. 3i, a major source of venture capital and management buyout finance for entrepreneurs, provides a range of related information, and contact details of relevant organizations, on 'The Land of Success' section of its website (www.3igroup.com).

Corporations that have themselves undergone a process of transformation may be keen to help their supply chain partners and key customers to do likewise. In so doing, many are redefining relationships and boundaries.

Citibank has adopted a global virtual model of operation. There are shared services, non-core activities are outsourced, and operations and responsibilities are located and relocated according to where they can be most cost effective. The bank also helps its corporate clients to identify appropriate change options and transformation partners.

Local, regional and national governments often provide a variety of services, ranging from information on new contract and public tender opportunities and advice on various matters, to suitable 'start-up' premises and financial assistance aimed at the new and smaller business.

The European Commission has introduced various initiatives to promote adaptability, employability and enterprise. Incentives, services and support structures are available to make it easier for people to set up and run small businesses, and establish co-operative links and joint venture partnerships.

Increasingly, single access points are being provided to facilitate business access to relevant and needed information, advice or support. For example, Hartlepool Council was one of the first Local Authorities to set up a one-stop-shop service to help individuals and businesses to negotiate their way through the complicated maze of planning and development regulations.

Certain information, advice and consulting services and finance, may be available at subsidized rates for companies that satisfy stated criteria, for example by being of a certain size or as a result of planning to create new jobs. There may be special incentives for additional employees that are taken on, or for siting a new enterprise or activity in particular geographic locations. Some entrepreneurs have established successful businesses whose purpose is to help others understand the many schemes and possibilities on offer.

When considering various incentives and subsidies, the objectives of an enterprise should be kept in mind. The availability of support at advantageous rates can sometimes lead to erroneous judgements. For example, an ongoing penalty in the form of higher transportation costs might have to be born as a consequence of picking a location purely in order to obtain certain initial support.

Managing Network Relationships

Mutual support networks can reduce risk and uncertainty. They can help people to adapt to new ways of working. Individuals can share their experiences of adjusting to the loss of 'position power', reacting to independent operation from home or managing to cope without the administrative support of a large organization.

Network relationships may be needed to replace those with former work colleagues. Physical and psychological support can be especially important. Employees may be covered by a range of income support and healthcare arrangements, but what about people who change direction? If they become ill or incapacitated, will they find themselves alone? Should they be unable to work, how will they meet their regular payments or look after their families?

While insurance cover for the loss of earnings is available, and may be advisable, this should be complemented by a conscious effort to remain fit. A healthier diet, periodic check ups, regular exercise and more of a balance between work and leisure, should accompany the assumption of greater personal responsibility.

In many parts of the world, the co-operative form of organization is well-established. An appreciation of the benefits of collaboration is passed from one generation to the next. Suppliers pool their resources to achieve objectives of which individual businesses might only dream. On occasion, their combined strength can match, or even exceed, the local capability of the largest international firms and eclipse their efforts.

The craft sector encompasses scattered 'micro-enterprises', many of which only consist of a single painter or potter. The funds available to such businesses may be limited to what one or two individuals can afford. Their knowledge of information and communications technologies might be almost non-existent. Yet, even in such unpromising circumstances, collective effort behind a shared vision can transform business practice.

Electronic ordering systems are a good example. Given the right business concept, and collaborative action, painters and potters can create 'solutions' to fundamental business problems that are far more imaginative than those installed in multinationals by high-flying MBAs who earn mega-salaries and are advised by leading firms of management consultants. The power of collective action and a single focus can be irresistible.

Learning and Transformation Partners

Traditionally, and from time to time, entrepreneurs have sought relevant financial and management services. Greater emphasis needs to be given to securing forms and types of assistance, which are more tailored to the requirements of an individual enterprise.

Whereas specific inputs may be purchased as and when required, more holistic support may be needed upon a continuing basis. Many firms cannot stand the cost and disruption of inducting a new supplier each time a major exercise needs to be undertaken, nor may an enterprise be able to afford to employ skills that may only be required upon an intermittent basis.

Consultants should be treated with caution. Once admitted through the door, some seem to spend most of their time trying to make a host company dependent upon them. Their focus is upon selling further services, rather than dealing with immediate issues. Their main concern is with their own future revenues, rather than the present problems of clients.

Consultancy resources can be expensive, unless a company is setting out to achieve a knowledge transfer. Up to 50 or more different consulting firms may be at work within a large corporation, with perhaps no one knowing their full and overall cost. Shell has a specialist team to advise those who are purchasing external support. London Electricity has central unit which buys in services. It is able to keep a tab on how much is being spent.

Start-up companies should watch every penny from day one. External consultants should not be allowed to emerge as powerful stakeholders with an inside track. Some of them manage to secure preferential access to corporate cash flows before a balance is struck to determine what can be distributed to other interested parties.

A learning and transformation partner, who understands the rationale and purpose of an enterprise the motivations of its owners, and who shares the vision and can be called upon when required to provide independent and objective advice, is invaluable. Ambitious entrepreneurs seek them out and sign them up.

Too many advisers devote a significant proportion of client contact time to self-promotion. In contrast, the ideal learning and transformation partner maintains ongoing relationships by only providing what is needed and doing this as cost-effectively as possible. The emphasis is upon pragmatism and value for money rather than gold-plating. The focus is upon selecting a relevant combination of elements, rather than pushing those particular building blocks which the supplier happens to offer.

Opportunities in Cyberspace

Joining a support network can enable an entrepreneur to secure flexible links and relationships with those who can help and advise at a price which a start-up company can afford.

The Networking Firm offers a range of advisory, counselling and mentoring services which are aimed at both individual entrepreneurs and corporate boards. They can be accessed via the internet (www.ntwkfirm.com). The focus is upon personal and organizational transformation. The network provides a forum for those who are establishing and operating virtual teams and grappling with the practical problems of managing and co-ordinating them.

Another network, which offers learning and transformation services, and is accessible through the internet, is Webtrain (www.webtrain.co.uk), which was established to support the training, development and change management community. Its discussion groups and virtual facilities bring together in-house staff, experts on various aspects of learning and self-employed consultants.

Many entrepreneurs are attracted to the possibilities offered by the World Wide Web. A diversity of potential collaborators around the world are accessible via the internet. The entry cost of achieving an effective presence appears relatively low. However, before jumping in, people should think through what they are seeking to achieve and who they are trying to reach. Is the aim to increase awareness, provide information and support, or achieve sales?

Any service which is offered on, or via, the Web needs to be positioned against, and differentiated from, competing sites. To achieve repeat visits, and become the focus of a virtual community, on-line notice boards, cyber-cafes and discussion groups must both attract and retain interest.

Those who take the plunge should keep a careful watch upon the, easily overlooked, expenses of maintaining and developing an effective Web presence, such as equipment, hosting and time costs. The latter can rise dramatically when surfing the net becomes addictive.

There are many people around the world who enjoy communicating for its own sake. The discussion group exchange is an end in itself. Intending entrepreneurs need to distinguish the time wasters from the 'doers'. Wealth creators have finite resources and there are only so many hours in each day. Whatever is available should be carefully guarded and used wisely.

A team of collaborators should not be over large. Each member must be allowed space to breath. When there is a limited supply of air in a blocked mine shaft, and too many individuals draw upon it, all may die. And yet, without some help, it may not be possible to dig through a barrier of rubble and debris in order to reach sunlight and freedom.

Checklist

1. What additional help do you need personally? Who, or what sort of person, is missing from your core team?

2. Have you prepared a prioritized inventory of the support which your proposed business needs? Have you identified and approached possible sources of supply?

3. How much do you know about the state of your health? When did you last have a comprehensive medical check-up?

4. Have you built regular exercise, and a balance between work and leisure activities, into your plans? Have you profiled the lifestyle that would enable you to give of your best, and avoid 'burn out'?

5. Have you explored the various forms of assistance that might be available from public sources or from professional, occupational and trade associations?

6. Are there interest groups, and relevant mutual help and support networks, which you could join? Have you thought through the benefits which you are seeking to derive?

7. What are you prepared to offer in order to secure what you need? Do the possibilities include an equity stake?

8. Have you developed a strategy for retaining control of your business? Where are you most vulnerable to a loss of control? Do your cash flow projections reveal a future danger point?

9. What are the possibilities for mutually beneficial collaboration? Would collective commitment and joint action enable additional activities to be undertaken and further innovations and new developments to be achieved?

10. What elements of the opportunity which you have identified would you be willing to share?

11. Are other people aware that you are seeking to move in a new direction? Do they know that you are open to entrepreneurial suggestions and looking for colleagues and partners?

12. Are there people within your family and social network who might be able to help?

13. Have you fully explored the possibilities for collaboration with your current employer?

14. Is there a potential corporate patron that might be interested in providing support? What would such an organization be looking for? Could you put together an acceptable business case?

15. Who else 'out there' might be willing to share your dreams and help you to realize them?

14

HOW DO I GET STARTED?

*The dog with dew on its paws
sinks its teeth into the rat.*

It is never too late to change direction or establish a new enterprise. Nor does one necessarily need to be rich, exceptional or lucky in order to succeed. Customers are not aliens that demand or expect the impossible. They are individual human beings that may have a variety of needs that are not met by the standard offerings of established businesses.

Increasingly, bright and ambitious people start to prepare themselves for entrepreneurship from the moment they leave university or business school. With many companies cutting out layers of management, their chances of reaching senior positions and achieving levels of remuneration, which might compensate for a lifetime in an unexciting sector, are greatly reduced.

Hence, many energetic and talented people avoid the majority of industrial corporations in favour of joining consulting practices, accounting firms or investment banks that can offer them a greater variety of experience and equip them with skills likely to be of value to an entrepreneur. Or, they seek out 'hi-tech' companies, such as Hewlett-Packard and Intel, which invest in their people and allow individuals some control over their career development.

Choosing the Moment

Some, such as Michael Dell of Dell Computers, Bill Gates of Microsoft and Charles Wang of Computer Associates, start young. By getting in early, they are well placed to benefit from the future growth of a particular sector which they themselves help to develop. In fields as varied as biotechnology, knowledge engineering and leisure and lifestyle options, individual pioneers are busily positioning themselves to ride future whirlwinds.

An entrepreneur does not always need to venture where no person has been before. Tailoring an existing product or service to personal requirements, providing access for further groups of consumers or introducing a modified form of something which is available elsewhere into a particular locality, can all generate additional value for new people. Each could result in improvements in their quality of life for which they are prepared to pay.

Nor does every wealth creator need to shoot for the moon or 'mortgage themselves up to the hilt'. Many individuals have derived enormous satisfaction and self-fulfillment from establishing quite modest enterprises and running them for a relatively short period of time. While doing so, they have attained their desire for independence. Their endeavours have enabled them to adopt and experience a different, perhaps long-coveted, lifestyle.

Those with savings can buy into an existing business. This might create a launch pad for further development. Being able to act does not mean that one should do so. The right opportunity needs to comes along. A hare has power and speed, but is also alert and has acute senses. It knows when to watch and wait, and where to anticipate and act. Similarly, a discerning venture capitalist may examine dozens of opportunities before selecting one in which to invest.

David Barber bought into Halma. He did not found it. However, by making around 100 acquisitions of small but specialist businesses, he has built the enterprise into a diversified engineering group. Although the company has grown, it remains a collection of family-sized businesses, each of which is given considerable discretion to run its own affairs.

Those without funds can minimize their risks by offering a personal service built around their own skills. But if premises and other people are involved, getting started may mean taking a gamble. Tim Waterstone borrowed three-quarters of what it took to open his initial Waterstone's bookshop in Old Brompton Road, London. The first book he sold was a copy of *The Koran*.

Tim Waterstone found that his business took longer to become established than he had anticipated. He soon had to borrow more – twice as much as the original figure – by way of an overdraft secured upon his house. This is the harsh reality of launching a business that requires start-up capital. The experience is one that so many other ultimately successful entrepreneurs share. Eventually, Waterstone's gamble paid off. By being different from other booksellers, and opening late, the Waterstone's chain soon attracted a loyal following of customers.

Others who lack finance but see an opportunity, for example to use information technology to create personalized clothes or furniture, go out and actively look for partners with the funding or technical capability which they lack. Thus Rodenstock teamed up with Specialist Data Solutions to develop a computer-assisted dispensing and patient care system. Together, they accomplished what neither could have achieved alone.

Staying in the Game

Older people can stand up and be counted. Not all entrepreneurs are precocious and brash yuppies. People of all ages 'have a go'. In fact, for certain opportunities maturity may be an advantage, as this may result in greater empathy with certain categories of customer. Waiting for the right moment is a critical aspect of the entrepreneurial process.

We are continually assailed with television, magazine and billboard images of young, tanned, good-looking, healthy, happy and smartly dressed people, proudly displaying the latest version of whatever it is that is being marketed. In real life, human beings have warts and wrinkles and bruises and bulges. We also know that consumption of itself does not necessarily lead to greater happiness. It can be transitory and unsatisfying. Those who eat too much may be physically sick.

Many individuals take to enterprise relatively late in life. Perhaps they are more conscious of their own mortality and become curious to sample what lies on the other side of the fence. They may experience an urge to live twice or thrice, effectively starting again, but on a different journey. Having spent long enough chasing phantoms, and working and providing for others, they now want to do something for themselves. Some

will have wearied of competing with others and may now want
to challenge themselves.

Sometimes an old lifestyle has to be let go so that a new one
can be created or grasped, just as some companies need to die
so that people and resources can be freed to join more promising enterprises. Struggling to keep an entity alive, which has
lost its sense of drive and purpose, can both destroy value
and prevent the realization of dreams.

Creating can be more rewarding than receiving. The spoiled
child, pampered youth and indulged partner may lack an inner sense of worth. Satisfied customers make their suppliers
feel valued. Good ideas can assume an existence of their own
and, as with the mouse, icons, windows and pull-down and pop-
up menus developed at Xerox PARC, may secure widespread
adoption with or without the later involvement of their initia-
tors and pioneers.

Successful businesses have been set up by people well past
the normal age of retirement. For one reason or another, there
were other things that preoccupied them, or which they wanted
to do, prior to the moment they felt ready to take the plunge.
Perhaps to have acted earlier would have been premature in
relation to the readiness of the market to accept whatever it
was that they were proposing.

Whereas hired hands may be fired simply for being over 40
or 50, owner-managers can carry on, should they wish to do so,
until they drop. G&H, a manufacturer of optical components,
was floated over 50 years after its formation with Archie Gooch
one of its two original founders remaining at the helm as an
active executive chairman. The company is still based in the
small country town where it was first established, even though
most of its sales are now to a variety of overseas markets. Adolf
Zukor became honorary chairman of the board of Paramount
Pictures at the age of 100.

Scale and Scope

The establishment of an Indian summer, autumn or third-
age enterprise could be linked with a fundamental, and perhaps irrevocable, change of lifestyle. An example would be
relocation to another area, possibly from the hectic bustle of
the city to the slower pace of country living. A combination of
down-scaling requirements, and moving to where property

prices are lower, might enable someone to raise enough capital to stake a new venture.

There is little point jumping out of a frying pan into a fire. Many small-scale entrepreneurs secure and enjoy a higher quality of life than those who become slaves to the building of a larger enterprise. People should not become obsessed with league tables and other comparisons. They should focus upon personal fulfillment, doing what is right for them.

Additional staff, more associates and an army of subcontractors can all fuel growth, but they also need to be managed. Sorting out people's problems can be distracting, while dealing with the disputes that could arise from a variety of different forms of contractual relationships can be wearing and costly.

'Teamwork' has a thousand champions and social beings have a habit of congregating together like Canadian geese. However, colleagues can sometimes be more trouble than they are worth. People can get under each others feet and create extra work.

In relation to the organizations visited during the course of research for this book, staff employed by smaller enterprises were regularly found to be having more fun, and deriving greater satisfaction, at their place of work. Some of those who watched a film clip of an ASK location on television's *The Money Programme* thought the company was a holiday camp. Creative work should be enjoyed. Inspiration should light up the eyes as well as the mind.

Major corporations are recognizing the inflexibility of scale, and the suffocating nature of bureaucratic controls. ABB, like Halma, has broken itself down into a host of distinct businesses. Each of these are of a size appropriate to its market. Considerable power is decentralized. Companies are expected to do what is right for their particular situation. Individual employees are encouraged to be entrepreneurial in relation to meeting the needs of their customers.

Failings Should not Deter

People who perceive an opportunity to create value should not necessarily be inhibited or deterred by deficiencies or failings. Many of these may not be relevant to what needs to be done. In any event, everyone has limitations of some form. Even the largest of corporations finds it impossible to be world class at everything. Perfection is unattainable even for artists.

Inadequacies can always be dealt with so long as they are recognized. Required skills, extra finance, relevant contacts or further capabilities can always be accessed, or obtained, through collaborative relationships. People can simply work with those who have what they lack.

There are those who place too much emphasis upon formal planning. They become unbending and constrained and less open and sensitive to what is happening around them than those who adopt a more flexible approach. Defining early roles in great detail can be a mistake and counter-productive. It can inhibit learning, particularly that about and with customers whose changing needs and requirements should drive a business forward.

Others draw too tight and rigid a distinction between preparation and action, to the extent that they stop questioning and challenging during implementation. Entrepreneurs need to reflect and achieve. They should also ensure that business teams contain both thinkers and doers.

Barriers to entry are not what they used to be. One by one they are falling away or can be circumvented. No one should feel automatically excluded from an opportunity they have recognized and which they understand. Individuals may opt not to become involved, but they should not necessarily consider themselves obliged or compelled to stand aside. Should some form of licence, permission or qualification be needed to supply a service, then those who have, or can obtain, what is required are obvious collaboration prospects to approach.

Too many people are needlessly inhibited by their lack of knowledge, previous jobs or the views which others have of them. They rule themselves out. They do not pick up the gauntlet. They lurk in dark alleys and enclosed courtyards, rather than venture into the daylight and the chaos and confusion of the streets. They stand aside, or defer to those who may have more of the requisite contacts, but less of the necessary talent and application to succeed.

People are sometimes unduly constrained by their past failures and privations. These could well prove beneficial, providing that one learns from them. Most individuals have their 'ups and downs'. The paths of new ventures do tend to undulate. It is almost impossible to take risks in business without making some mistakes.

Events are often cyclical. The darkest clouds and the sharpest showers are sometimes followed by the brightest rays of sunshine. They may appear that way, because on breaking through they come as such a relief from what has gone before. It is when people are at rock bottom that they often have the best prospects of improvement.

Golden lives from cradle to grave are rare. Many of those who are concerned with aiding or supporting new and growing businesses are tolerant of mistakes. Some venture capitalists go as far as to be reluctant to lend large amounts to those who have not experienced past failures and 'grown' because of them. If someone has not been tested, others cannot be sure about their reaction to challenging situations? Will the person concerned cope or fold?

Assessing Timescales

Corporate managers are often obsessed with short-term performance, even though pension funds may hold on to particular stocks for longer than many of them imagine (in the UK, around eight years is the norm). Dealing costs and stamp duties are incurred whenever investors change their holdings. Smart savers select wisely and hold their positions.

Those who are used to the 'knee-jerk reaction', 'wanted yesterday' and 'sound bite' cultures of major corporations often underestimate the distance that may be required to slow down and change direction. Something so important should not be rushed. People may not know what they do not know. For example, within a year or so of leaving a large corporation, a person may have a very different view of minimum income requirements or the advantages and drawbacks of employing others rather than operating alone.

Discussing what is proposed with family and friends, restructuring one's commitments, and examining opportunities for collaboration with a current employer, all take time. A distinctive business concept may evolve over a period of months. Those with whom one is exploring various possibilities may or may not have something in mind for the next financial year.

Some find that invitations and proposals which they cannot resist come 'out of the blue'. A much cited example is Steve Jobs' question to John Sculley of whether he wanted to stay at PepsiCo and sell 'sugar water' or join Apple and 'change the world'. Those contemplating a change of direction should think about how they would answer such a question. Many people carry too much baggage to react quickly.

An entrepreneur needs to strike a balance between being alert to windows of opportunity, while at the same time laying the foundations for longer term development. Encouraging learning and innovation ensures continuing growth. Many of the founders of Victorian companies continued until late in life to initiate activities that would bear fruit generations later. Their time horizons extended beyond their own existence. Their industry ushered in the modern age.

Exercise: Voyage Analysis

Before people leave port they should ensure they have everything that is likely to be required for the first leg of whatever journey they intend to make.

Is everything that you may need on board? What else should you take? Which items do you require now and what could be picked up later en route? Will your planned provisions keep or might they deteriorate and become stale during the journey? When the tides and other conditions are expected to be most favourable, will you be ready to set sail?

Making the Transition

Some people favour a clean break in order to concentrate single-mindedly upon a business venture. Others adopt a more cautious approach. They prefer to phase in a new life, perhaps taking time to learn additional skills and develop a network of useful contacts. Rearranging family finances, or co-ordinating a move with developments that involve other members of the family, may take months rather than days. The longer and more carefully one prepares for a change, the more successful it is likely to be.

Where an area of opportunity is embryonic, or when someone is proposing to become a pioneer, there may not be anyone who has relevant previous experience. The field concerned may be new for everyone. What is fresh can be risky. As the tide goes out, later arrivals can follow the footsteps of earlier visitors to a beach. From the pattern of tracks they may be able to avoid getting their feet damp by walking around the wet patches.

Many of those who 'have a go' find they are 'naturals' for the frontiers they cross or into pastures which they move, particularly when they follow their instincts. Interests, drives and preferences are often the result of a conscious or unconscious appreciation that one has what it takes. People are attracted or lured because they sense it is right for them.

Rather than conform to the stereotyped, and possibly mistaken, impressions of others, individuals should determine their own agendas. Those who simply 'follow and fit' tend not to stand out. To have an impact one needs to be noticed by potential collaborators and customers. For example, when so much information is accessible to all by means of the internet, it may be necessary to have a distinctive voice or 'angle' in order to register and attract attention.

It may be helpful to let it be known that one is 'available' or 'on the market'. Some people are so adept at playing a current game that it would not occur to others, including those who most value and respect them, that they would consider moving in a new direction. Others who would like to benefit from their advice do not ask. Because they are not thought to be 'open to offers', they do not receive them.

Many people face a difficult choice. They would like to move in a more entrepreneurial direction, but they also value their current role. They are reluctant to send out signals that might prejudice a present job. Corporations that are seeking to encourage intrapreneurship and risk taking, and which have a strategy of expansion through more collaborative activities, should recognize such dilemmas. They should also take steps to identify individuals with business instincts and longings for independence.

Enterprising companies initiate measures to tap the latent capability which they may have to establish, launch and manage new ventures. Many are well-placed to work with the grain of both individual aspirations and public policy. There are many programmes at local, regional, national and European level, to encourage such developments and various forms of assistance for new job creating activities in certain geographic areas. An organization could simultaneously help itself; fulfill its people; please its customers, partners and shareholders and benefit local communities.

Self-assessment

Personal qualities, such as sensitivity to customer requirements, or being shrewd where money is involved, can be more
important for wealth creation than past credentials. Many of
those with impressive job titles, including holders of top management positions in large companies, may not be, necessarily, better equipped to run an entrepreneurial business than
junior staff. Many senior executives have budgets to live
within, rather than cash flows to generate and manage.

It is worth really thinking through what one is particularly good at. Thus, someone who is inwardly motivated, persistent and tenacious, and with a preference for continuity
and building upon firm foundations, could concentrate upon
areas of opportunity in which it may take time to break in,
but a reputation that has been acquired can result in a continuing flow of business.

In contrast, another person might be more outward looking. Individuals who like to monitor what is happening around
them, and flit from pillar to post, could focus upon quick responses to fashionable trading opportunities. There are many
dealing activities which can be performed from an office at
home. These range from long-established pursuits, such as developing a share portfolio, to the creation of a new electronic
market for a particular service.

People should be realistic about their attention span and
stamina. Some businesses take time to become established.
Those involved in their formation may have to run ever faster
to stay ahead in competitive races. Where others are involved,
one needs to know how far to push them. Colleagues require
both encouragement and support. While they might be inspired
by values, they may also have to be focused and channelled by
appropriate frameworks and guidelines.

The entrepreneur needs both an eye for detail and an awareness of the 'big picture'. Sensitivity to immediate issues and
priorities is also required. At the same time, the wealth creator should maintain a strategic perspective and sustain a longer
term sense of purpose.

Getting started might involve a large leap for many of those
concerned. In contrast, subsequent development may require
a succession of small steps. There may be additional employees to hire and new customers to win, while existing staff

and patrons will still want to feel special. Many independent operators find it very difficult to develop further clientele while undertaking work for continuing clients and supporting current consumers.

Starting Small

Many professionals, from doctors and dentists to lawyers and accountants, have operated from 'front rooms' on first setting up in practice. A growing number of individuals now work at, or from, home. They run trading businesses, act as consultants who offer specialist advice and comment or provide various information services. All they need is a commercial concept, a PC connected, via a modem, to the internet and a cup of tea. Some succeed without the tea.

Product-based businesses can also have modest beginnings. A simple kitchen experiment initiated the development of the technology that would form the basis for the explosive early growth of Xerox. A young Marconi carried out tests and trials in his bedroom and garden. Apple computers did not start among the fountains, lawns and plate glass of a science park, but in a humble garage.

A family business, or a friend seeking help, could provide an enterprise entry point. When such opportunities arise, some hesitate for so long that they miss the boat. Others are psychologically better prepared. They pounce upon what is offered as a first step which might lead to a more extensive involvement.

A part-time, or consultancy, engagement can sometimes grow into a deeper relationship. Rather than become over anxious, it may be wise to concentrate upon doing good work and allowing nature to run its course. Fresh shoots may branch into new directions, as tasks accomplished result through word of mouth recommendations in additional assignments.

There might be a choice between width and depth, for example, undertaking similar projects for various other organizations or building a more lasting arrangement with a particular one. An initial customer/supplier contract might evolve into a continuing link, such as some form of joint venture or partnership, or even an equity stake and a seat on the board.

Life as Preparation

We begin and end our lives as dependents. The challenge is to secure as much independence as possible during the interval between the onset of maturity and such warning signs as a diminution of energy or the beginning of senility.

Successful wealth creators often harbour a desire to establish or acquire a business for many years before they take the plunge. From a young age, they notice trade and commerce, whether the corner shop or the supermarket. They register the chink of money changing hands, the swipe of the credit card and the satisfaction which both parties can derive from a transaction. One obtains something that was wanted, the other is rewarded for providing it.

Although family or other commitments may postpone the moment of decision, the experience of life need not be wasted. During years in the wilderness, people can prepare. They can use a wide range of incidents in their daily existence to identify, and learn about, areas of opportunity. They can obtain the insights, develop the instincts and forge the tools that will allow them to think and act like an entrepreneur.

Students at leading business schools pay many thousands of pounds, and forgo one or two years earnings, to learn from 'examples' or the results of 'research'. Yet, every day we are surrounded by real-time cases. We can undertake our own enquiries. For example, why do some shops attract more visitors than others? What is the relative importance of location, service, price or atmosphere? Sights and sounds are sustenance for the entrepreneurial soul.

With any activity, whether travelling to work in the morning, 'popping out' during the day, collecting a take-away in the evening, or calling a chemist at night, one could reflect upon how a customer experience might have been improved. What did the body language or the expressions on the faces of those involved, reveal? Questions could be put to those encountered. A simple 'how's business?' might elicit an illuminating response.

Those who open their eyes find there is a great deal going on around them. Some people keep notebooks handy in which to record any unusual practices they observe which appear to work. So much may be captured that time might need to be put aside each week to review what has been learned. While backseat drivers do sometimes annoy, and armchair strategists can irritate, the closet entrepreneur may, inexorably, become the real thing.

Finding the Right Business Concept

The inclination may be present, but not the opportunity. All the talent, burning desire and start-up finance in the world is of little relevance if someone has failed to identify a gap in the market or spot a customer requirement. Goods and services cannot be forced upon people.

Dead ends should be avoided. Frustration leads some citizens to fall for the lure of 'get rich quick' ideas peddled by the unprincipled. In most cases, the advice which is offered, wrapped, and arrives through the post, turns out to be worthless. When opportunities are well-signposted, so many people may sniff around them as to make it unlikely that particular individuals will derive any distinct benefit.

Caution should also be exercised when considering packaged business concepts. A formula might appear to work, but for how long? It may only do so until the bubble bursts due to over supply or a change of fashion occurs. Many people rush to climb aboard bandwaggons when it is already too late. Their dreams turn into nightmares.

Some unscrupulous characters prey upon the genuine desires of others to do something more positive with their lives. Their deceptions can be well-organized and relatively sophisticated. Each year, new generations of people are burned by a variety of scams that take advantage of the innocent and the unwary. Pyramid schemes feed equally upon gullibility and greed until they implode. Those who manage to exit with a positive return, generally do so at the expense of the misery of many others.

It is worth saving one's emotional and financial resources for when the 'big one' comes along. There is no substitute for a winning business concept that is rooted in the real needs of others. Ideally, once the product or service in question is launched, people should find it difficult to conceive of it ever having not been available. They should exclaim 'How did we cope before?'

If a proposed enterprise is not started, someone somewhere should miss out on something which would have improved the quality of their life. If no one else would benefit or be disadvantaged, by the existence or otherwise of a venture, then a question to ask is whether its establishment would be an exercise in vanity.

Drives and Motivations

Some ideas or suggestions for businesses are daringly ambitious, while others are relatively modest. People should not jump to conclusions about whether or not a particular proposal is sufficiently stretching, without first understanding the drives and motivations of those involved.

While some might want an enterprise to expand and continue as a form of living memorial after their death, others may have more limited expectations. They are 'tryers' rather than tycoons. In any event, who remembers those who founded the constituent parts of most of the major companies with which we are so familiar? The only evidence of their existence might be a portrait in a corridor leading to the boardroom, at least until the next review of office decor.

In some cases, the identity of an individual may form part of an organization's name. Other companies are the products of a succession of mergers and acquisitions. Many memorable corporate logos and titles have emerged from market research exercises or legal investigations of what is available for international use.

Many of the companies whose founders once graced their signs and letterheads have been renamed with an acronym or single word that is thought to travel more easily across national borders. Those who seek to leave behind monuments should perhaps look at other alternatives such as prizes or endowments.

A modest proposal is perfectly valid, as is an intention to form and operate a venture for a limited period only, perhaps the natural span of a concept. Some people go into commercial situations with a view to committing a certain number of years to them, rather than the whole of their life. There are also serial entrepreneurs who found, and subsequently dispose of, more than one business.

People sometimes worry, and become inhibited, concerned and frustrated, because they feel that a business concept lacks certain elements that would sustain growth. This may well be so, but at the same time, the conditions might exist for a profitable operation to be run for a number of years. In any event, those involved may not be able to maintain the interest and commitment, or supply the required levels of energy or finance, to extend the activities of an enterprise beyond a watershed or decision point.

A business could be expressly established to operate for a fixed-term. During this time it may deliver value and satisfaction to all those who associate with it, and thus enrich their lives.

Next Steps

Success rarely comes to those who simply wish for it. The hungry hawk does not dither or dawdle. It spots and swoops. While there is little virtue in being naïve or unprepared, opportunities should not be analyzed to death. Intuition and instinct may tell people that a particular concept is a runner.

Some launch too soon. A critical consideration is whether or not there are customers for what is being proposed. Good ideas can be ahead of their time. Whether through market research, direct contact or by judging the strength of interest and depth of feeling, the extent of the likely market should be assessed.

Never forget that it is customers who create a business. They can be much more difficult than costs to acquire. A restaurant draws groups of people who sit together, eat and drink and subsequently tell others of their experience. An empty room of tables and chairs is just that. It is not recommended to friends. Putting out a sign or a brass plate and opening up is one thing, attracting interest is something else, while securing paying customers and repeat visits is quite another matter.

Due to enthusiasm borne of a desire to triumph, people sometimes declare victory too soon. Customers have to be retained as well as won. Those establishing a new enterprise, or taking over an existing one, cannot be certain of success until customers return for subsequent purchases and settle their bills.

A considerable interval may elapse between supplying a customer and a requirement for a repeat or replacement purchase coming around again. In some sectors, it may be years before one can be confident about the future viability of an enterprise. Such a long period of uncertainty can put a severe strain upon relationships.

Those with responsibilities for others are sometimes inhibited by the fear of the possible impact of failure upon their families. This is the time to be open and to discuss the possibilities. Many of those who do talk with the people closest to them are surprised by their positive reactions.

A partner who is truly fulfilled can be more fun to be with than those resigned individuals who feel trapped by duties and responsibilities and are unable to be themselves. To want to live according to one's own rules should not be regarded as selfish. The lack of courage to have a go denies many people the opportunity to bury boredom and share an exciting journey. Challenge and adversity can bind collaborators and family members more closely together.

Certain, over-cautious people worry about letting a good idea 'out of the bag'. While there are garrulous individuals who let others snatch opportunities from under their noses, some new business teams exaggerate the degree of novelty of their insights.

In itself, an idea may have little value without the commitment and capability to effect its implementation. It may also not be unique. The potential market might be able to absorb the initial offerings of a great many different suppliers. At some stage, if support, collaborators and potential customers are to be attracted, a concept will need to be fleshed out, articulated and shared.

Intriguingly, many of the creative innovators whose inventions formed the foundations for the subsequent development of major multinational corporations had to struggle for some time before 'lift off' occurred. Like prophets, they wandered in the desert while seeking to capture the attention of a disinterested world. To take an example, with the benefit of hindsight it is difficult to believe that Chester Carlson, who discovered the plain copier process, found it so difficult to interest others in his ideas. He showed people the future. They showed him the door.

Exercise: Lift-off Analysis

Some ventures are easier to get airborne than others. Many people remain desk bound and stay grounded. Yet, in various walks of life, there are those who have managed to transcend the limitations of their circumstances. They have made their childhood dreams a reality. People should identify what is holding them back and work out how to secure additional lift. They should actively investigate how to take off and stay aloft.

How close are you to getting airborne? Is there any dead weight which you could jettison? Have all the restraining ropes been cut? Is someone holding back the throttle? Have you thought of a winch, tow or catapult? How might you get some extra power or increased lift?

Taking the Plunge

For the inveterate procrastinator, the time is never ripe. Resolutions are made one day and undone, or forgotten, the next. There is always another excuse for inaction. While the conditions may not have been perfect, enterprises have been conceived on hospital beds and behind prison bars. In some cases, these differing forms of confinement have given people the time to think things through. They find or rediscover a sense of purpose.

To be forever seeking instant gratification and quick returns can prevent significant accomplishments. A particular venture may require careful planning. However, a person should not delay for so long as to miss a window of opportunity. One can over-prepare. When all the surfaces are silky smooth they may not grip. People sometimes slide over promising possibilities.

Entrepreneurs don't wait for other people to give them permission to do things. They act as catalysts and seize the initiative. They move positively and engage decisively, making it clear what they expect from other people. They prioritize and are able to focus upon both short-term objectives and longer term goals. They do not look the other way or put a finger in the dyke. They bring concerns and conflicts into the open, so that they can be addressed and resolved.

Taking the plunge may be less wearing than struggling on. While people are young, they are less aware of the relentless pace and ravages of time. They may feel that there will always be another day. Sooner or later there are no tomorrows. Long before such a point is reached, individuals may find they no longer have sufficient energy or the efficiency to do what is necessary to succeed. As the level of reserves in the tank falls, the power of the flow declines.

To be confronted with the realization that one has left it too late, or avoided an opportunity, can be frustrating. It may lead to regrets, speculation, rumination and fantasies about what might have been. Better perhaps to venture forth and start to accumulate 'real' memories of the trials and tribulations of launching an initiative that may have a positive impact upon others.

Even failure can bring its rewards. Provided one has not been irresponsible or foolish, a flop can be a learning and character-building event. On looking back over their lives, people often find that many of the most vivid experiences they have had are associated with business and personal crises. Surviving accidents, coping with challenges, handling difficulties, holding a team together, extracting oneself from a market trap, can all give rise to a greater sense of self-worth than lazily consuming the fruits of easy success.

The satisfaction that comes from knowing that one has 'had a go' or battled with adversity can be intense. It may last for a lifetime. Chris Moon lost his right leg when a landmine exploded. Two years later he successfully completed the Sahara marathon over 230 kilometers of some of the most inhospitable terrain on earth. His message on finishing was: "The only limits we have are those we put on ourselves."

The act of jumping into a marketplace need not be final or forever. It might feel so at the time, but with the perspective of years, it may represent but one phase of life, and an experience that did not necessarily preclude others.

Many people exaggerate the opportunity costs of the time and resources devoted to a new venture or a fresh direction. Such calculations sometimes represent self-deception. Often, what was foregone would have been more of the same, rather than something which is different, broadening and exhilarating. The familiar can lack novelty, challenge and excitement.

Having committed to change, a venturer should periodically review the progress made in relation to the original goals that were set. If the initial aim or purpose was to create more balance and harmony, or to introduce a degree of spontaneity into a lifestyle, the question of whether or not this has been achieved should be asked.

People should confront reality. Are they fulfilling more aspects of themselves than was previously the case? Do they have a better understanding of who they are? Does their world consist of human relationships or plans, possessions and figures? Do they feel more in control?

Negative answers should be addressed. Some individuals are 'quitters' who will cut and run. Others pursue their quest. They will try again or explore new avenues of opportunity. They have metamorphosed and have become entrepreneurs, the creators of value and fulfillers of dreams.

Checklist

1. Can you remember your childhood dreams or youthful ambitions? Could they yet be achieved?

2. Have you mapped out your life? Have you prepared adequately for the transition which you seek? How realistic are your plans and the assumptions upon which they are based?

3. Will your proposed venture and intended lifestyle enable you to contribute something of value to others and allow you to be true to yourself?

4. Who, or what, is holding you back from changing direction and having a go? What are the major inhibitors, obstacles and constraints? How might they be overcome?

5. How well prepared are you financially? Could you and your family survive the lean years of an economic famine? Do you need more time to restructure your finances?

6. Are those who are closest to you supportive of what you would like to do? Have you involved them? Have you discussed your business plans and personal intentions with them?

7. How compelling and distinctive is your service offering or business concept? Can it be easily communicated and shared?

8. Who will benefit? Why should they be interested? Do they care?

9. How easily could your ideas be copied and emulated by others? How might they be protected?

10. If the right moment to act or commit has not yet come, why is this? What would speed matters up?

11. Is there a particular window of opportunity? Will your ideas date or mature?

12. Who or what is missing? How might the remaining pieces of the jigsaw puzzle be secured and assembled?

13. Do you have access to the competencies and capabilities that are needed for successful implementation?

14. What would happen if you do not follow your instincts and pursue your quest? Would people be able to get something similar from someone else? What would you miss or lose?

15. Do you feel more human, more fulfilled and more in charge of your own destiny as a result of the steps which you have taken? Have you already metamorphosed into an entrepreneur, or are you about to?

Conclusion

THE ENTERPRISE MANIFESTO

Let the scent lead you to the honeysuckle.

The 21st century could become an era of unprecedented creativity, entrepreneurship and personal fulfilment. During our historical evolution, we have moved through periods in which a substantial proportion of those at work have been hunter-gatherers, farmers and industrial workers. Now it is time for the citizen/entrepreneur to take centre stage.

Inclusive and challenging visions are required that will widen participation in the innovative process, and span the private, public and voluntary sectors. We need business entrepreneurs to create new sources of commercial value that will reward and satisfy themselves and deliver benefits to others. We require social entrepreneurs who will discover better ways of bringing together voluntary effort and public provision to further improve the quality of our lives.

But first attitudes have to change. In some quarters, there verges upon an obsession with failure. People chip away at reputations and records until downsides and defects are revealed. Too much attention is devoted to exposing, debunking and dragging down. Dig deep enough and there may be some exploitation and greed to be found, but they are not the primary motivations of most entrepreneurs.

There are modern 'merchants of death' who peddle danger, despair and decay on dingy and dirty street corners. But there are also champions of new ways of working, and providers of open routes to lifelong learning. There are contemporary pioneers of the arts and sports, creators of healthier diets, and instigators of more balanced lifestyles. There are also advocates of enlightenment, entrepreneurs of aspirations, feelings and values. Wherever and whenever it is free to operate, enterprise is at work.

Insufficient effort is applied to lifting our sights, raising our spirits, and increasing our awareness of new choices and options for living and learning. There are abundant, fresh and exciting possibilities for scaling and sharing, healing and caring, and building and providing. Greater priority should be given to the development and dissemination of positive case studies that reveal hitherto hidden qualities, illustrate active contribution, and demonstrate achievement and success.

Negative motives and drivers have had far too much of the limelight. Literature and films are overly concerned and excessively preoccupied with 'escaping' or 'taking from, rather than 'giving to' or the 'building of'. Destruction, horror and violence are more dramatic than the peaceful tranquillity of reflection. Quick cutting between the brash and the bizarre is more 'pacey and racey' than lingering, and featuring the silent and solitary act of thinking.

The process of creation can, on occasion, be painful and protracted. Yet it is natural and noble, and the consequences can be inspiring and profound. A succession of innovative breakthroughs within an extensive family of technologies allows the sounds, images and drama of a momentary incident to echo within seconds around the world. An instant can be captured for all time.

Exploration and learning can both challenge and liberate. External discovery, and a growth of internal awareness, may occur together. Each becomes a catalyst of the other. Design, development and building are intensely rewarding. Moreover, everyone could experience them. They are not reserved activities that are only prescribed for a favoured few.

People toil underground to extract diminishing returns from reluctant seams that are almost worked out, when above them are rivers teeming with fish. We could all become entrepreneurs on our own terms; and in ways that suit our preferences and personalities, and also enable us to serve others. Learning, leisure, lifestyle and healthy living all represent rich frontier lands beyond which are lush forests of opportunity.

The pursuit of illusion could, and should, be replaced by the sense of satisfaction and fulfilment which results from the reality of achievement. Protest, criticism and reaction against needs to give way to the resolution of disputes, the restoration of harmony between contending forces, and the presentation, selection and construction of preferred alternatives. There are momentous opportunities for creative ditheists to reconcile individuals and teams, people and organizations, and town and country. The fruits of enterprise can reach across a myriad of divisions and benefit both 'haves' and 'have nots'.

The various problems that concern so many people, such as noise and pollution, plundered resources, insecurity, inner emptiness and doubt, represent exciting and intriguing opportunities for the sensitive, intuitive and alert to react, investigate, tackle and solve. They present endless possibilities for enterprising people.

One could offer improved physical insulation and greater financial security, or introduce measures to safeguard, protect and enrich the environment. One could discover new means of sustainable development, create alternative lifestyles or provide more balance and deeper meaning. The options, permutations and combinations abound.

Mere survival and sullen accommodation represent a denial of human potential and a default on fulfilment. There is no need for people to wallow perpetually in quicksand and mud when they could take off along a causeway that leads to firmer ground and supportive relationships. Chaos and uncertainty reign because too many people lack the courage to drive stakes into the ground and build the groynes that would anchor shifting sands and prevent the further erosion of fundamental human desires and aspirations.

Too many people pick at sores rather than seize the moment. Left alone a scab may heal, but promising possibilities and the best chances of success can be as fleeting as the flicker of a candle in a drafty corridor. Ignore them and they may pass on by. Heavy-lidded onlookers and retiring bystanders do not cause economic, social, scientific or technological revolutions.

We should champion exemplars and role models from all walks of life who display passion and exude energy and enthusiasm. We should celebrate their competence and capability, along with the loyalty and commitment of those who help and support them. We should also treasure those who think and learn, and who care and share. We must encourage our citizen entrepreneurs to become ambassadors of enterprise who will actively inspire new generations of pioneers and contributors.

The various elements of what is needed to produce an explosion of creativity and enterprise, and fulfilment for the many, are all around us. What is needed in greater measure is the entrepreneurial will, motivation and persistence to fuse them together in new combinations that represent and deliver value to users, customers and clients.

Individuals should be true to their own unique personality and inner soul. They should set out to develop a particular mission and a special purpose. They should assume greater personal responsibility, and exert more control over their lives. Corporate and public leaders should support them, and act quickly, decisively and explicitly to create working, learning and living environments that will enable people to discover themselves, form venture teams, and give of their best.

The Future of the Organization[1] advocates the corporate adoption, and the individual and collective observance, of ten essential freedoms.

- Freedom to dream, aspire, build and create.
- Freedom to enter into mutually beneficial relationships.
- Freedom to do what is necessary to deliver value and satisfaction to customers.
- Freedom as a customer to seek new sources of benefit and value.
- Freedom to initiate debates, explore, question, challenge, innovate and learn.
- Freedom to understand one's self, be true to one's self, and to develop and build upon natural strengths.
- Freedom to work at a time, location and mode that best contributes to desired outputs.
- Freedom to use the most relevant technology, tools and processes depending upon what it is that needs to be done.
- Freedom to confront reality, identify root causes and tackle obstacles and barriers.
- Freedom to learn according to one's individual learning potential.

These freedoms 'should become the basis of a new social contract or charter with key stakeholders', creating both rights and obligations, and 'turning the hard protective shells of companies into open arenas of opportunity'. Members of organizations, networks, families and other groups should cherish and

1. Colin Coulson-Thomas, *The Future of the Organization: Achieving Excellence through Business Transformation* (London: Kogan Page) 1997 hardback and 1998 paperback, p. 123.

actively propagate them. Fundamental freedoms are critical enablers of mass enterprise, and those who practice them are likely to be among the major beneficiaries.

New life and a fresh purpose needs to be breathed into many of our corporations and public bodies, along with most associations and neighbourhoods. They should be transformed into enterprise communities, fertile incubators and breeding grounds for individual and collaborative ideas, initiatives and ventures.

Obstacles to innovation, creativity and freedom must be confronted and removed. Barriers to the acquisition, development and application of information, knowledge and understanding must be identified and broken through. These challenges must be tackled with urgency, vigour and determination.

The clock is ticking: for some the sand is running out. There has never been a more promising time to be proactive, or a more opportune moment to reflect, assess, network, prioritize, focus and act. People of all ages and abilities should consider venturing forth and 'having a go' at becoming an entrepreneur. Simply to try is to join a 'great game'. Those who pursue their dreams often discover their inner selves and can forge lasting friendships. By following their stars they attain inner peace, achieve fulfilment and secure self-respect.

Appendix

INDIVIDUALS AND ENTERPRISE RESEARCH PROGRAMME

The Individuals and Enterprise Research Programme has drawn upon extensive discussions with entrepreneurs, a variety of consultancy projects for growing businesses and a continuing set of investigations (see the diagram on page 296, which presents an overview) into the requirements for successful entrepreneurship which are being led by Professor Colin Coulson-Thomas. The latter exercises are examining the main areas which need to be addressed in order to win and retain customers, deliver value to them in a competitive marketplace and remain capable and relevant.

A number of other books, and various research reports, based upon the work which has been undertaken to date have already been published.

Achieving Business Excellence

The Future of the Organization: Achieving Excellence through Business Transformation by Colin Coulson-Thomas, Kogan Page (Tel: +44 [0]171 278 0433; Fax: +44 [0]171 837 6348), hardback 1997 and paperback 1998, provides a range of approaches for implementing more holistic and people-centred approaches to management and business transformation.

Establishing and Maintaining Strategic Direction

Creating Excellence in the Boardroom by Colin Coulson-Thomas, McGraw Hill Europe (Tel: +44 [0]1628 23432, Fax: +44 [0]1628 770224), hardback 1993, examines the strategic role of directors in building and transforming businesses. It represents a guide to shaping directorial competence and board effectiveness.

Individuals and Enterprise Research Programme

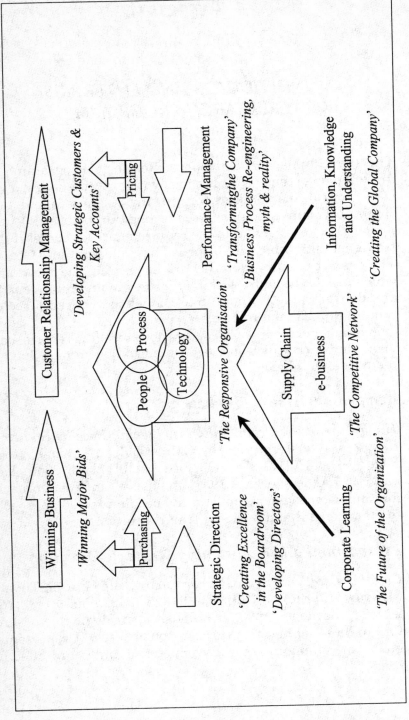

Developing Directors: Building an Effective Boardroom Team by Colin Coulson-Thomas, McGraw Hill Europe (Tel: +44 [0]1628 23432, Fax: +44 [0]1628 770224), paperback 1993, is concerned with the development of more competent directors and more effective boards. It provides a range of practical exercises which can be used by individual directors and boardroom teams.

Winning and Retaining Customers

The report 'Winning Major Bids: the Critical Success Factors' by Carol Kennedy and Matthew O'Connor (editor Peter Bartram and executive editor Colin Coulson-Thomas) Policy Publications (Tel: +44 [0]1234 328448, Fax: +44 [0]1234 357231), 1997 draws on the experiences of 293 companies. It examines processes and practices for winning business in competitive situations and contains case studies of successful approaches.

A related report 'Developing Strategic Customers and Key Accounts: the Critical Success Factors' by John Hurcomb (editor Peter Bartram and executive editor Colin Coulson-Thomas) Policy Publications (Tel: +44 [0]1234 328448, Fax: +44 [0]1234 357231), 1998, examines the experiences and key customer relationship practices of 194 companies.

Creating a More Flexible and Responsive Organization

The three volume set of reports 'The Responsive Organisation: Re-engineering New Patterns of Work' (executive editor Colin Coulson-Thomas) Policy Publications (Tel: +44 [0]1234328 448; Fax: +44 [0]1234 357231), November 1995, comprises a re-engineering methodology manual, 21 case studies, briefings on teleworking, and notes on 101 re-engineering techniques.

Supply Chain Management

The report 'The Competitive Network' by Peter Bartram (executive editor Colin Coulson-Thomas and associate editor Lee Tate) Policy Publications (Tel: +44 [0]1234 328448; Fax: +44 [0]1234 357231), April 1996, provides a methodology for the re-engineering of supply chains through the enabling technologies of electronic commerce/e-business. It includes nine detailed case studies.

Transforming Corporate Peformance

Business Process Re-engineering: Myth and Reality (edited by Colin Coulson-Thomas) Kogan Page (Tel: +44 [0]171 278 0433; Fax: +44 [0]171 837 6348), hardback October 1994 and paperback September 1996, provides a critique of business process re-engineering and its use in improving corporate performance.

Transforming the Company: Bridging the Gap Between Management Myth and Corporate Reality by Colin Coulson-Thomas, Kogan Page (Tel: +44 [0]171 278 0433; Fax: +44 [0]171 837 6348), paperback October 1992, examines the practical problems of implementing corporate re-engineering or transformation to create a more flexible, responsive and 'network' form of organization.

International Business Development

Creating the Global Company: Successful Internationalisation by Colin Coulson-Thomas, McGraw Hill Europe (Tel: +44 [0]1628 23432, Fax: +44 [0]1628 770224), hardback 1992, provides guidance on the strategic, organisational and people aspects of internationalization and global operation.

Additional research reports are concerned with purchasing, pricing, the winning of business in particular sectors, corporate learning, and information and knowledge entrepreneurship. Further information can be obtained from Professor Colin Coulson-Thomas (Tel: +44 [0]1733 361149; fax: +44 [0]1733 361459; e-mail: adaptation@compuserve.com).

Bibliography

J Birkinshaw, "Corporate Entrepreneurships in Network Organisations How Subsidiary Initiative Drives Internal Market Efficiency" *European Management Journal* (June 1998) Vol. 16, No. 3, pp. 355-364.

S Birley & D F Muzykal, *Mastering Enterprise* (London: Pitman in association with the *Financial Times*) 1997.

B Bygrave, "Building an Entrepreneurial Economy Lessons from the United States" *Business Strategy Review* (Summer 1998) Vol. 6, No. 2, pp. 11-18.

R F Cammarano, *Entrepreneuirial Transitions: From Entrepreneurial Genius to Visionary Leader* (Glendale California: Griffin) 1994.

D Carson *et al*, *Marketing and Entrepreneurship in SMEs: An Innovative Approach* (Hemel Hempstead: Prentice Hall) 1995.

P S Cohan, "Lessons from Hi-tech Companies" *Journal of Business Strategy* (November/December 1997) Vol. 18, No. 6, pp. 10-13.

J C Collins & W Lazier, *Beyond Entrepreneurship: Turning your Business into an Enduring Great Company* (Englewood Cliffs, NJ: Prentice Hall) 1992.

C Coulson-Thomas, *The Future of the Organization: Achieving Excellence through Business Transformation* (London: Kogan Page) 1997 & 1998.

D Deakins & M Freel, "Entrepreneurial Learning and the growth Process in SMEs" *Learning Organization Journal* (1998) Vol. 5, No. 3, pp. 144-155.

D Deakins, P Jenkins & C Mason (eds), *Small Firms: Entre-preneurship in the Nineties* (London: Chapman) 1998.

P A Galagan "Smart Companies" *Training and Development* (December 1997) Vol. 51, No. 12, pp. 20-24.

J W Halloran, *Why Entrepreneurs Fail: Avoid the 20 Fatal Pit-falls of Ruining your Business* (Blue Ridge Summit, Pa: Liberty Hall Press) 1991.

J Harrison & B Taylor, *Supergrowth Companies: Entrepre-neurs in Action* (Oxford: Butterworth Heinemann) 1996.

R D Hisrich & M P Peters, *Entrepreneurship* (Boston Mass: Irwin/McGraw Hill) 1998.

D E Hussey (ed), *The Innovation Challenge* (Chichester: John Wiley) 1997.

K Inomori, *A Passion for Success: Practical Inspriational and Spiritual Insight from Japan's Leading Entrepreneur* (New York: McGraw Hill) 1995.

J P Kotter, *Matsushita Leadership: Lessons from the 20th Cen-tury's most Remarkable Entrepreneur* (New York: Free Press) 1997.

C Lewis, *The Unemployables: How Top Entrepreneurs Achieved Success* (Didcot: Management Books) 1994.

P Lorange, "The Internal Entrepreneur as Driver of Business Growth" *Perspectives for Managers* (special issue, July 1998) Vol. 49, No. 8.

A E Mann, "Entrepreneurship to Succeed in Business by Really Trying" *EFMD Forum* (1998) No. 1, pp. 68-72.

M McCrimmon, *Unleash the Entrepreneur Within: How to Make Everyone an Entrepreneur and Stay Efficient* (London: Pitman) 1995.

M E McGill & J W Slocum, *The Smarter Organization: How to Build a Business that Learns and Adapts to Marketplace Needs* (New York: John Wiley) 1994.

M J C Martin, *Managing Innovation and Entrepreneurship in Technology-based Firms* (New York: John Wiley) 1994.

D Molian & B Leleux, *European Casebook on Entrepreneurship and New Ventures* (Hemel Hempstead: Prentice Hall) 1997.

N Nicholson, "Personality and Entrepreneurial Leadership a Study of the Heads of the UK's Most Successful Independent Companies" *European Management Journal* (October 1998) Vol. 16, No. 5, pp. 529-539.

D Oates, *Complete Entrepreneur* (London: Mercury Books) 1990.

D Potter, "Entrepreneurship Psion and Europe" *Business Strategy Review* (Spring 1998) Vol. 9, No. 1, pp. 15-20.

D Robinson, *Naked Entrepreneur* (London: Kogan Page) 1990.

W J Stolze, *Start Up: An Entrepreneur's Guide to Launching and Managing a New Business* (Franklin Lakes NJ: Careeer Press) 1996.

M Wright, K Robbie & C Ennew, "Serial Entrepreneurs" *British Journal of Management* (September 1997) Vol. 8, No. 3, pp. 251-268.

The Shape of Things to Come:
Business in the New Millennium

Colin Coulson-Thomas

The Shape of Things to Come is a futuristic, cutting edge appraisal of what organizational development in the early years of the new millennium will be like. It looks at current organizational and management trends and predicts how things may develop. Using models and futuristic examples, business guru Colin Coulson-Thomas shows what organizations will be like if the trends that are happening today - globalization, flexible forms of working, Internet developments and other technological advances, changes in people management, organizational development and holistic approaches to management - continue unabated.

The author ultimately suggests that rather than organizations becoming even more de-personalised, the technological advances that will take place will enable more personal interaction and certainly more personal growth and development than has previously been the case. People will be able to build up business networks and operate competitively from the comfort of their armchair, and if organizations are to continue to attract people they will have to recognize that individual talents must be nurtured and allowed to prosper within an organizational environment.

This is the latest in a series of dynamic, futuristic books from Colin Coulson-Thomas. Its importance for the business market of the early millennium years cannot be overestimated. It shows clearly what things will be like, and how we all need to change - in both corporate and individual terms - to cope with the new century.

The Author:
COLIN COULSON-THOMAS has written extensively on business and management topics. Recent books include *The Future of the Organization* (Kogan Page), *Transforming the Company* (Kogan Page) and *Individuals and Enterprise* (Blackhall Publishing).

360 pages
1-901657-87-6 £27.50 hbk: October 1999

The above books can be purchased at any good bookshop or direct from:
BLACKHALL PUBLISHING
26 Eustace Street
Dublin 2.
Telephone: +44 (0)1-677-3242; Fax: +44 (0)1-677-3243;
e-mail: blackhall@tinet.ie

The Shape of Things to Come:
Business in the New Millennium

Colin Coulson-Thomas

The Shape of Things to Come is a futuristic, cutting edge appraisal of what organizational development in the early years of the new millennium will be like. It looks at current organizational and management trends and predicts how things may develop. Using models and futuristic examples, business guru Colin Coulson-Thomas shows what organizations will be like if the trends that are happening today - globalization, flexible forms of working, Internet developments and other technological advances, changes in people management, organizational development and holistic approaches to management - continue unabated.

The author ultimately suggests that rather than organizations becoming even more de-personalised, the technological advances that will take place will enable more personal interaction and certainly more personal growth and development than has previously been the case. People will be able to build up business networks and operate competitively from the comfort of their armchair, and if organizations are to continue to attract people they will have to recognize that individual talents must be nurtured and allowed to prosper within an organizational environment.

This is the latest in a series of dynamic, futuristic books from Colin Coulson-Thomas. Its importance for the business market of the early millennium years cannot be overestimated. It shows clearly what things will be like, and how we all need to change - in both corporate and individual terms - to cope with the new century.

The Author:
COLIN COULSON-THOMAS has written extensively on business and management topics. Recent books include *The Future of the Organization* (Kogan Page), *Transforming the Company* (Kogan Page) and *Individuals and Enterprise* (Blackhall Publishing).

360 pages
1-901657-87-6 £27.50 hbk: October 1999

The above books can be purchased at any good bookshop or direct from:
BLACKHALL PUBLISHING
26 Eustace Street
Dublin 2.

Telephone: +44 (0)1-677-3242; Fax: +44 (0)1-677-3243;
e-mail: blackhall@tinet.ie